IMAGES
of America

STEEL PIER

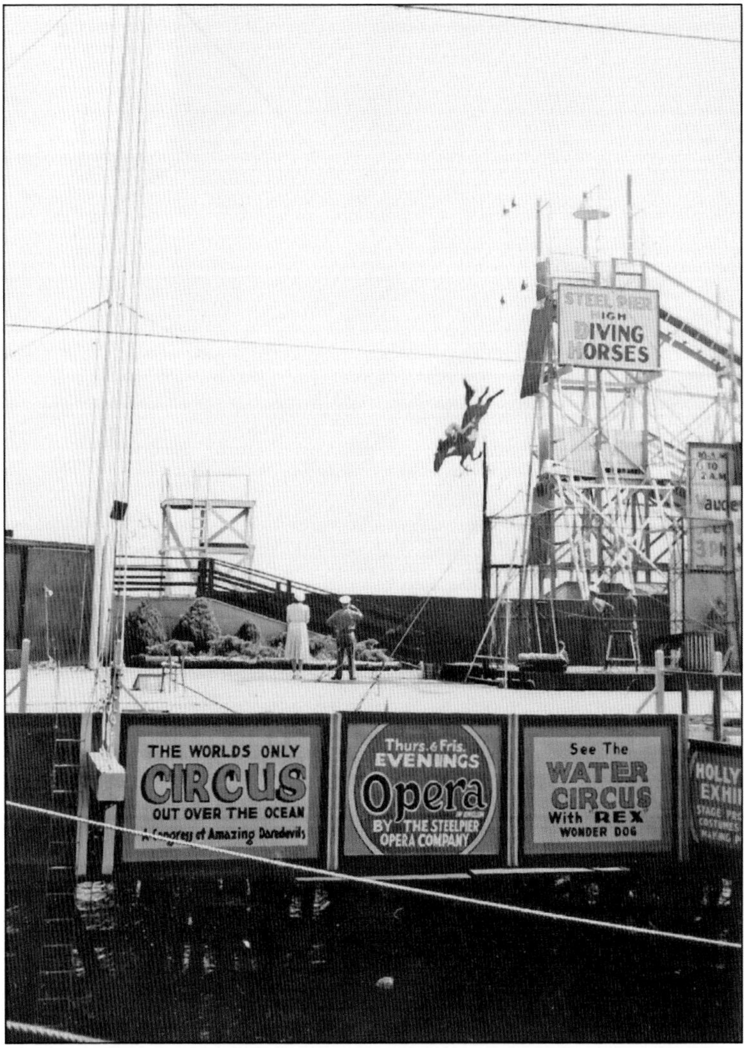

The Diving Horse was the icon of Atlantic City, proudly displayed on billboards and magazines throughout the United States. The act began accidently when W.F. "Doc" Carver, a renowned marksman, came upon a damaged bridge in Nebraska in 1881 while on horseback. As he attempted to cross, the bridge collapsed, with the horse diving into the water some 40 feet below, and an idea was formed. The act came to Steel Pier in 1929 and was presented until 1945. It returned after an eight-year hiatus and remained thereafter on the pier until it closed in 1978. Due to persistent rumors throughout the years, it must be noted that the horses were never pushed, shocked, or mistreated, nor was there a platform that collapsed. If that were the case, the female riders who sat on the horses would have been injured more than the horse. The SPCA made it a priority to arrive unannounced and never found a problem. This 1938 photograph touts the Water Circus and opera performances. (Author's collection.)

ON THE COVER: The crowds are bundled up in their finest as they stroll past the Steel Pier on Atlantic City's famed boardwalk during Easter weekend in 1940. The pier would annually open for the holiday and then close until Memorial Day. Big names such as the Mills Brothers and Kay Kyser and his orchestra were booked to accommodate the big holiday crowd. (Author's collection.)

IMAGES
of America

STEEL PIER

Steve Liebowitz

ARCADIA
PUBLISHING

ISBN 978-1-4671-1600-8

Published by Arcadia Publishing
Charleston, South Carolina

Printed in the United States of America

Library of Congress Control Number: 2015953482

For all general information, please contact Arcadia Publishing:
Telephone 843-853-2070
Fax 843-853-0044
E-mail sales@arcadiapublishing.com
For customer service and orders:
Toll-Free 1-888-313-2665

Visit us on the Internet at www.arcadiapublishing.com

To the late Frank P. Gravatt, George A. Hamid, and George A. Hamid Jr.: thanks for creating the world's greatest entertainment complex

Contents

ACKNOWLEDGMENTS

Most of the pictures and photographs in this book are from my personal collection of Atlantic City and Steel Pier items that seems endless; however, images not mine are credited. I would like to thank employees who worked on the pier during the 1960s and 1970s for their invaluable snapshots. Without the love they have for the legacy of Steel Pier and the friendships with each other still to this day, the spirit of Steel Pier would not continue. These individuals include Jim Schilling (aka Jim Craine), Terri Tyrrell, Roxy Grant, the legendary Ed Hurst, Marty Morley, Ann Miles, Alan "Woody" Woodin, Lou Plocher, Sarah Hart, John Carney, and so many, many more incredible people who have made me jealous with their stories of performing, singing, diving, and just hanging with rock groups and celebrities on Steel Pier. This was considered work?

I learned an incredible amount about Atlantic City and Steel Pier from my friend, the late research and history guru Allen "Boo" Pergament, and from the late great George Hamid Jr., who would take my phone calls and explain to me how Steel Pier operated, the idiosyncrasies of each building, and how he always regretted not signing Elvis Presley to a contract when he had the chance.

I also wish to thank the folks at Arcadia Publishing, most notably acquisitions editor Katie McAlpin-Owens, for suggesting I do another Steel Pier book totally different from my first, title manager Matt Todd, and title management coordinator Jeff Reutsche.

And finally, a big thanks goes to my wife, Andrea, who has had to cope for a long time with all of my research materials and obsession with Steel Pier and Atlantic City, but also understands the importance of a book such as this.

INTRODUCTION

Atlantic City, New Jersey, was the top destination for vacationers across the United States until the 1940s. Newlyweds honeymooned there, Broadway shows held their tryouts on the boardwalk in palatial theaters, and politicians, bankers, and movie stars lined the high-quality stores and bought high-priced furs, suits, and jewelry as their names appeared in society columns. Fresh seafood eateries were always crowded with customers patiently awaiting a table, and beer gardens were filled with revelers. Being open year-round did not hurt either, as the boardwalk beckoned visitors to take a hearty walk and breathe in the fresh, cold salt air that Atlantic City offered.

Countless books tell the story of how the barren lands off of Absecon Island on the New Jersey shore were slowly improved by use of the trains that hurried day trippers from the hot urban sidewalks of Philadelphia and New York to the breaking waves of the Atlantic Ocean.

Atlantic City was incorporated as a municipality on March 3, 1854. Gradually, fine hotels were built to enable the excursionists to stay longer, thus allowing them to partake of the unique charms that prevailed as well as helping the economy grow. The first of Atlantic City's many boardwalks was built around 1870 and was just a footpath that was rolled up for the winter. Today's boardwalk, the fourth one assembled, dates from 1896.

The wide, wooden walkway became the catalyst for the businesses that followed. Originally, small piers such as the West Pier in 1880 extended from the boardwalk out over the ocean and provided dancing and amusements. The beaches next to the piers would draw curious visitors, the majority donning suits and full dresses, who would relax and watch those who bathed. This was the simple 19th-century world that ushered in the next generation of progressively larger amusement piers that would enrich and entertain the masses and extend out farther into the Atlantic Ocean—some for almost a mile.

Piers have been a part of the beach resorts of Great Britain since Victorian days, built with elaborate music halls and restaurants. When the great piers began being constructed in Atlantic City, it was a direct linkage to the British piers that influenced their design and entertainment offerings.

Howard's Pier opened in 1882 and was considered the first true amusement pier, chiefly because it presented the first carousel in the country. A few storms, however, put the flimsy structure away for good in 1889.

This opened the challenge of building a better pier, one which would hopefully withstand storms and fires. As the hotels with names such as Traymore, Haddon Hall, and Blenheim rose from their original wooden cottages to massive "castles by the sea," so did the piers, each different in personality and offering members of the public strange and incredible exhibits, animals, and performers they had never before experienced.

Other piers were built before June 18, 1898, the day Steel Pier opened. The Iron Pier, later renamed Heinz Pier (as in pickle and ketchup fame), opened in 1886 at Massachusetts Avenue and the boardwalk. The great hurricane of 1944 pretty much destroyed this delicate structure.

Applegate's Pier opened in 1884 at Tennessee Avenue and became the first pier to offer multiple amusements. In 1891, a young businessman named John L. Young, along with his partner Stewart McShea, purchased Applegate's. Young bought out McShea in 1897, and the renamed Young's Ocean Pier existed until a major fire destroyed most of it in 1912. In 1922, it merged into the Central Pier, which still stands today—with its Moorish facade and much shorter in length.

Young, however, had already built a second pier at Arkansas Avenue in 1906. His crowning achievement, the Million Dollar Pier, named for its cost, barely lasted until the early 1980s, hanging on even when most of its structures had been destroyed by fire or by deterioration. It was then rebuilt as Ocean One, an indoor shopping mall and food court.

Steeplechase, only a block away from Steel Pier, opened as the Auditorium Pier in 1899. When George C. Tilyou of Coney Island's Steeplechase Park fame bought it in 1902, he turned it into a fun place full of mirth and excitement. Steeplechase burned down on Valentine's Day 1932 and languished as rubble for some years. After World War II, it was rebuilt as a shorter pier filled with rides and amusements. Closing in the 1980s, Steeplechase eventually was demolished.

In 1913, the classy Garden Pier opened between Steel and Heinz Piers. Landscaped flower beds and gardens occupied the center of the pier, and a large theater sat at its ocean end. Vaudeville and Broadway shows played the theater until 1944, when the hurricane that destroyed the Heinz Pier shortened its life. Torn down in 1950 and rebuilt as a community outdoor gathering place with a band shell and seats, Garden Pier remained popular until the early 1970s. With the band shell now gone, Garden Pier is the home to the Atlantic City Historical Museum and Arts Center.

So many piers! But what made Steel Pier so different? Why a book focusing on just this one Atlantic City attraction?

The fact that it was open only 13 weeks of the year, Memorial Day to Labor Day and Easter weekend, and presented the biggest stars and bands in the country during that short span could have something to do with it. Maybe paying one low price for everything, including movies, stage shows, exhibits, vaudeville, big bands, rock groups, Motown acts, a diving bell, a diving horse, and a complete water circus, might also weigh in.

Atlantic City piers came in different lengths and with distinctive identities that sustained them for over 80 years, and it must be remembered that television did not exist during most of these piers' lives. The American public had only radio, newspapers, and newsreels to actually know what current events were going on in the world, so when people could witness a diving horse or aerialists dangerously teetering over the ocean or a dog enjoying a romp on water skis, it was something exciting and unique that they had never seen.

What killed off the piers was a combination of a jaded public, changing tastes, and the deterioration of Atlantic City itself. But in their day, these structures built of pilings and wooden planks were unlike anything in the United States.

But only one pier developed the aura and charisma that stood out from the rest and rose up to become the greatest entertainment complex in the world—that was Steel Pier.

One

A Star Is Born

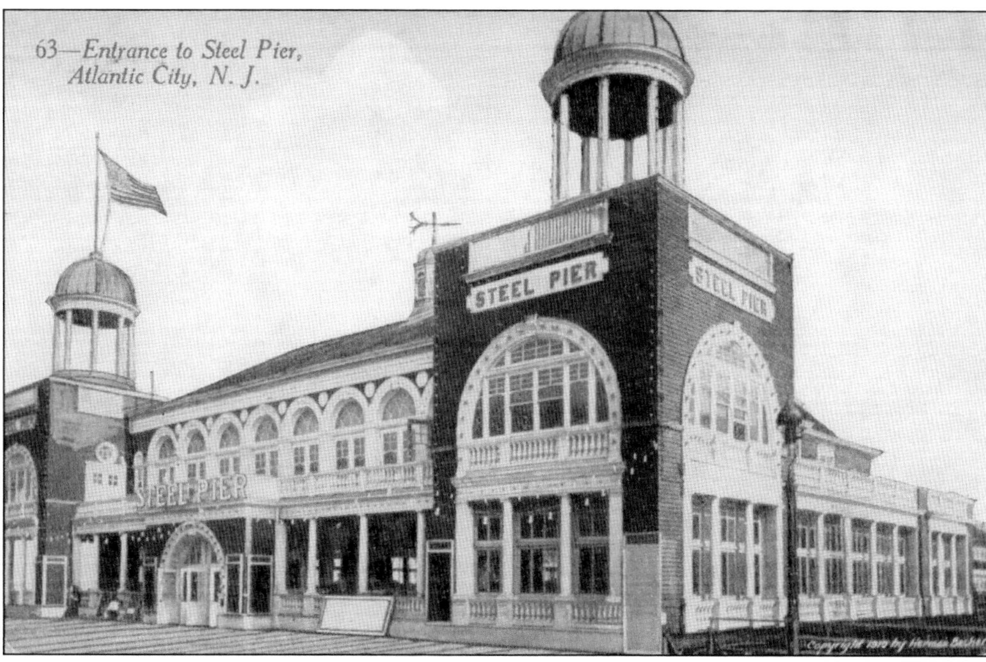

Steel Pier was an immediate hit when it opened on June 18, 1898, and this postcard from 1910 shows why. Designed by Philadelphia architect John T. Windram in a Colonial style, its majestic front Casino building features arched windows, open-air lobbies, and cupolas on each side, framing the entrance. No other pier in Atlantic City offered visitors such elegance and refinement.

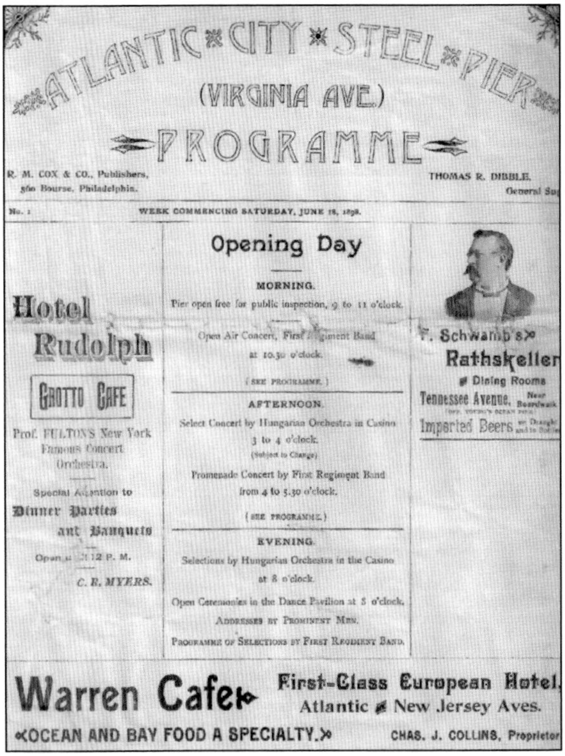

ATLANTIC CITY STEEL PIER
(VIRGINIA AVE.)
PROGRAMME

R. M. COX & CO., Publishers,
560 Bourse, Philadelphia.

THOMAS R. DIBBLE,
General Su

No. 1

WEEK COMMENCING SATURDAY, JUNE 18, 1898.

Hotel Rudolph

GROTTO CAFE

Prof. FULTON'S New York Famous Concert Orchestra.

Special Attention to
Dinner Parties and Banquets

Open until 12 P. M.

C. E. MYERS.

Opening Day

MORNING.

Pier open free for public inspection, 9 to 11 o'clock.

Open Air Concert, First Regiment Band at 10.30 o'clock.

(SEE PROGRAMME.)

AFTERNOON.

Select Concert by Hungarian Orchestra in Casino 3 to 4 o'clock.
(Subject to Change)

Promenade Concert by First Regiment Band from 4 to 5.30 o'clock.

(SEE PROGRAMME.)

EVENING.

Selections by Hungarian Orchestra in the Casino at 8 o'clock.

Open Ceremonies in the Dance Pavilion at 8 o'clock.

ADDRESSES BY PROMINENT MEN.

PROGRAMME OF SELECTIONS BY FIRST REGIMENT BAND.

F. Schwamb's Rathskeller
Dining Rooms
Tennessee Avenue, Near Boardwalk
Imported Beers on Draught and in Bottles

Warren Cafe
First-Class European Hotel,
Atlantic New Jersey Aves.
OCEAN AND BAY FOOD A SPECIALTY.
CHAS. J. COLLINS, Proprietor

The opening-day program promises concerts by military bands, a Hungarian orchestra, the Elite Operatic Minstrels, a children's novelty ball, and a plantation cakewalk. It was a very sedate affair and continued in that fashion for the first 27 years of the pier's existence. Coverage was included in major newspapers, including the *Washington Post.*

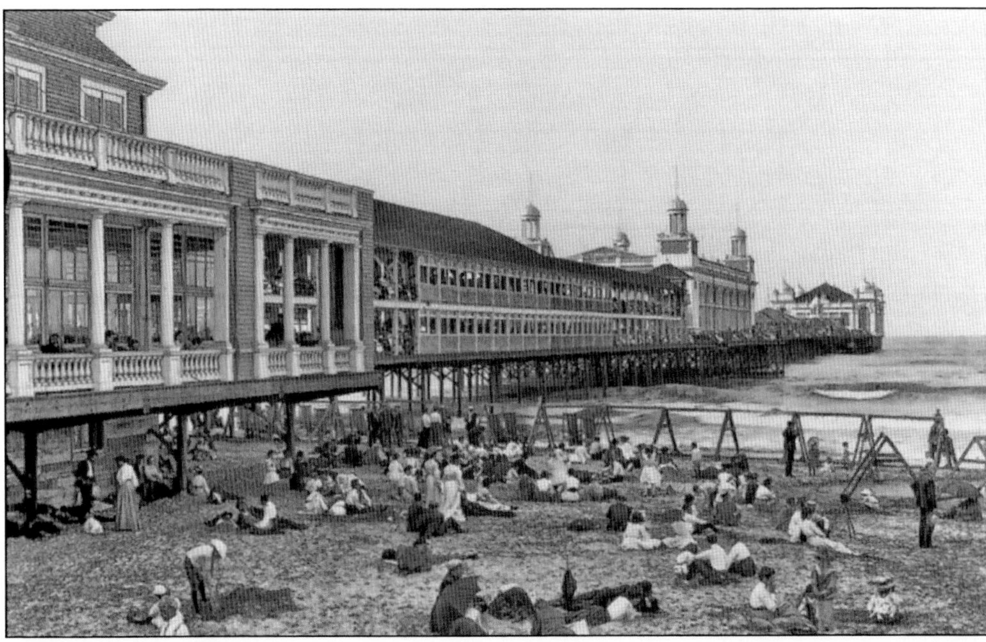

The length of Steel Pier and its buildings is seen from the beach in 1904. The structure at far left held the lobbies and Casino auditorium, home of the minstrels. To the right of the Casino is the two-story, open-air pavilion where patrons relaxed on rocking chairs and benches while enjoying a concert. The Dancing Hall is the square building with four towers, and at the end of the pier is the vast Music Hall with room for thousands of dancers.

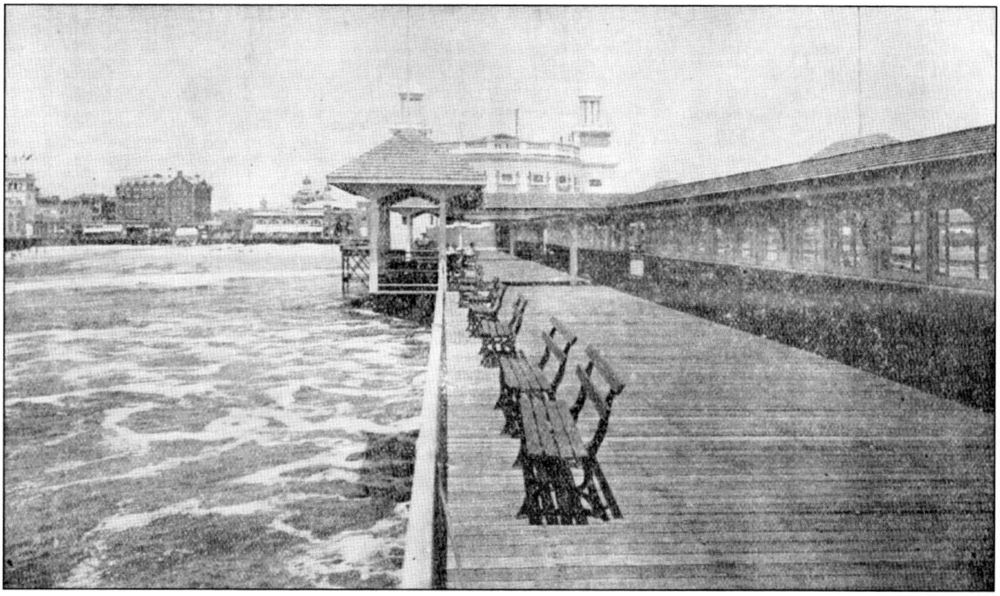

This view from 1904 was captured on the pier and looks back toward the boardwalk. A lengthy promenade for strolling was located between the back end of the Dancing Hall and the front of the Music Hall located at the pier's ocean end. Patrons were very content just to sit on benches and enjoy the view, with many visiting Atlantic City for therapeutic and health reasons.

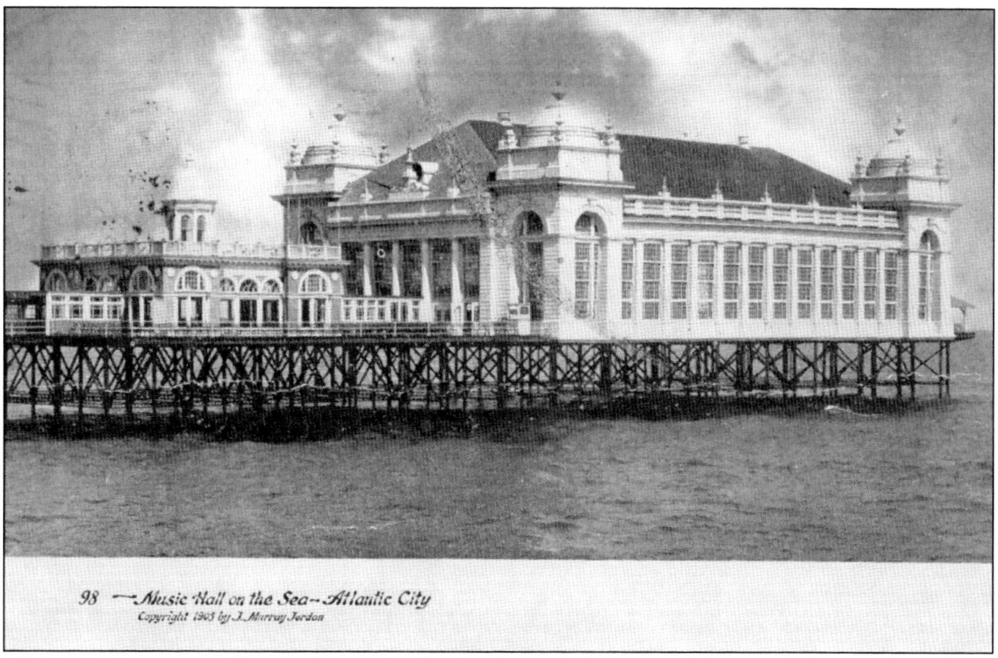

The ornate Music Hall, seen here, was later renamed the Marine Ballroom. To make it more confusing, the middle Dancing Hall was later renamed the Music Hall. To the Music Hall's left is the also ornate Sun Parlor. The iron piles and steel girders can be seen quite clearly, thus giving the pier its distinctive name. Walkway areas were also later built around the Music Hall for safety reasons.

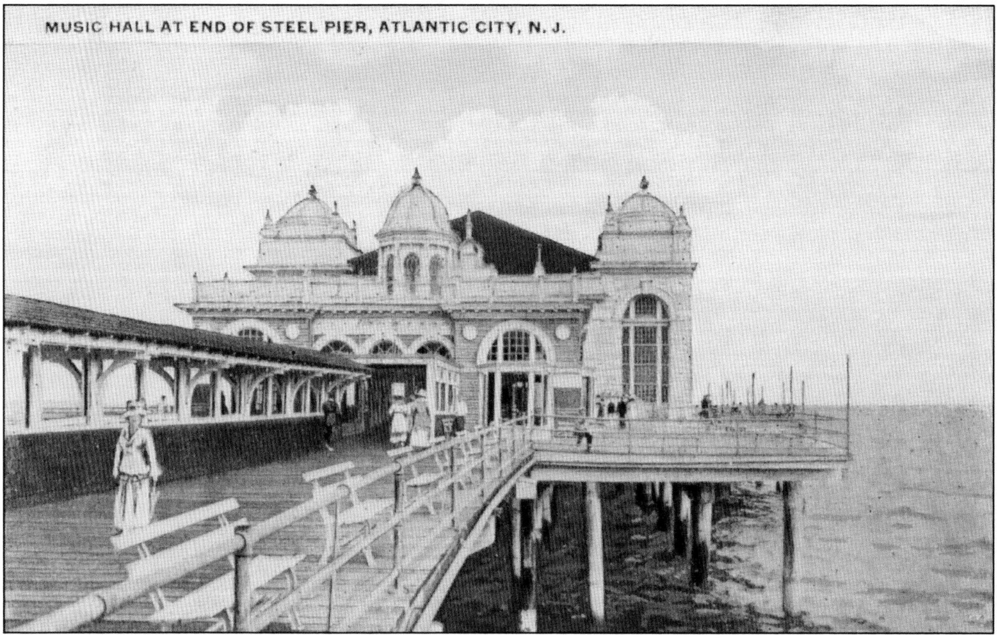

This later view of the Music Hall and Sun Parlor shows off the grand designs that made Steel Pier a major desirable attraction for Atlantic City visitors. The added walkway seen around the Music Hall was useful in later years for those going to the Water Circus area, which was later constructed behind the building.

THE PIER

Daily Schedule

Hungarian Band Concert	11 A. M.
Farce and Vaudeville	11.15 A. M.
Seals Fed	12.30 A. M.
Minstrels	3.30 P. M.
Hungarian Band	3.30 P. M.
Innes and his Band	4 30 P. M.
Farce and Vaudeville	4 30 P. M.
Hungarian Band Concert	7.30 P. M.
Seals Fed	7.30 P. M.
Farce and Vaudeville	7.30 P. M.
Minstrels	8.15 P. M.
Cake Walk, Tuesday and Friday	8.30 P. M.
Children's Carnival, Thursday	8.30 P. M.

Dancing Every Night

Innes and his Band	9.00 P. M.

Additional features specially announced.

A daily schedule from 1899 shows that the pier was open from at least 10:00 a.m. until probably midnight. Patrons could spend all day listening to various bands and orchestras, catching vaudeville or a minstrel program, or just enjoying the seals that were fed twice a day. It was a formula that was simple: offer a little of everything for the whole family to enjoy.

Two

THE COMPETITION

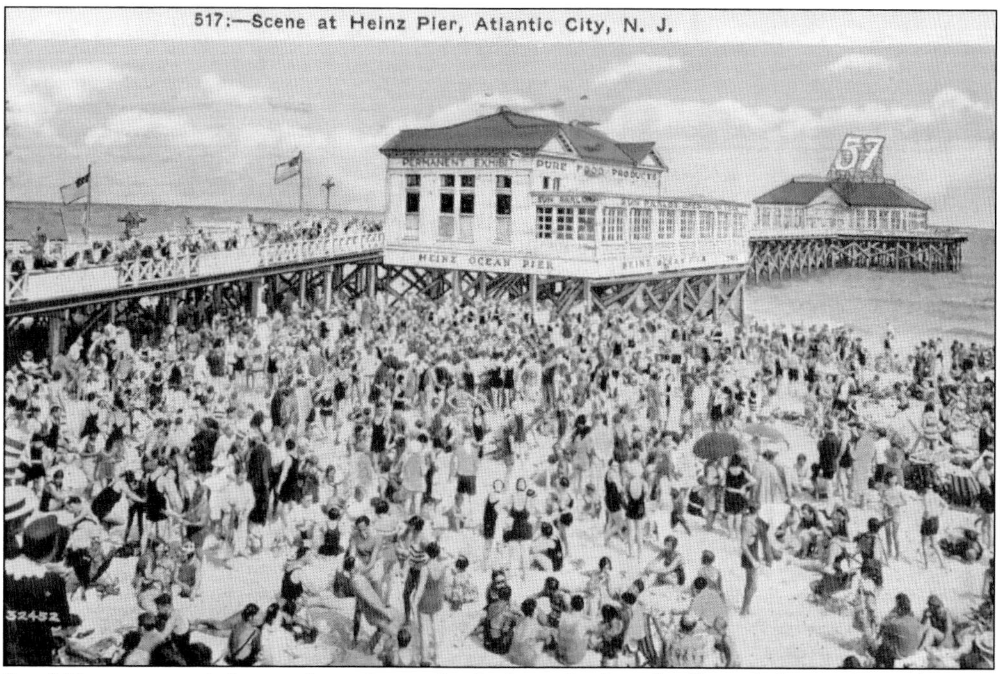

Steel Pier was certainly not the only pier built along the boardwalk in Atlantic City. The Iron Pier opened on April 25, 1886, at Massachusetts Avenue near the boardwalk's north end. About 1898, the H.J. Heinz Company of Pittsburgh, known for its ketchup and other condiments, bought the pier and introduced a very popular promotional pin shaped like a pickle that was given away to visitors. This postcard from 1928 displays a small front building, which held exhibits and a sun parlor. The ocean building was noted for its large neon "57" sign, proclaiming Heinz's popular advertising slogan.

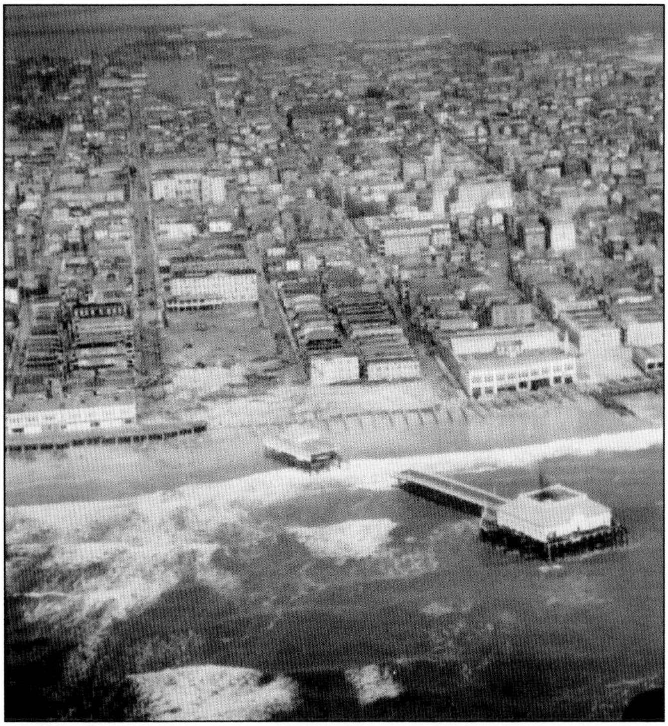

An airplane view of Heinz Pier after the September 1944 hurricane shows almost complete destruction. The pier was the smallest, oldest, and probably the most delicate of the piers existing at that time. Taking into account the fact that Heinz Pier was situated away from the other piers and received less foot traffic, it was easily decided not to rebuild. It was demolished a short time thereafter.

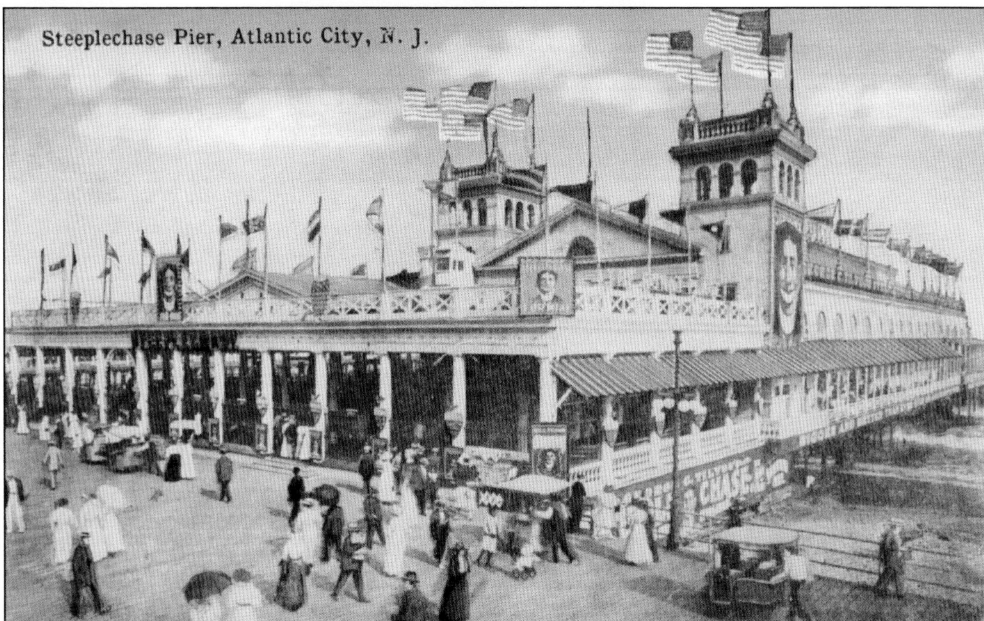

Auditorium Pier opened on August 25, 1899, a year after Steel Pier. It was located just one block away at Pennsylvania Avenue, perhaps a little too close for comfort. But it was an entirely different type of pier. When George C. Tilyou of Coney Island's Steeplechase Park bought and renamed it, the pier became known for hijinks and amusements. On this 1918 postcard, one can easily see the display of the famous broad smiling face and showy teeth of Tilyou's caricature that could also be found on the Palace Amusements building in Asbury Park.

This 1931 ad explains the whole purpose of Steeplechase Pier. It was all about fun and frolic—basically the same formula that held true to Steeplechase Park in Coney Island. It offered rides, fun houses, and a "Babyland" for the kiddies within its 51 attractions.

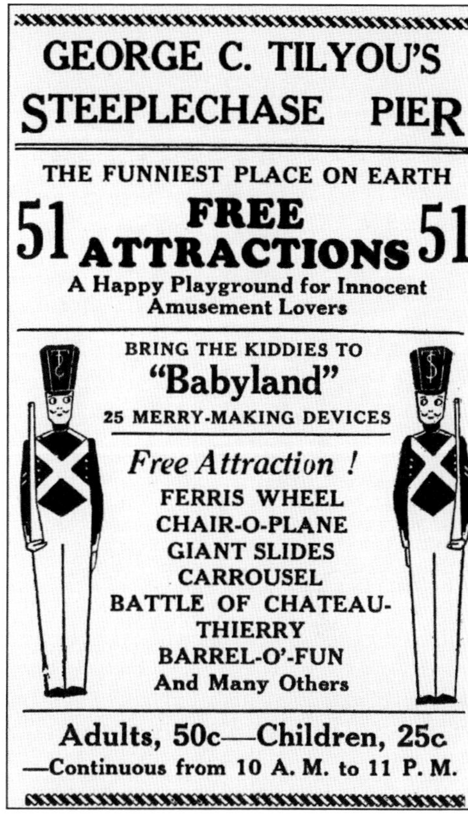

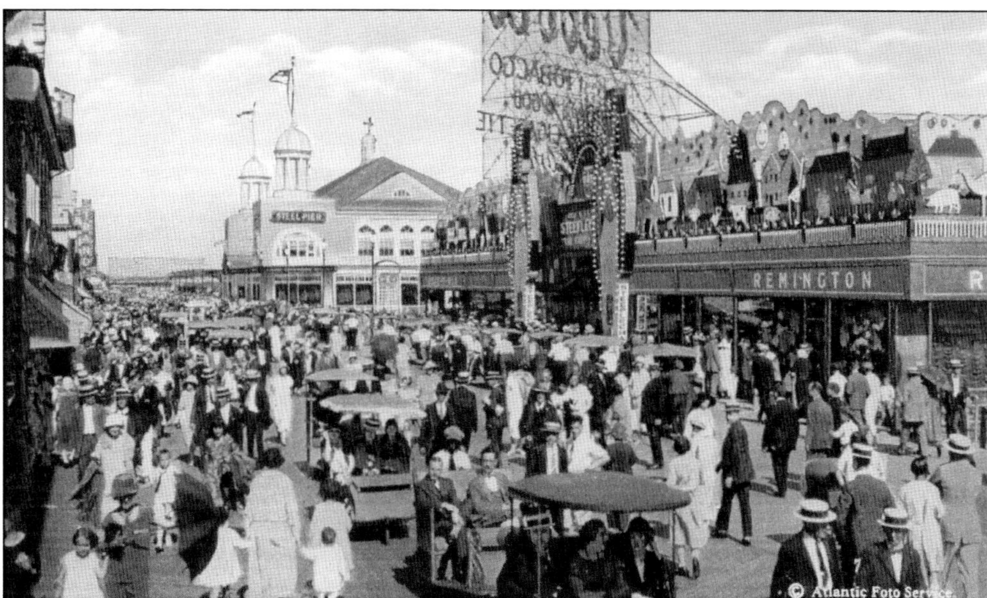

Steeplechase and Steel Pier were friendly neighbors for decades. As seen around 1930, Steeplechase is promoting Remington typewriters in one of its boardwalk lobbies. Companies such as Dupont, General Motors, Crane, and Texaco promoted their products along Atlantic City's boardwalk during this time as educational exhibits designed to produce more sales.

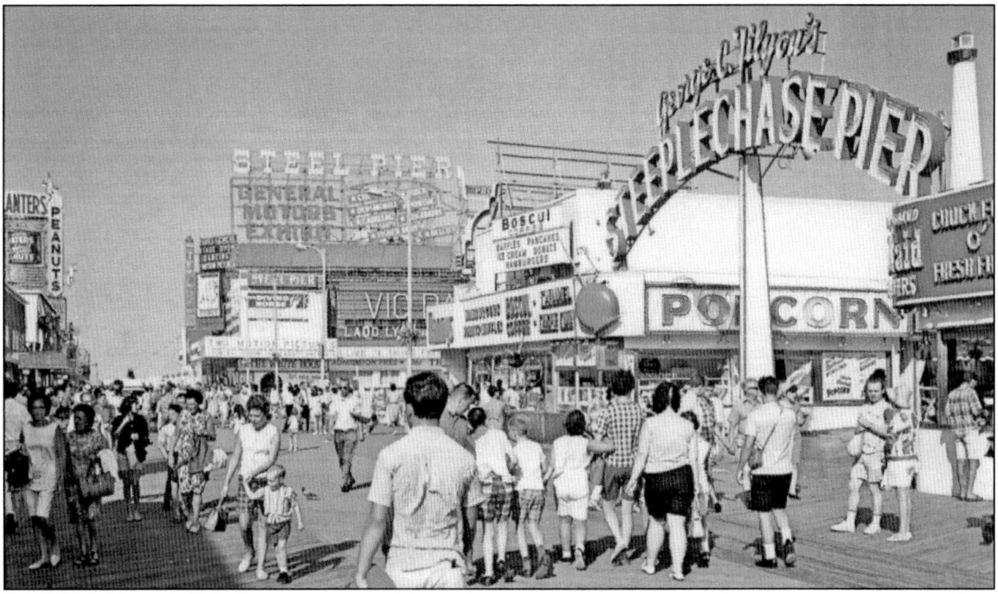

Steeplechase unfortunately burned to the ground on Valentine's Day 1932. It remained rubble for a few years and then was partially rebuilt as a long thin pier named Calvert Pier, due to the giant neon sign of the same name displayed on its front. Finally, after World War II, Steeplechase was rebuilt as a shorter, open-air amusement pier. This picture from 1965 shows the carnival-like front of Steeplechase.

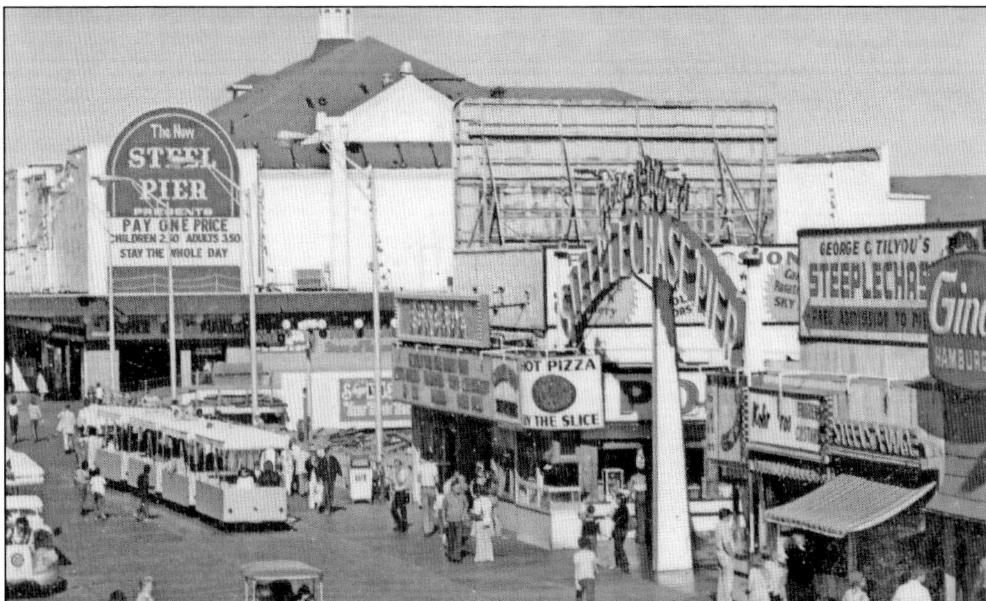

Here is a similar shot from 1977. Steel Pier was in its last years, the familiar signage from the 1930s already stripped away, exposing the Casino building as it pretty much looked at its 1898 opening. Steeplechase itself would last into the 1980s. The old structure was finally closed due to safety concerns in 1986, and the remainder burned down in December 1988. A small portion of the fun pier's platform remained connected to the boardwalk years after. Today, a beach bar and restaurant stands in its place.

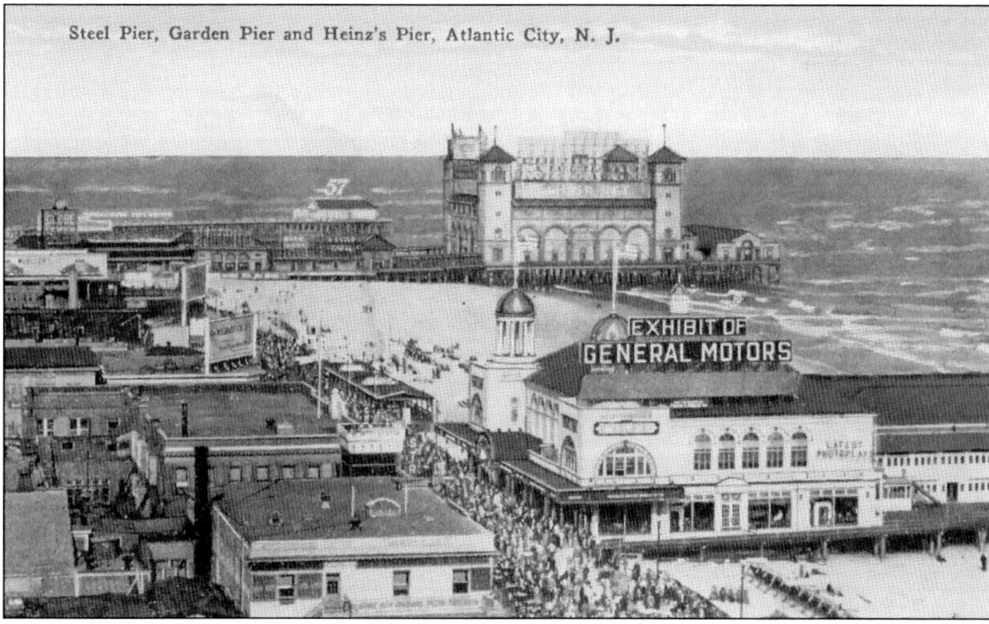

The unique Garden Pier was a latecomer to the boardwalk. Opening July 19, 1913, Garden Pier was simply that, with landscaped gardens throughout the center of the structure. This 1927 view depicts Spanish-tiled exhibition buildings and a tremendous theater and ballroom. Not a long pier, it nevertheless offered big-time B.F. Keith vaudeville as well as dances with Cab Calloway and Fletcher Henderson's band. Rarely did African American bands play to white audiences in the early 1930s, due to Atlantic City's strict segregation policy. Only white bands played the piers, although Henderson did play Million Dollar Pier in July 1930.

This is a 1924 picture of the theater and exhibit areas on Garden Pier. The great magician Harry Houdini escaped from being shackled and bound and suspended upside down from the top of the theater's towers in 1917 while thousands watched from below and on the beach. A popular pier exhibit was the world's largest typewriter, built by the Underwood Typewriter Company, that stood 18 feet high and could hold a person on each key.

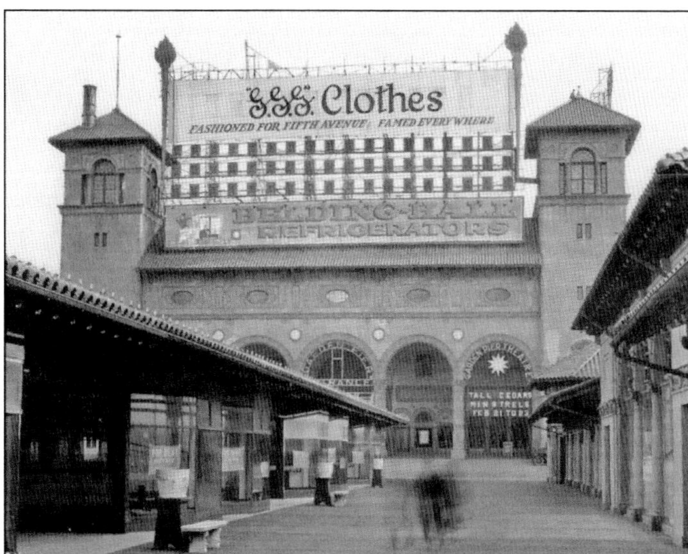

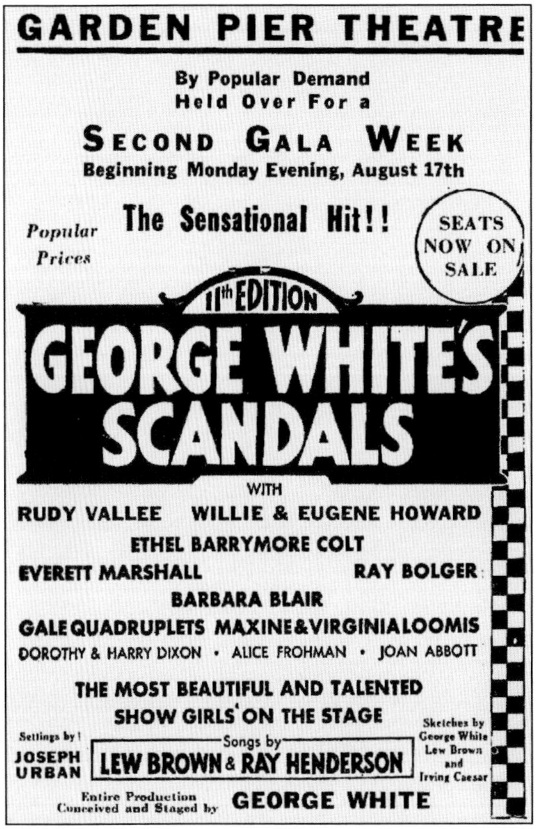

After vaudeville waned in the 1920s, Garden Pier's theater presented large-scale movies, such as Cecil B. DeMille's original *The Ten Commandments*. Pre-Broadway stage plays and musicals also abounded, with Al Jolson, Gypsy Rose Lee, the Three Stooges, and Milton Berle as the stars. This ad for the 1931 version of *George White's Scandals* presents a stellar cast. Garden Pier was badly damaged during the 1944 hurricane and was completely remodeled in the 1950s as an outside performance area with a band shell. Today, the much shorter pier is the location of the Atlantic City Historical Museum and the Arts Center. Curiously, the original 1913 pilings that held up the theater on the ocean end were still there until 2013, a hundred years later.

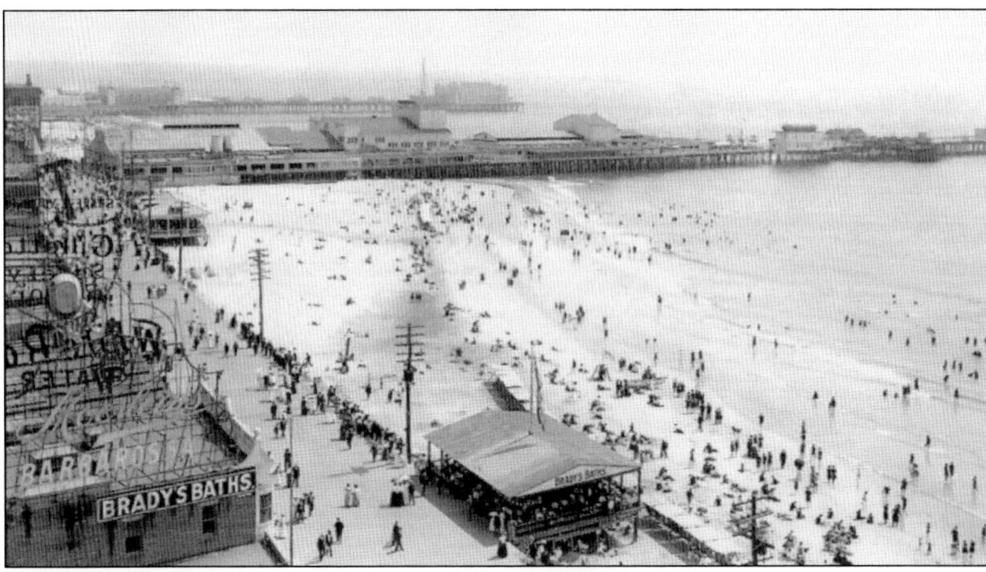

The old Applegate Pier at Tennessee Avenue was a small, early pier that opened in 1884. When entrepreneurs John L. Young and Stewart McShea bought it in 1891 and renamed it Ocean Pier, they built an almost 2,000-foot mega-monster that had something for everyone. Young, born in 1853 outside of Atlantic City in Absecon, was the first of the great boardwalk showmen. McShea retired in 1897 and left the pier to Young, whose creativity would make him a millionaire.

An 1899 ad for Young's Ocean Pier offers an idea of the variety of activities presented. Young began the novel net hauls, a twice-daily undertaking of large nets raising fresh fish and sea creatures out of the ocean. Young and his wife also lived right on the pier in an English Tudor–style cottage, where it was said he fished from his kitchen window. The pier had an enclosed ballroom for dances, a children's carnival, sacred concerts, and an exhibition of infant incubators. Sarah Bernhardt, the most famous actress of the day, appeared on June 6, 1906, for one night only in *Camille*. Tickets ranged from $1 to $3, an unheard of price. Nevertheless, the theater was sold out.

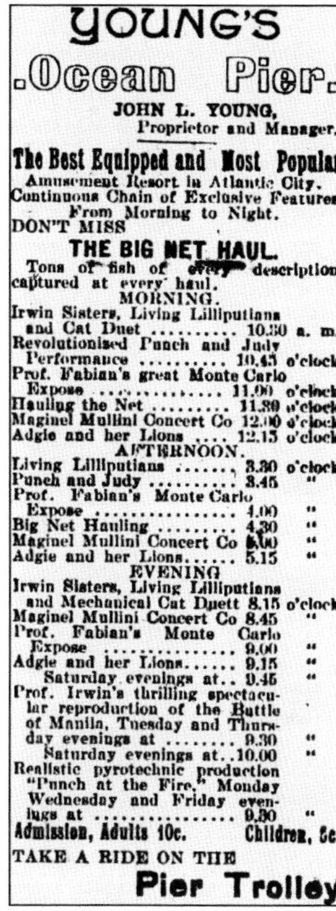

On March 29, 1912, most of Young's Ocean Pier burned in a large fire. The ballroom was rebuilt for movies and dancing, and, for the most part, the front remained in tack. The Old Pier, as it was now called, took on a new breath of life when it was bought by investors. This image from the early 1920s shows the morphing of Young's facade into the renamed Central Pier.

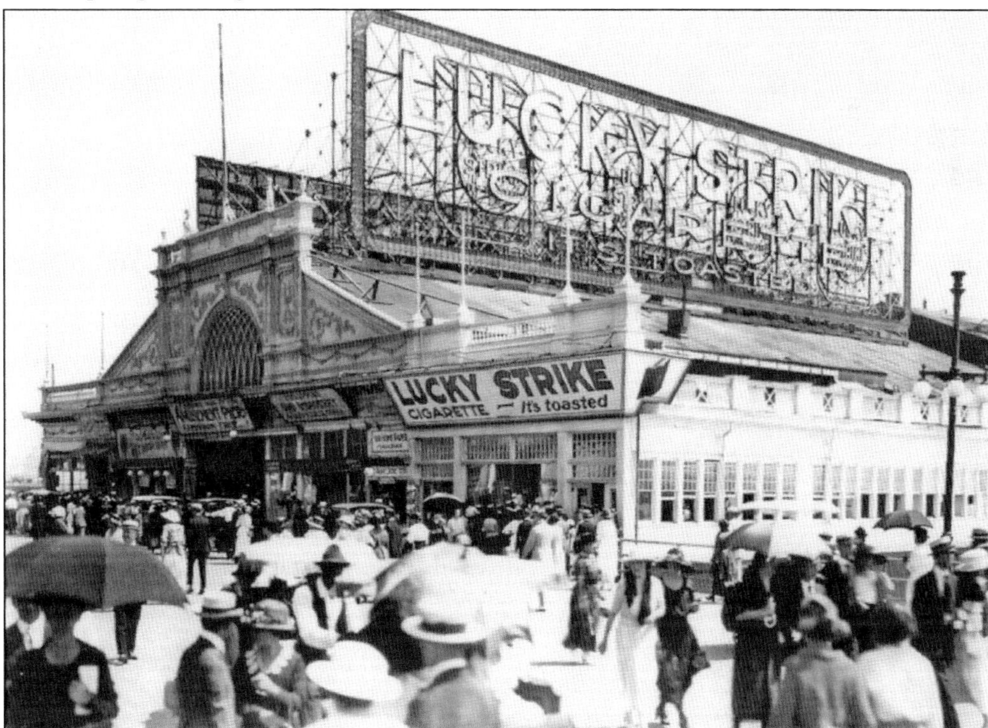

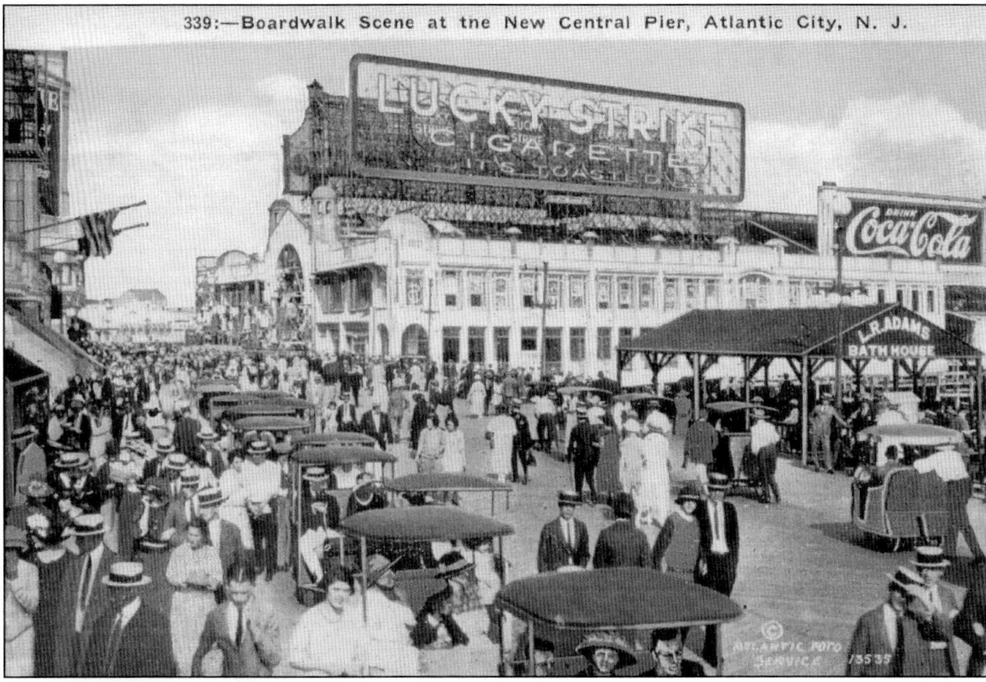

The new Moorish facade of Central Pier was built in 1922. Notice the Lucky Strike signage still in place from the previous picture. On a much shorter pier than Young's Ocean Pier, Central Pier's building had offices and exhibits on its two floors with rides added in the 1950s on the ocean end. The pier's facade looks exactly the same today and is the oldest pier architecture on the Atlantic City boardwalk.

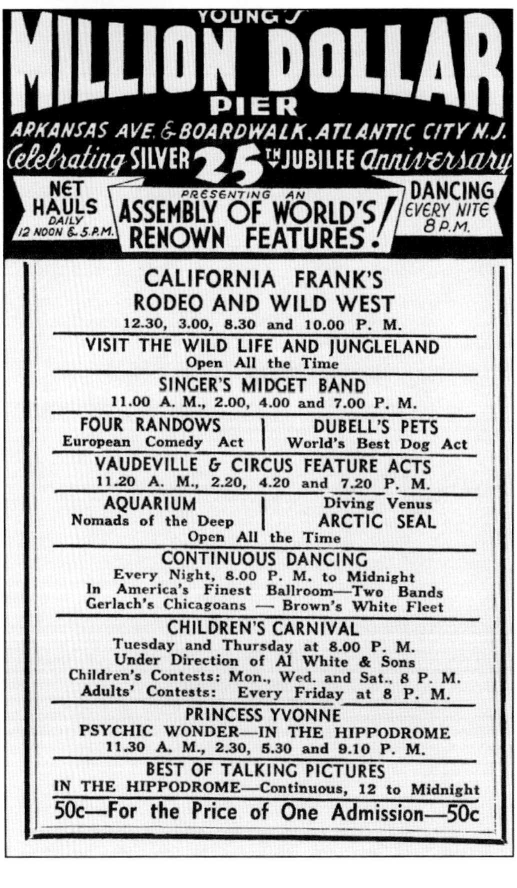

If Steel Pier had never been built, Young's new Million Dollar Pier would have probably been the pier most people would remember. It opened on July 26, 1906, and John Young spent a million dollars building the most extravagant pier yet for the masses. Architecturally much more pleasing to the eye than the boxy Ocean Pier, his new pier still featured net hauls, as seen in this 1931 advertisement, but also offered movies, vaudeville, and a circus.

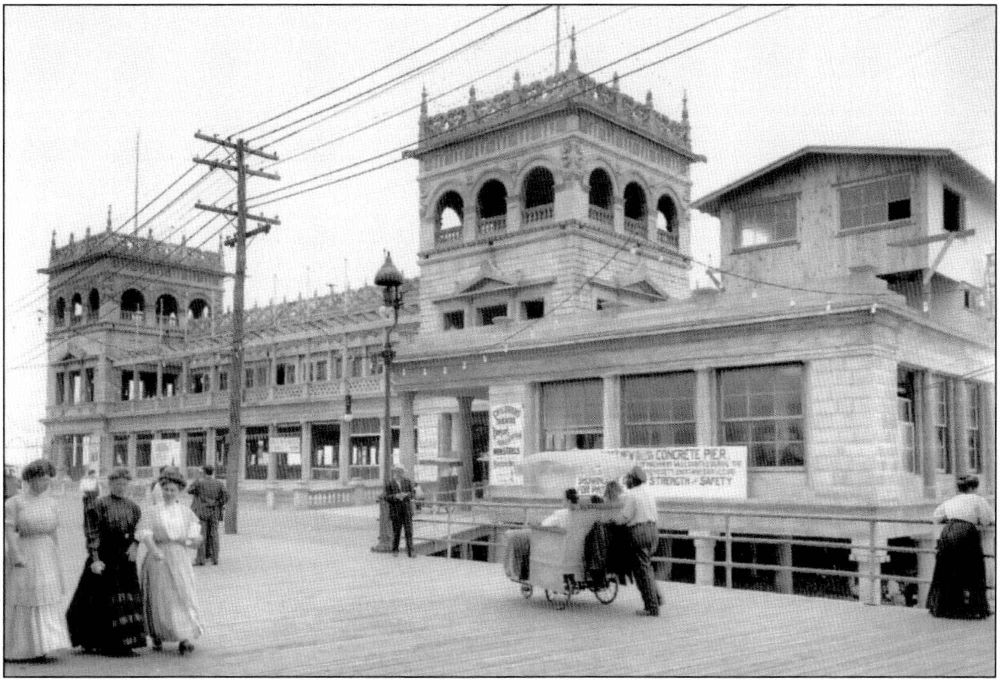

The Million Dollar Pier's ornate front is seen in 1908, when it was just two years old. Stretching 1,700 feet out to sea, the pier at Arkansas Avenue was the farthest south on the boardwalk. This front building contained the lobby and large ballroom, which was filled with thousands of ceiling lights and two bandstands.

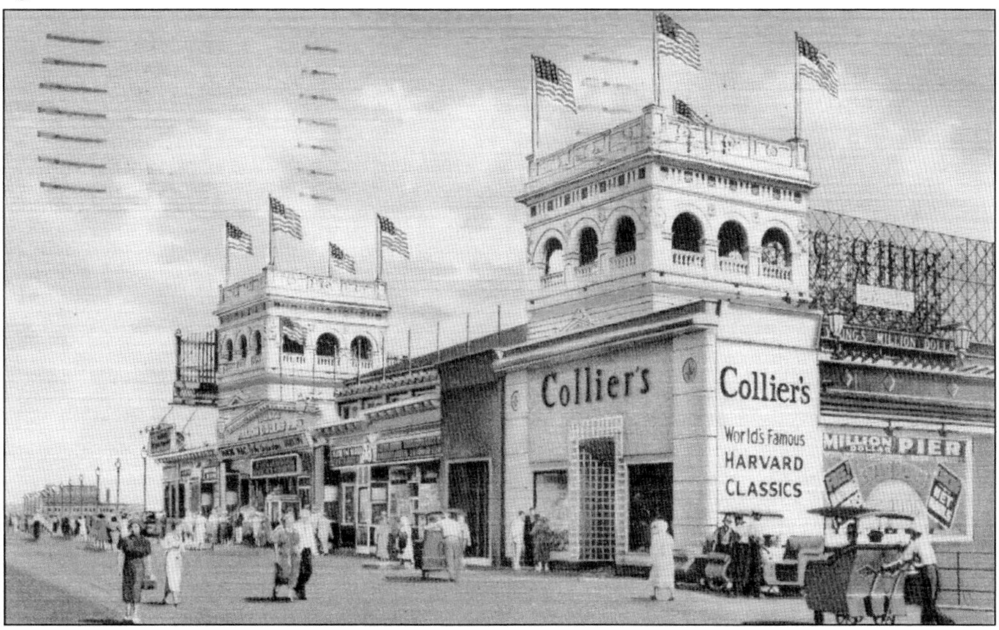

The same location is pictured in 1937, which was the last year the pier was under Young's supervision. By then over 30 years old, the front open porches were now built over and utilized by exhibits from *Collier's* magazine and other businesses. A bit of the ornamentation is also gone or modernized. As the piers' infrastructure aged, upgrades and remodeling were a common necessity.

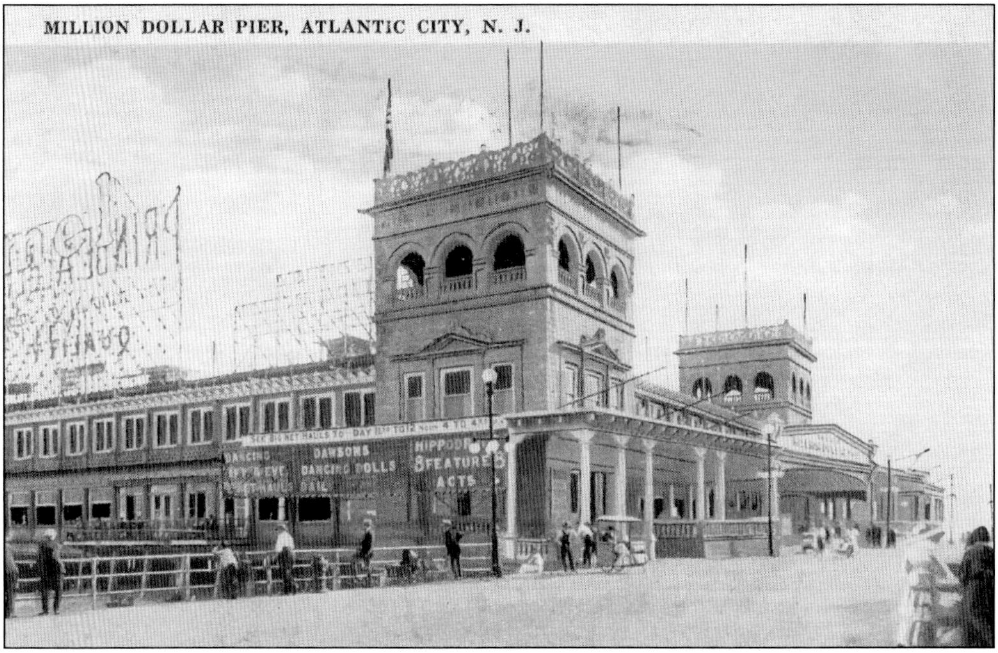

In a 1922 postcard, Million Dollar Pier's north facade still has the open porch and ornamentation from earlier years. Noticeable is the large Camel cigarettes sign, which could be seen far down the boardwalk. Simple signs announce the net hauls, dancing, and vaudeville in the Hippodrome theater.

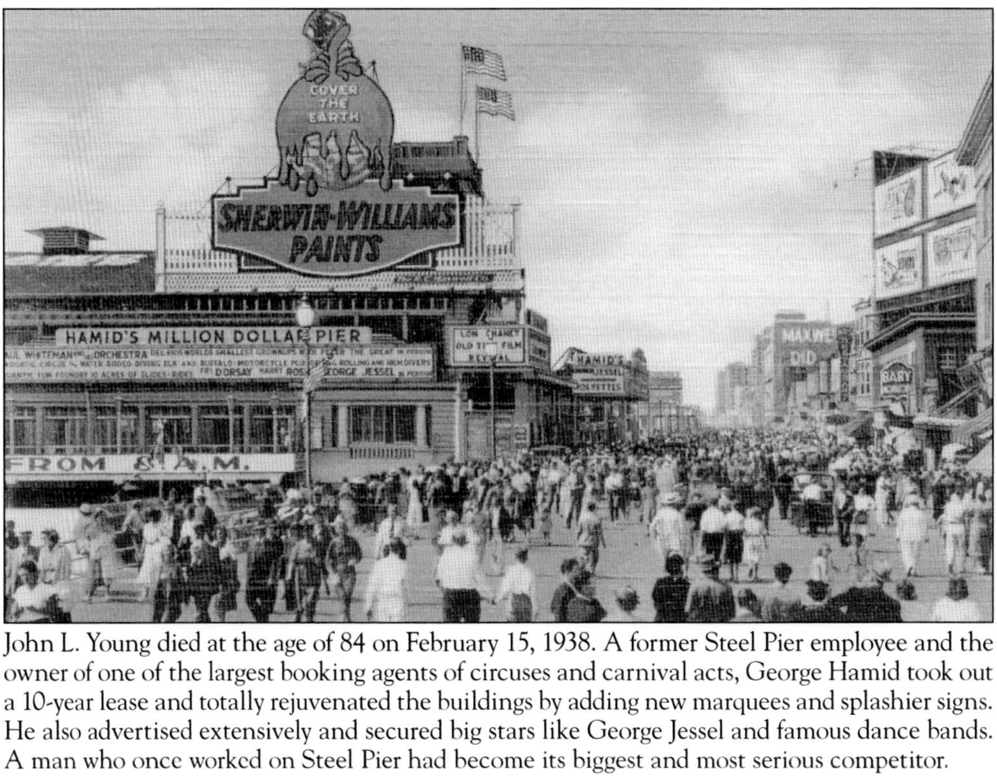

John L. Young died at the age of 84 on February 15, 1938. A former Steel Pier employee and the owner of one of the largest booking agents of circuses and carnival acts, George Hamid took out a 10-year lease and totally rejuvenated the buildings by adding new marquees and splashier signs. He also advertised extensively and secured big stars like George Jessel and famous dance bands. A man who once worked on Steel Pier had become its biggest and most serious competitor.

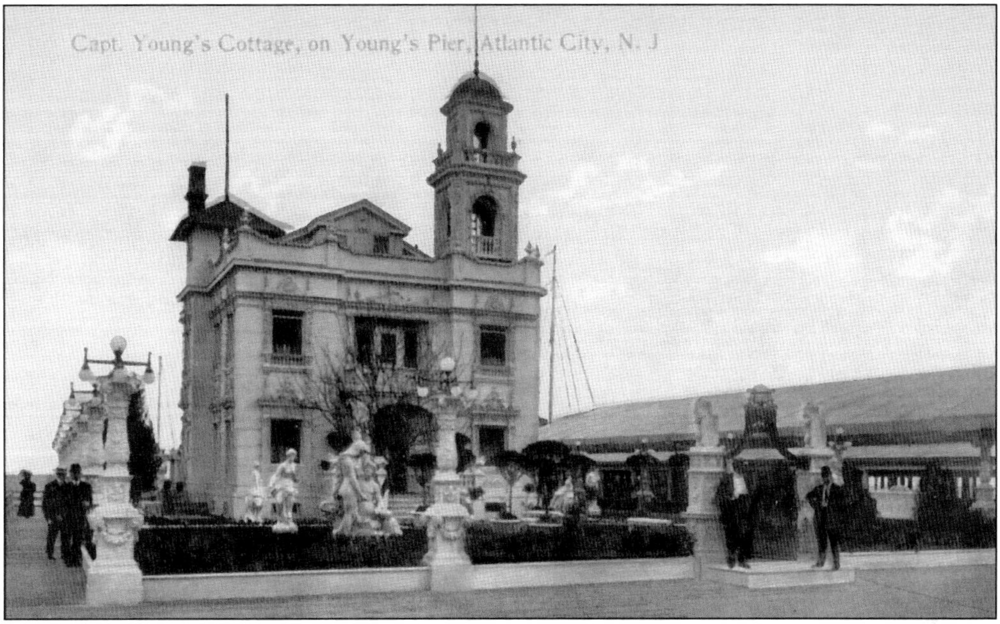

Young built a three-story, 12-room Victorian mansion on Million Dollar Pier, which he famously named No. 1 Atlantic Ocean. He and his wife lived there and welcomed guests such as Thomas Edison, composer Victor Herbert, and Pres. William Howard Taft. This postcard from 1912 shows the many statues from Italy that were displayed in the garden.

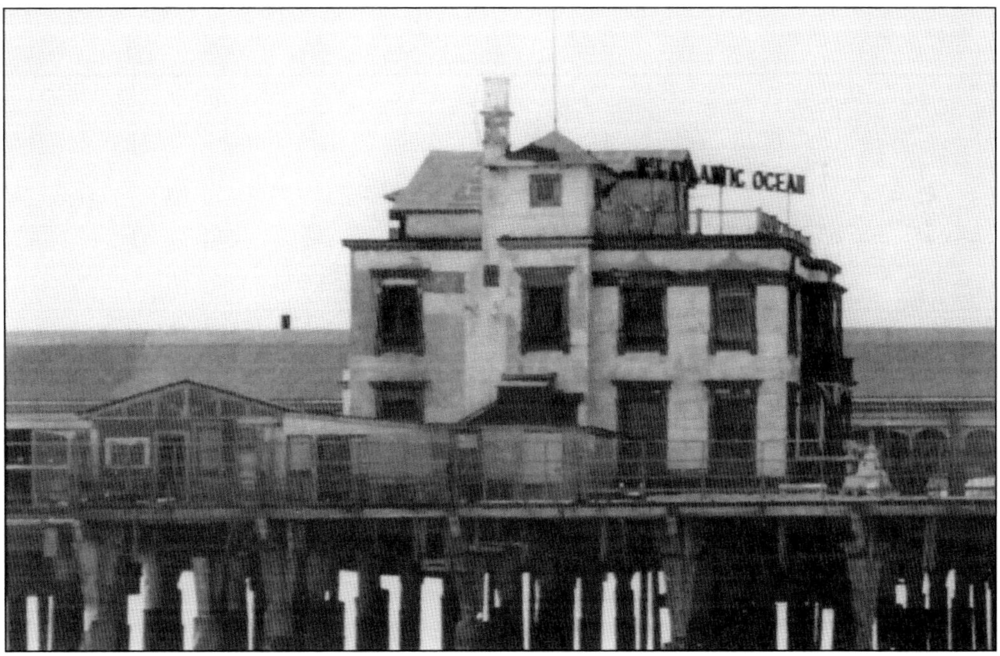

Seen here is the same No. 1 Atlantic Ocean in 1950 as a relic from a different era. With the mansion's cupola removed and the structure vacant, it was demolished in 1953. George Hamid and his family had lived there during the summers he leased the pier, but it was known to be damp as there was no subbasement. It was built right on top of the wooden boards, with the sea churning below.

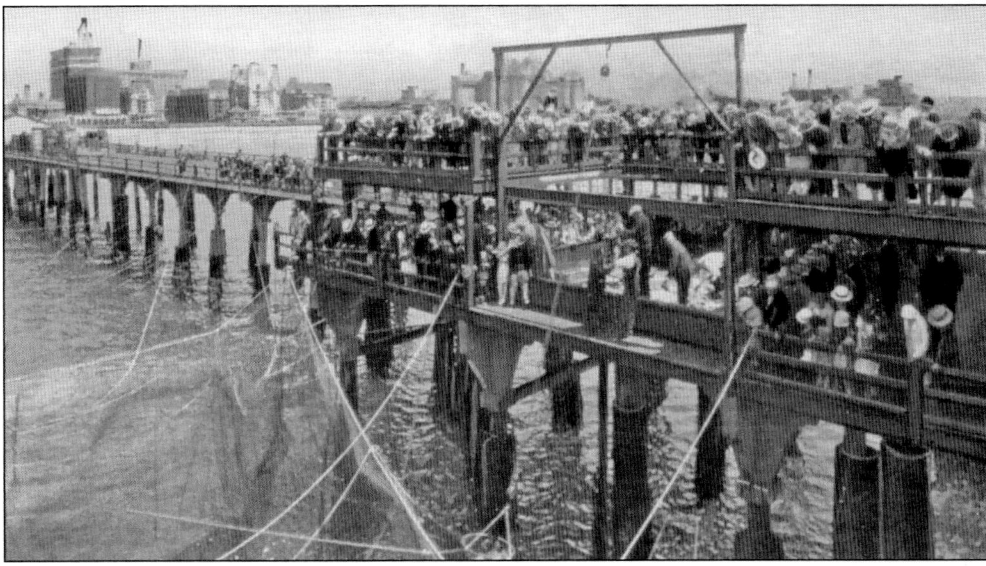

The famous net hauls located almost 1,700 feet out over the ocean at the pier's end were the top attraction on Million Dollar Pier. The practice lasted as late as 1956, until it was deemed unsafe due to pier deterioration. The twice-daily hauls enabled many of Atlantic City's fine restaurants to offer fresh seafood taken directly from the pier. John Young's nickname was "Captain" due to his expertise on sea life, and he would regularly participate in the net hauls and explain the various species of sea life caught.

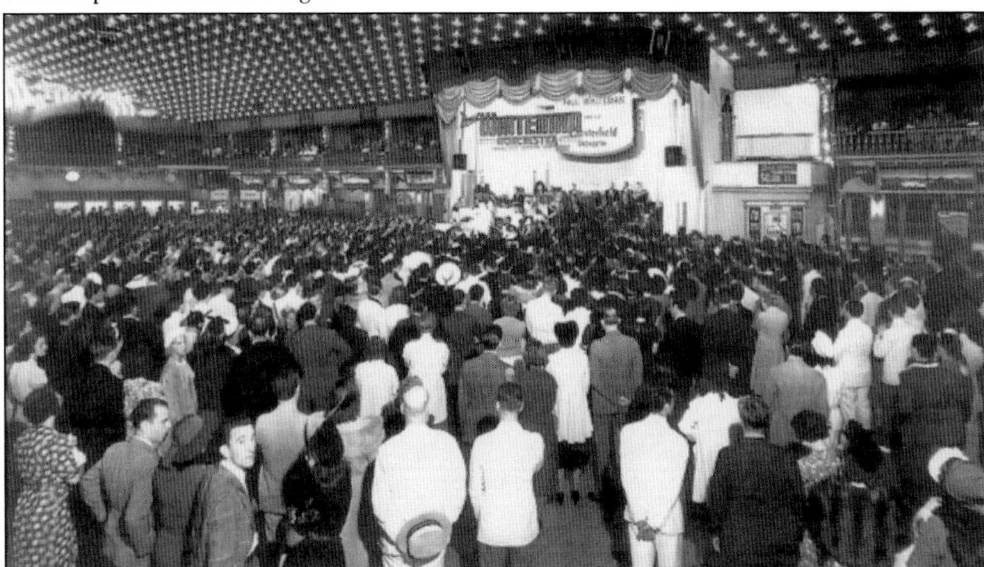

Paul Whiteman and his orchestra play in the Ballroom of States in 1938. The ballroom, located on Million Dollar Pier's front as opposed to the Marine Ballroom on Steel Pier's ocean end, was magnificent. It had not only a ceiling of lights, but also two bandstands facing each other on opposite walls. When the house band stopped playing, the name band began. Glenn Miller, Woody Herman, and Artie Shaw all played here, as did the Miss America Pageants in 1926 and 1927. Even still, its location on the front of the pier just did not offer the romantic vibe many had while dancing out over the ocean on Steel Pier.

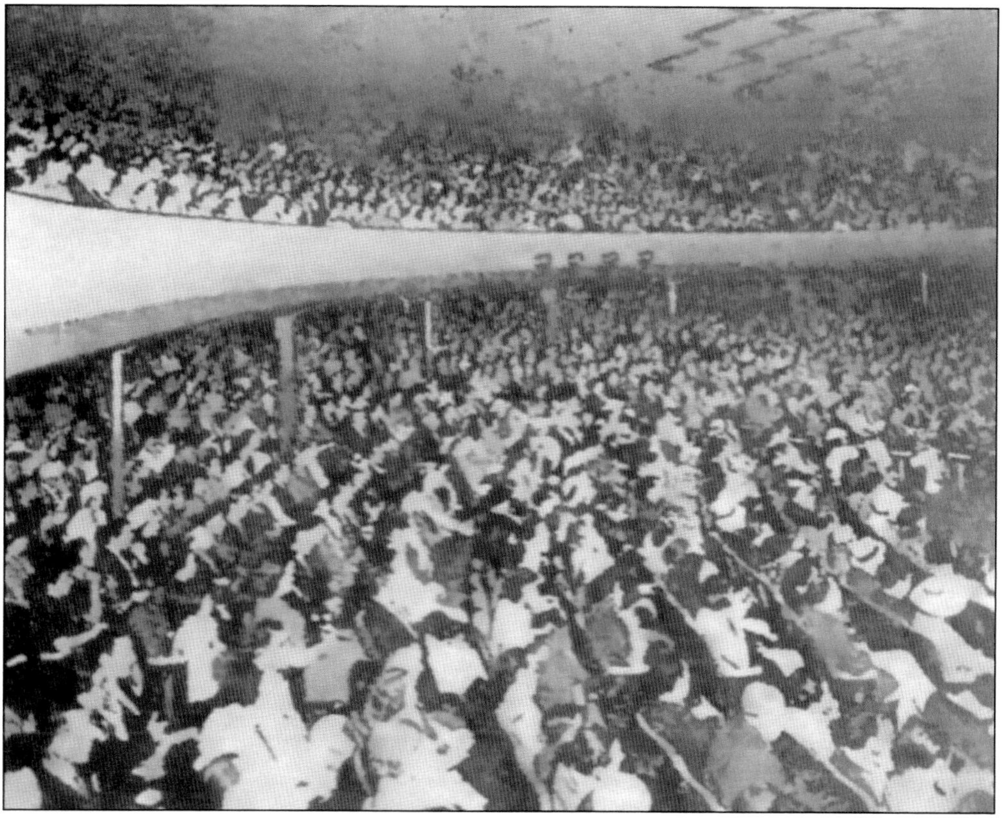

Pictures of Million Dollar Pier are not nearly abundant as those of Steel Pier. George Hamid remodeled the Hippodrome, the middle building on the pier, which boasted of 4,000 seats in 1922. Above is a very rare picture of the Hippodrome theater in 1938. This image is one of the few known to exist showing the interior of the venue. Many famous stars played here and it later hosted Broadway plays and revues, from 1950 to 1952. The ballroom was destroyed by fire on September 13, 1949, leaving a tremendous gap on the pier's boardwalk end, which was then filled with rides. The Hippodrome was gutted in the 1950s and became the popular Italian Village, as seen below in 1964. The structure sustained a major fire in 1969 and was almost entirely torn down except for the towers, seen here to the left of the Goldwater billboard. This last portion of the once-grand Hippodrome lasted until October 12, 1981, when fire again struck.

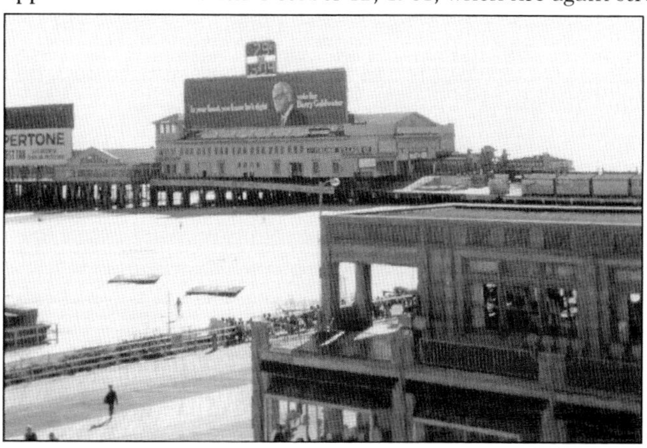

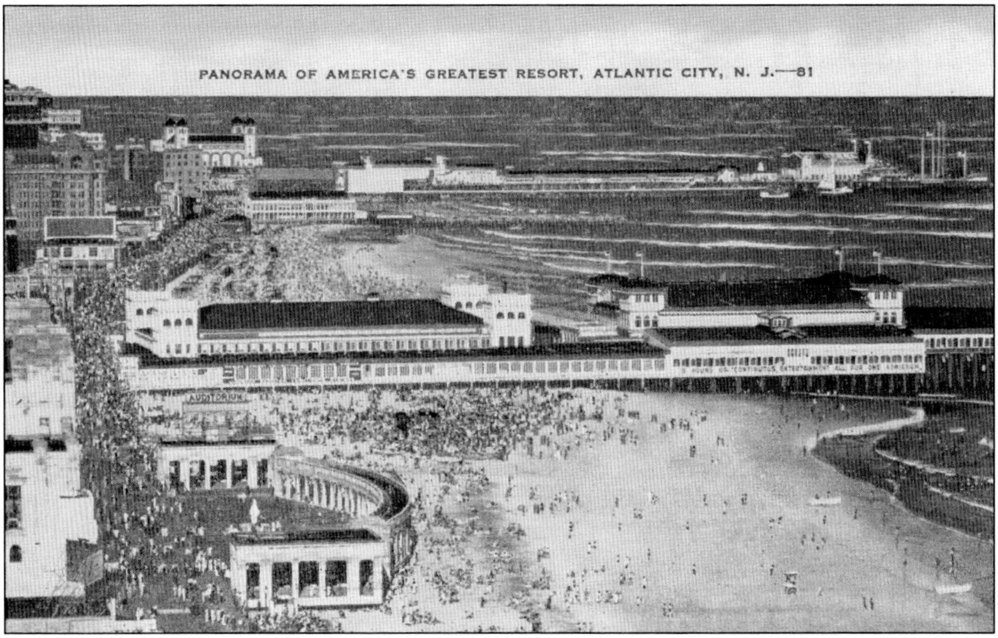

With Steel Pier in the background, Million Dollar Pier's majestic ballroom and Hippodrome buildings stand out. In the foreground to the left is the plaza of Convention Hall. The crowd on the beach next to the pier is probably made up of African Americans. Due to the segregation in Atlantic City, black people could only utilize this portion of the beach, which became fondly known as "Chicken Bone Beach" due to the abundance of picnic lunches. Sammy Davis Jr. and Nat "King" Cole were just two of the performers who were welcomed along this stretch.

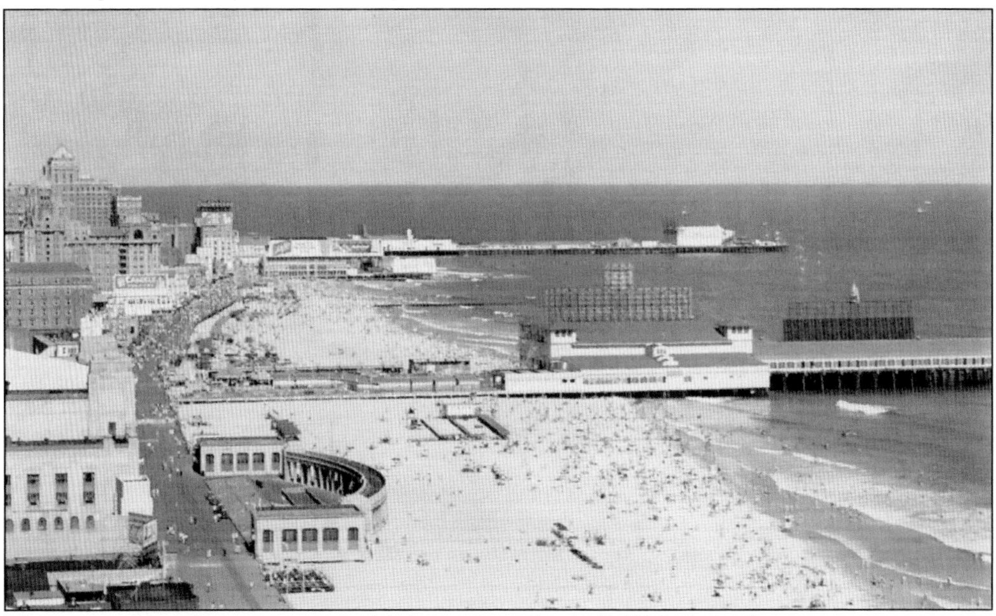

This picture shows the same section of Atlantic City after 1949. With the ballroom gone, amusements take up the open area. A well-remembered ride was the Orient Express, whose facade displayed a large overhanging dragon billowing smoke. The billboard on the right marks the location of Captain Young's mansion.

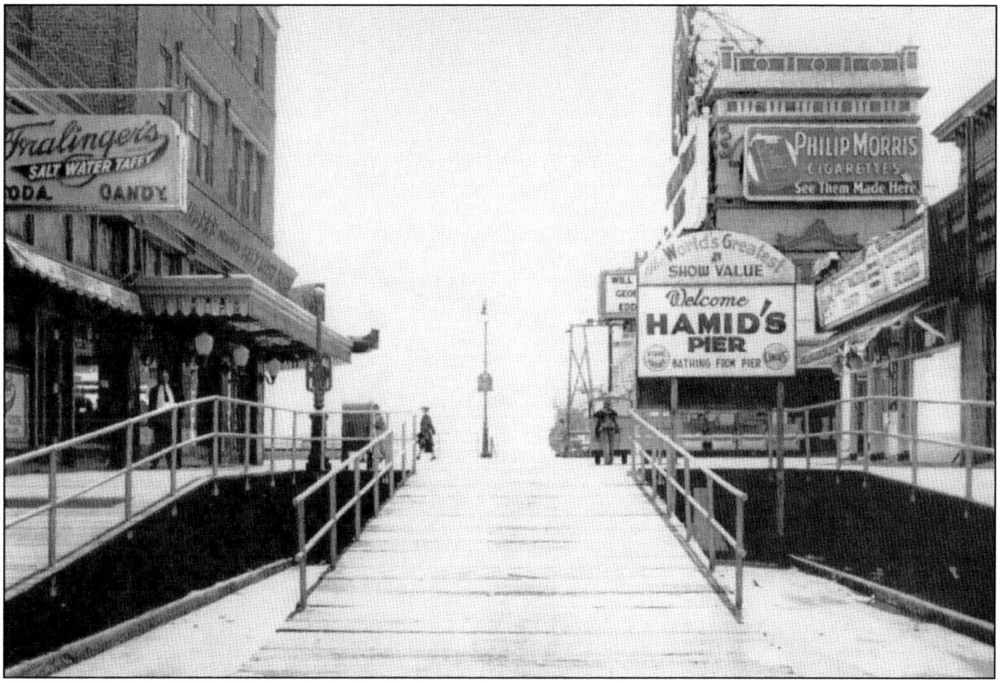

This view looks at Hamid's Million Dollar Pier in 1940 from the Arkansas Avenue boardwalk ramp. A Fralinger Salt Water Taffy store, one of many on the boardwalk since 1885, beckons on the left. The candy got its name from an early boardwalk merchant whose items were drenched with a large surf. Even though there is not salt water in any taffy, the name stuck.

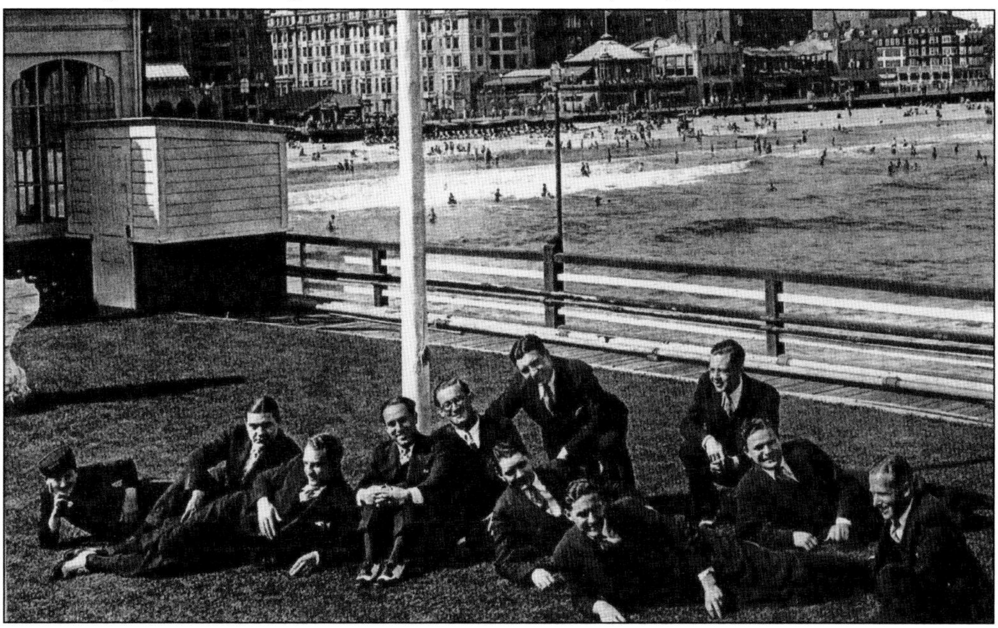

In 1928, the Ben Pollack orchestra lounges in the front yard of No. 1 Atlantic Ocean. Pollack is fourth from left, and rising star trombonist Jack Teagarden is second from left. The fellow stretched out in the foreground is a then unknown Benny Goodman. Many hot bands played the pier in the 1920s, including Isham Jones, Jean Goldkette, and Coon-Sanders.

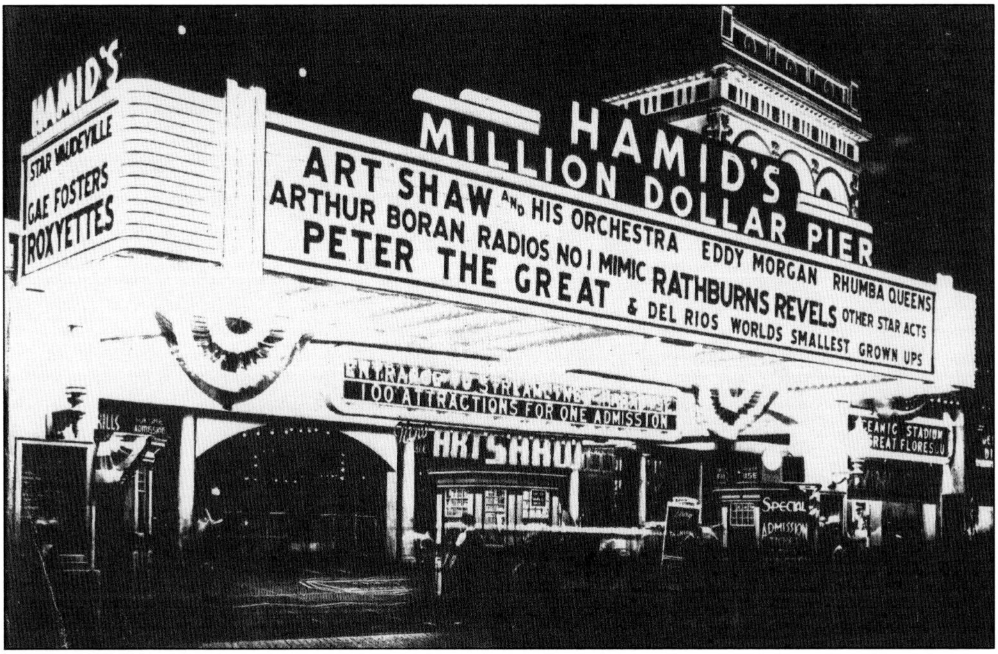

Million Dollar Pier is lit up like a million dollars in 1938, George Hamid's first year of supervision. Artie Shaw went by Art then, but when his version of "Begin the Beguine" became a big hit shortly after this picture was taken, he changed his name. Hamid spent a small fortune completely overhauling the pier and adding billboards to New Jersey roadsides.

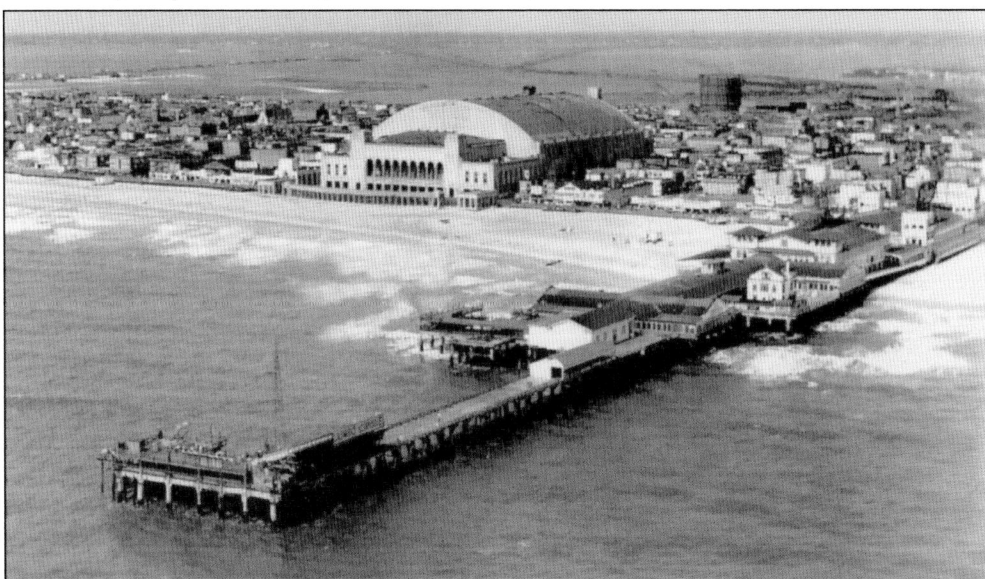

From the ocean, the pier's rectangular buildings narrow to a long walkway that ends with the net haul area. Young's mansion can be seen halfway down the pier on the right, and another net haul can be seen closer in. Hamid turned the outer area into a Jumbo Circus, erecting a large seating area. He searched around the world for his acts and always found unique animals and aerialists that would thrill audiences. Clyde Beatty, the famed animal trainer, led the circus in 1939. The massive Convention Hall is seen in the background.

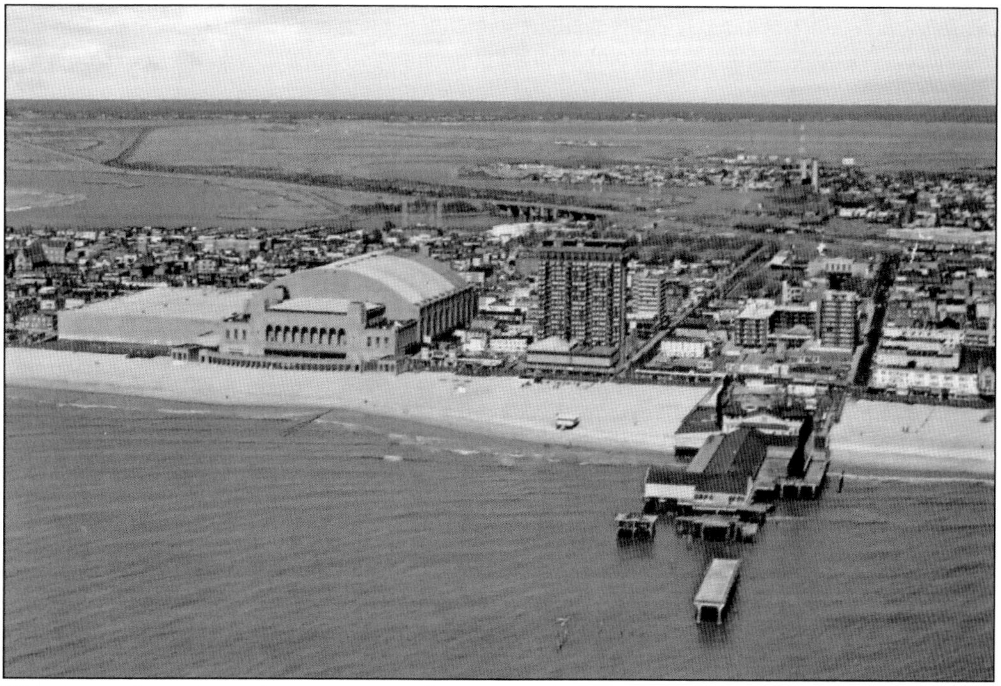

This is another picture from out over the ocean, this time in the early 1970s. The pier has deteriorated, with its long walkway eaten up by storms and the sea. The outlined remains of the net hauls are apparent, and the vacant space where No. 1 Atlantic Ocean stood can also be seen. With few renovations, the once-fantastic pier was now a decrepit memory. The tall square building is the new Holiday Inn, the first boardwalk hotel to be built in almost 40 years.

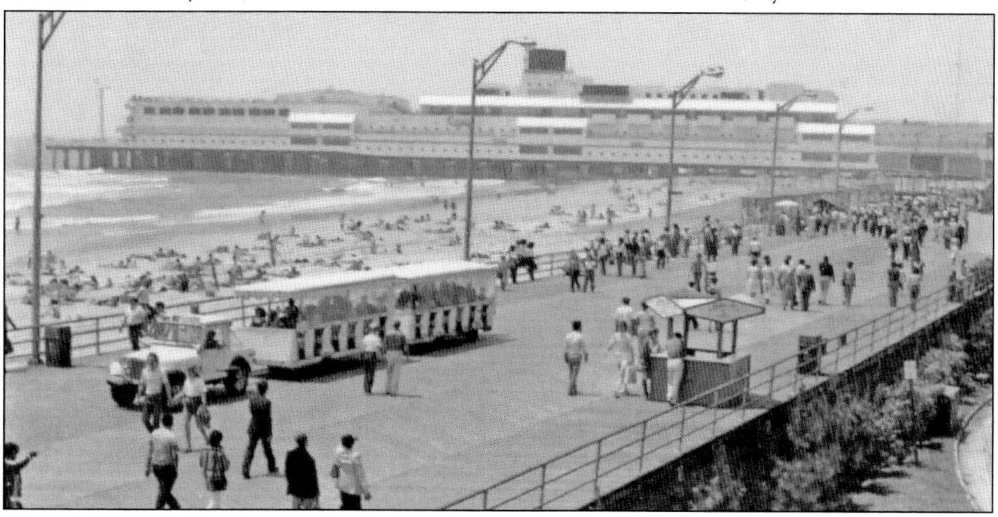

When Million Dollar Pier was finally demolished in late 1981, work began almost immediately to transform the structure into an upscale shopping mall that would feature stores, a food court, and an observation deck. The four-story, 900-foot-long Ocean One opened in 1983 and was promoted as part of Atlantic City's rebirth. After all, casino gambling had only been in existence for five years at that point. Tastes changed, however, and Ocean One was stripped to its skeleton in 2003 and replaced with the Shops at Caesar's, where Tiffany, Louis Vuitton, Gucci, and a floor of restaurants and clubs awaited. In 2015, the pier was renamed the Playground.

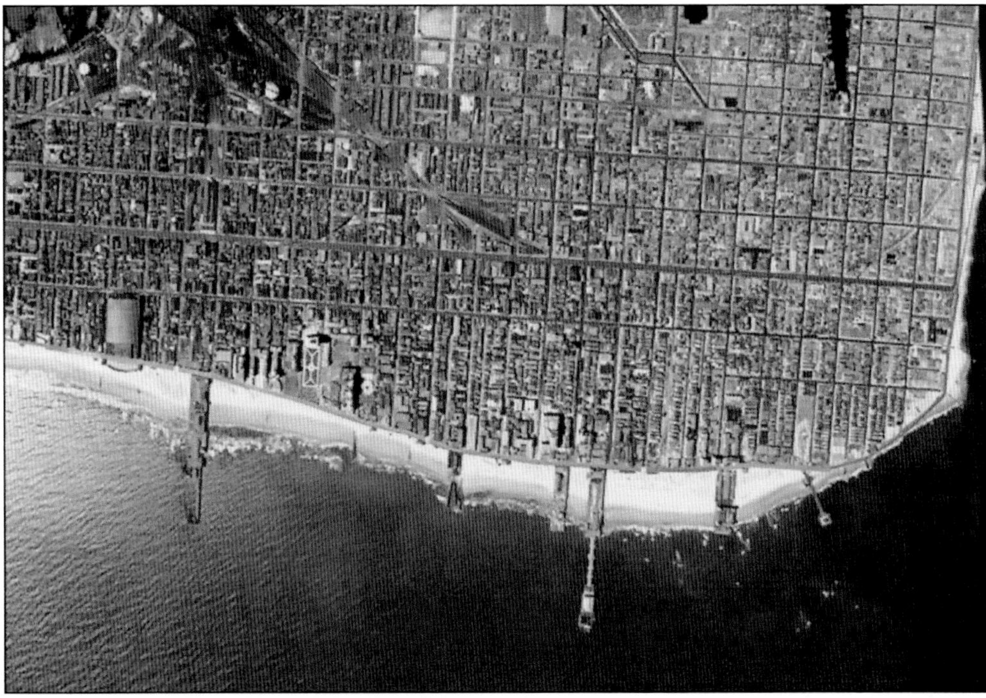

This aerial from 1944 shows Atlantic City's six piers. From left to right are the Million Dollar, Central, Steeplechase, Steel, Garden, and Heinz Piers. The 1944 hurricane would destroy Heinz, and as deterioration set in, many piers were demolished. Today, there are only four, much shorter in length than those in this picture.

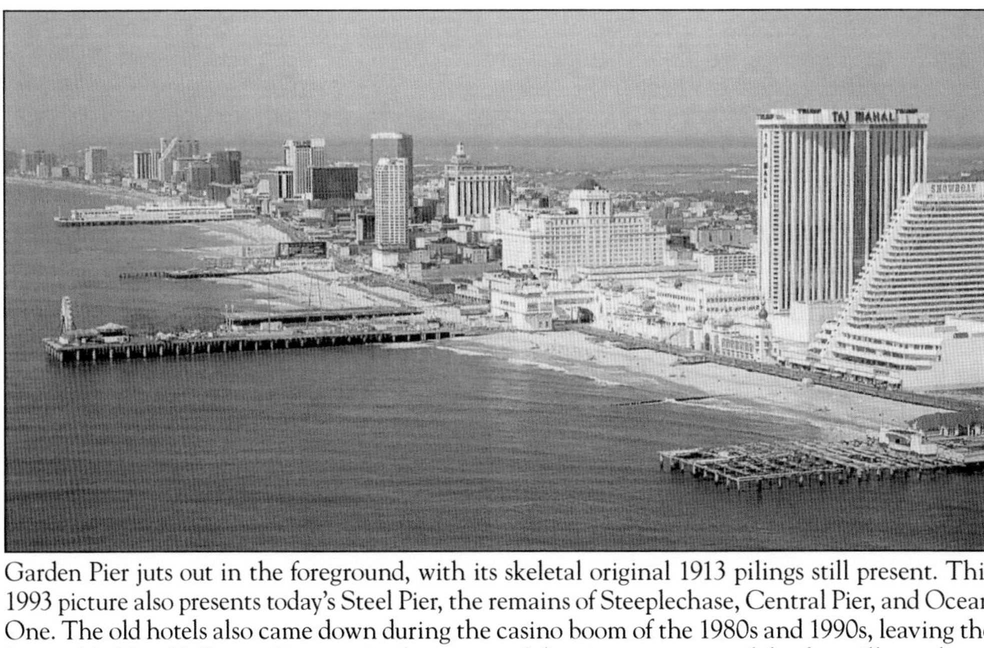

Garden Pier juts out in the foreground, with its skeletal original 1913 pilings still present. This 1993 picture also presents today's Steel Pier, the remains of Steeplechase, Central Pier, and Ocean One. The old hotels also came down during the casino boom of the 1980s and 1990s, leaving the former Haddon Hall, now Resorts, in the center of the picture, as one of the few still standing.

Three

And a Novice Shall Lead Them

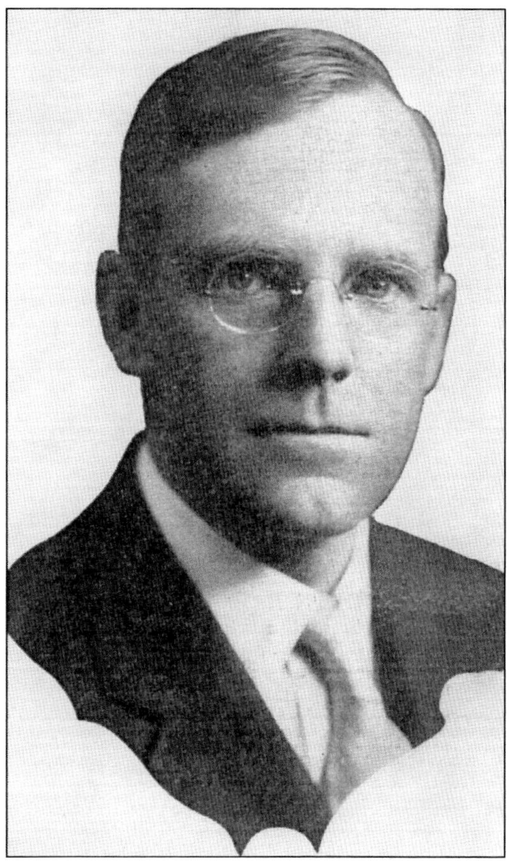

Steel Pier was sold to local businessman Frank Gravatt in 1925 for $2 million. An entrepreneur and a master in marketing and promotions, Gravatt made his money in transportation and real estate. He knew nothing about operating a pier, much less a moribund one whose only claims to fame were concert bands and rocking chairs. This portrait shows Gravatt two years after buying the pier.

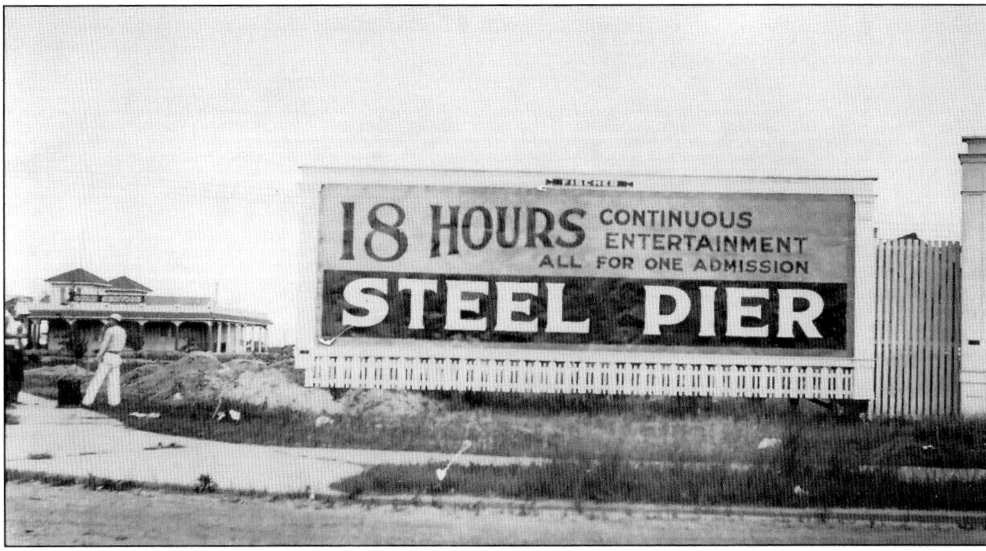

Gravatt made sure his pier would be well known and hired Philadelphia promotions man Harry Volk to oversee the advertising. Volk made sure the name "Steel Pier" would be seen along heavily traveled roadways and high-volume locations like New York's Times Square and Philadelphia's Market Street. This photograph was taken in 1934 outside of Atlantic City in Pleasantville.

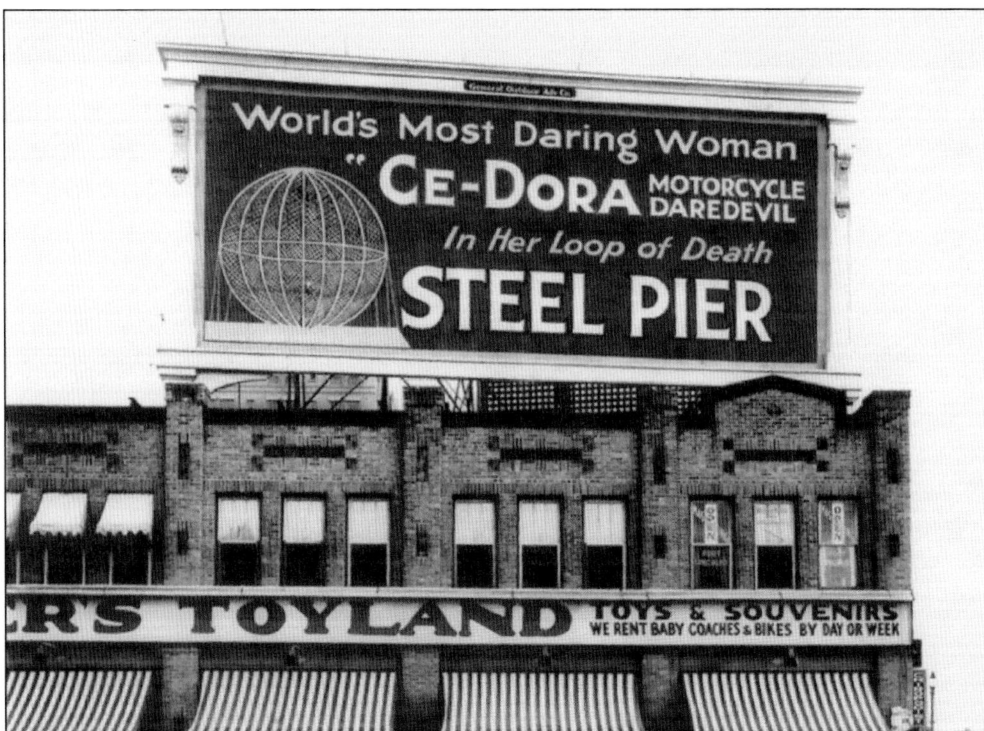

Another billboard from 1931 rises a block away from Steel Pier, above the roof of Taber's Toyland store on the boardwalk. It was rare to go anywhere in Atlantic City without seeing some sort of advertisement publicizing Steel Pier. Even public transportation was not immune.

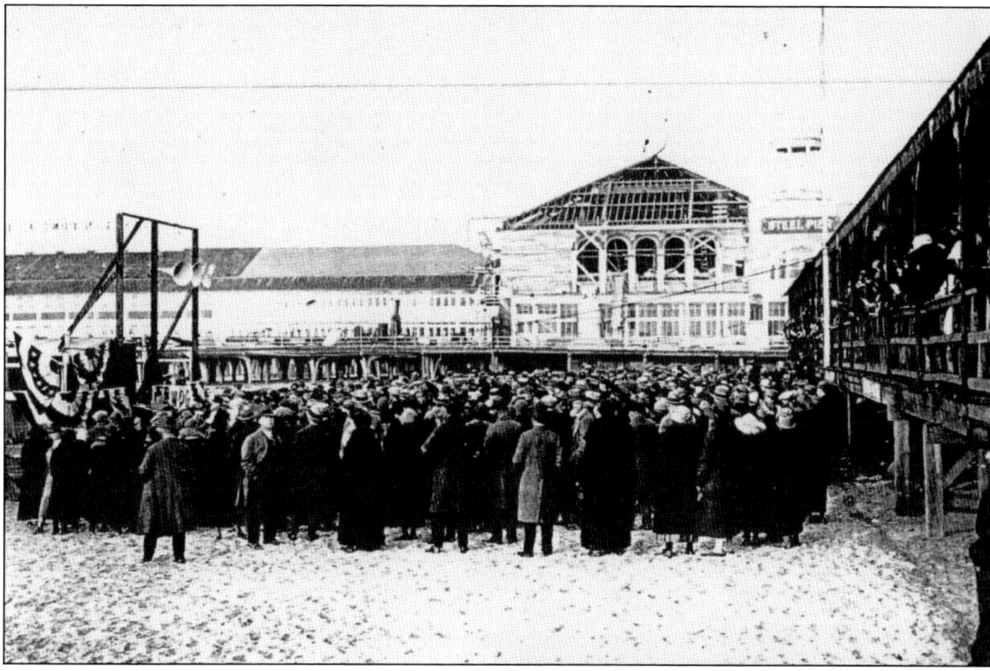

Gravatt did not waste time. In 1928, he unleashed a master plan to remodel the entire pier. Work continues on the front Casino building as seen here. Widened walkways, new theaters, a bigger ballroom, and a large water circus area were constructed, with seating for thousands.

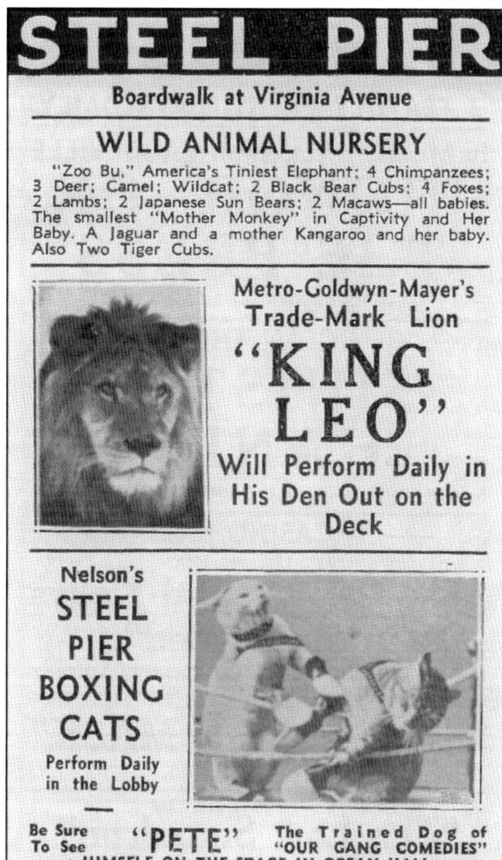

During Frank Gravatt's ownership, Steel Pier evolved into the world's greatest entertainment complex. Especially during the halcyon years of the 1930s, visitors could see the most unusual and preposterous subjects imaginable. Here is an advertisement from 1932 that displays the variety of animals on the pier. The MGM lion, King Leo, was present, as were the famous Boxing Cats. Even Petey, the lovable dog from the Our Gang movie shorts held court from 1932 until 1938. Today, concerned citizens would be picketing, but back then, it was an accepted, novel display of animals.

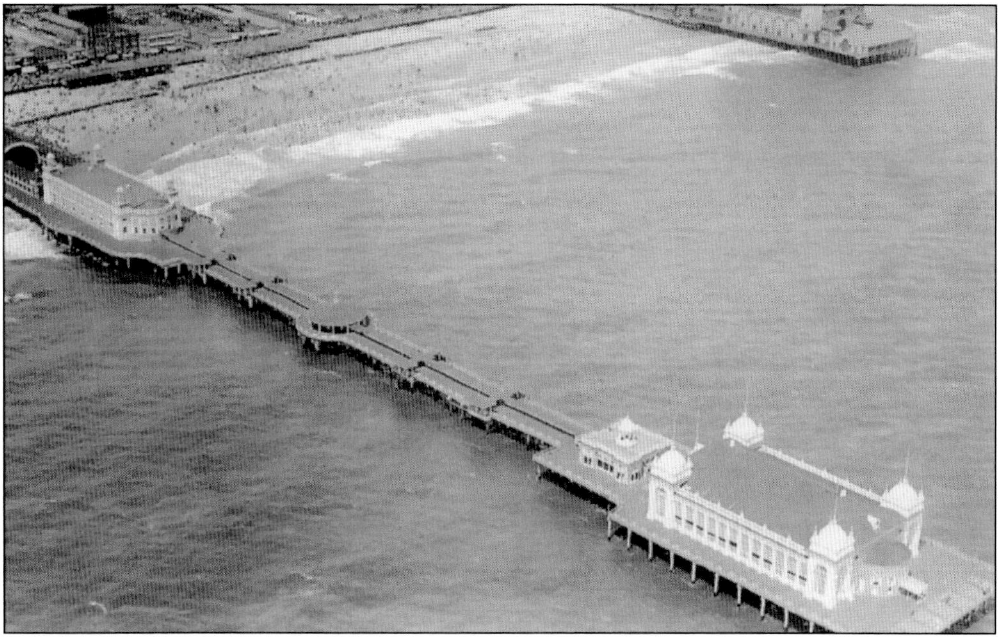

Before Gravatt improved the pier's structure, the area between the front Casino and the middle Music Hall was still open air. This rare picture shows the ocean sides of the Music Hall as well as the Marine Ballroom. Once Gravatt started his augmentations, the backs of these buildings would never be seen again.

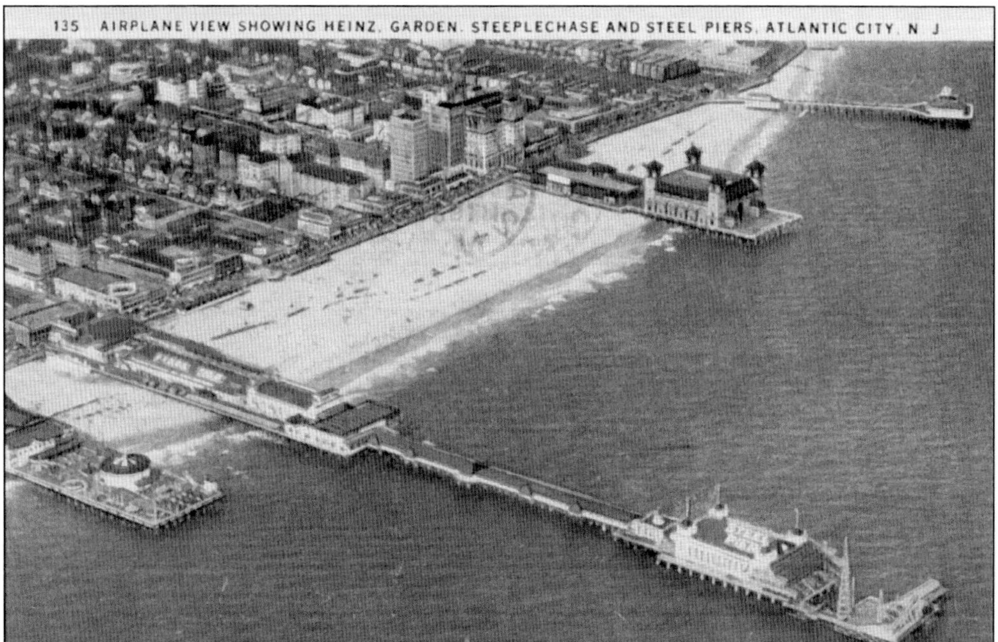

This 1930 postcard shows the new Ocean theater built in back of the Music Hall as well as the entire Water Circus seating, stage, and towers, which extended the pier out over the ocean even farther. The long promenade was also enclosed with exhibits and novelties.

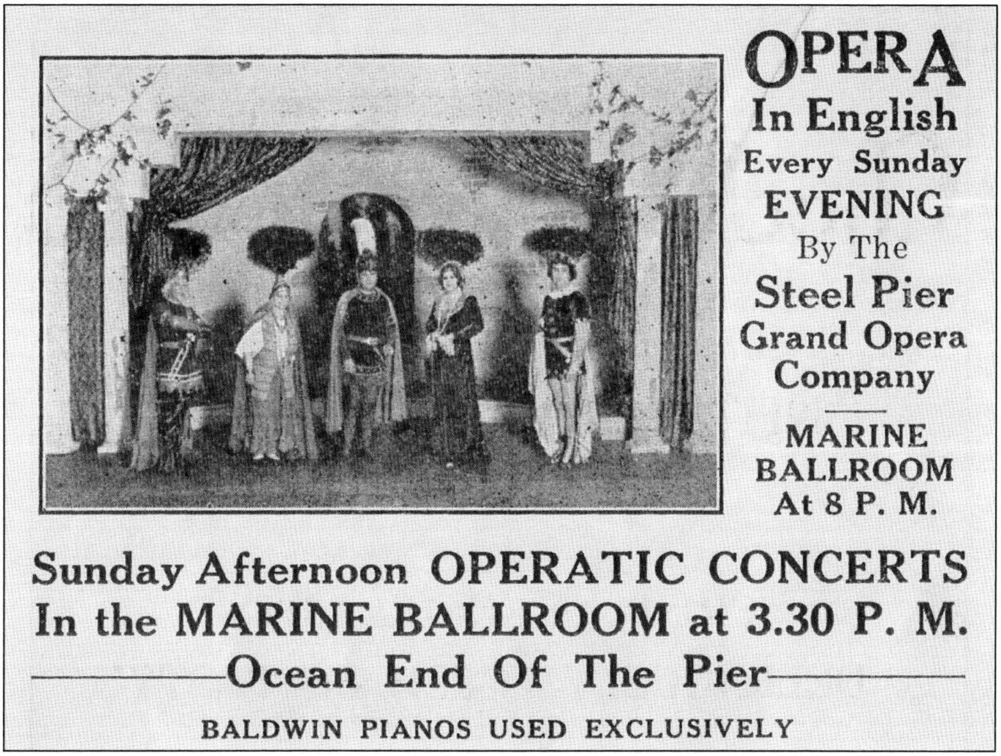

Culture was also a part of Gravatt's plan. He wanted to offer something for everyone, and a little bit of class would not hurt. From 1926 through 1938, familiar operas were presented Sundays in the Marine Ballroom. What makes this even more unusual was that they were all transcribed and sung in English. In fact, it was the only place probably in the world that Americans could hear *Pagliacci* in their native tongue.

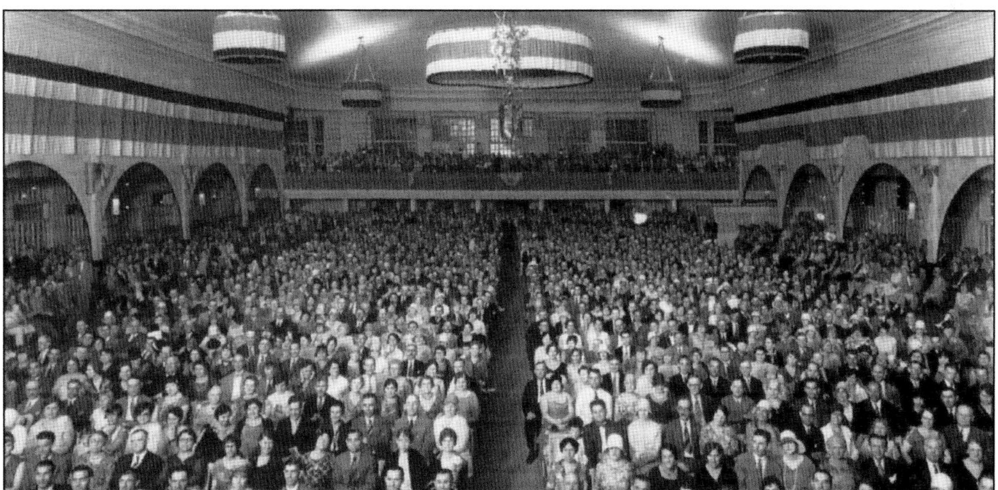

A packed Marine Ballroom awaits the beginning of an opera performance. Usually, the ballroom, one of the largest in the country, was filled with dancers listening to one of the nation's top bands, but on this day, high-brow entertainment replaced swing and "hot" tunes.

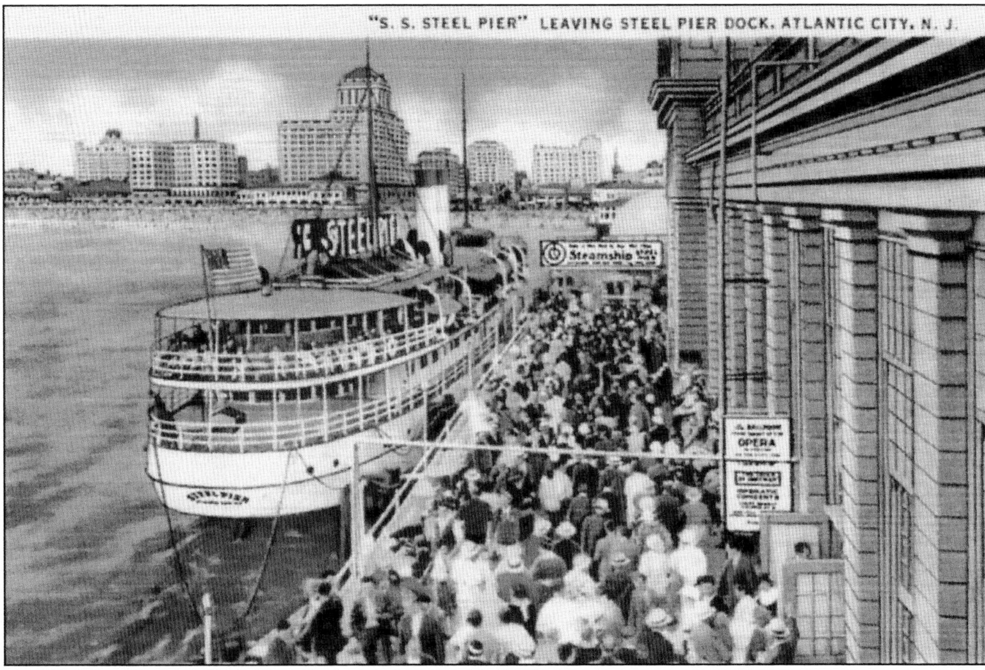

Gravatt was full of ideas. In 1932, he purchased a yacht for $100,000 that was once owned by Florida developer Henry Flagler and converted it into a passenger steamer for sightseeing. Visitors could dine and dance aboard the ship, named the SS *Steel Pier*, as it would slowly embark from the ballroom end of the pier. Two years later, Gravatt sold the ship to a New England steamship company.

"The Talk of the 'Walk"

Extraordinary Engagement

A. F. THAVIU

and his

EXPOSITION BAND

11.15, 3.30, 8.45 o'clock

IN THE MUSIC HALL

Dancing in Ball Room, Afternoon and Evening

Ted Weems' Orchestra

4:00 and 9:00 P. M.

Steel Pier Minstrels

Augmented and Better than Ever

3 and 8:30 P. M.—In the Casino

LATEST PHOTO-PLAYS

4 and 9:30 P. M.—In the Casino

Children's Carnival, Tuesday and Thursday Evenings, 8 o'Clock, Ballroom

STEEL PIER

Summer Home of WPG—Only Ocean Pier Broadcasting Station

ONE PRICE ADMITS TO ALL ATTRACTIONS

MORNINGS

Adults—25 Cents Children—20 Cents

AFTERNOONS

Adults—50 Cents Children—30 Cents

Steel Pier was also home to a radio station. WPG, for "World's Play Ground," first went on the air in January 1925 and was later broadcast from the only ocean pier studio in the country. Although it was home to famed broadcaster Norman Brokenshire, it never made money and folded in 1939. The next year, another station, WFPG, founded by Gravatt, went on the air and remained on the pier through 1981, three years after the pier itself had closed. This advertisement is from 1926.

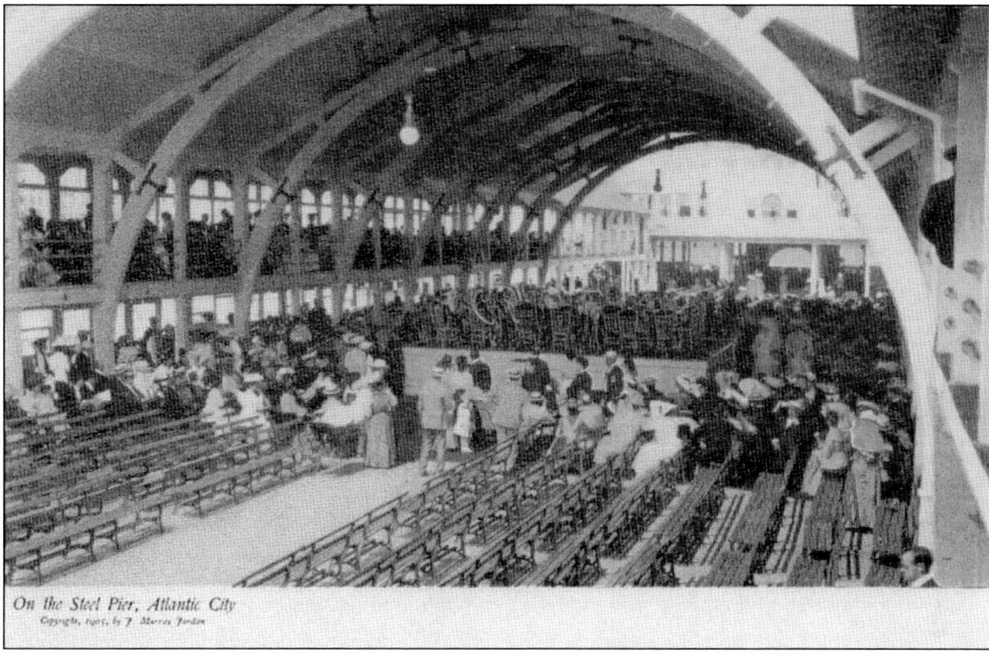

Frank Gravatt inherited a pier that needed help physically. Between the Casino and Music Hall stood an open-air section that regularly held concerts during the pier's early days. The view in this postcard from 1905 looks towards the future Music Hall entrance. Both levels of the pavilion would fill with patrons sitting on rows of benches and enjoying light classics and marches played by the Goldman Band or maestro Oreste Vessella.

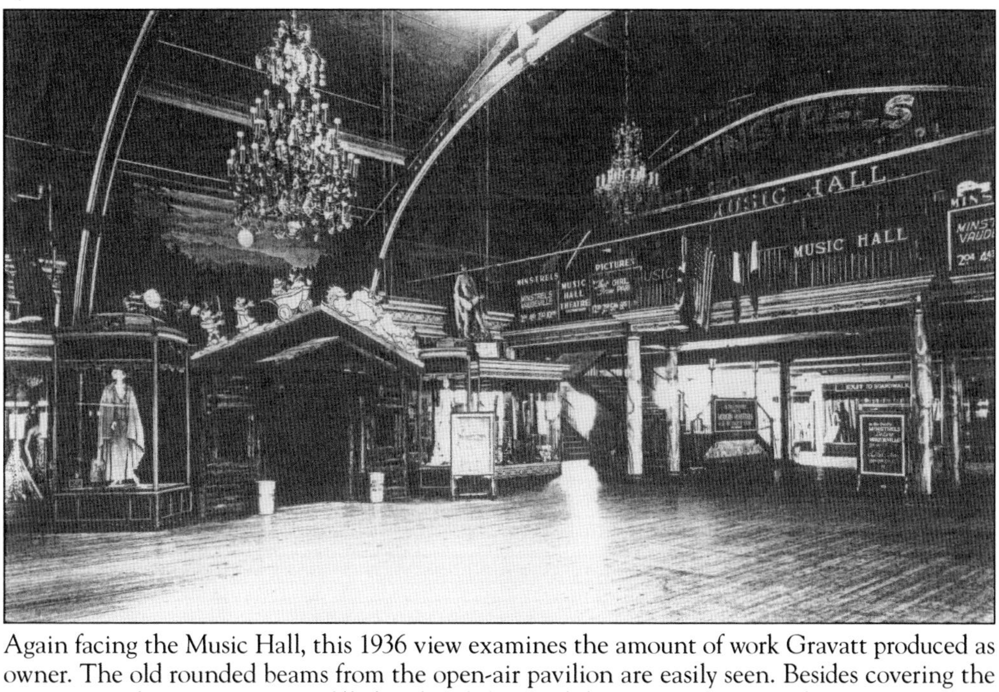

Again facing the Music Hall, this 1936 view examines the amount of work Gravatt produced as owner. The old rounded beams from the open-air pavilion are easily seen. Besides covering the entire area, the space was now filled with exhibits and shows. Center left is the entrance to the Little Theatre, where the children shows were performed.

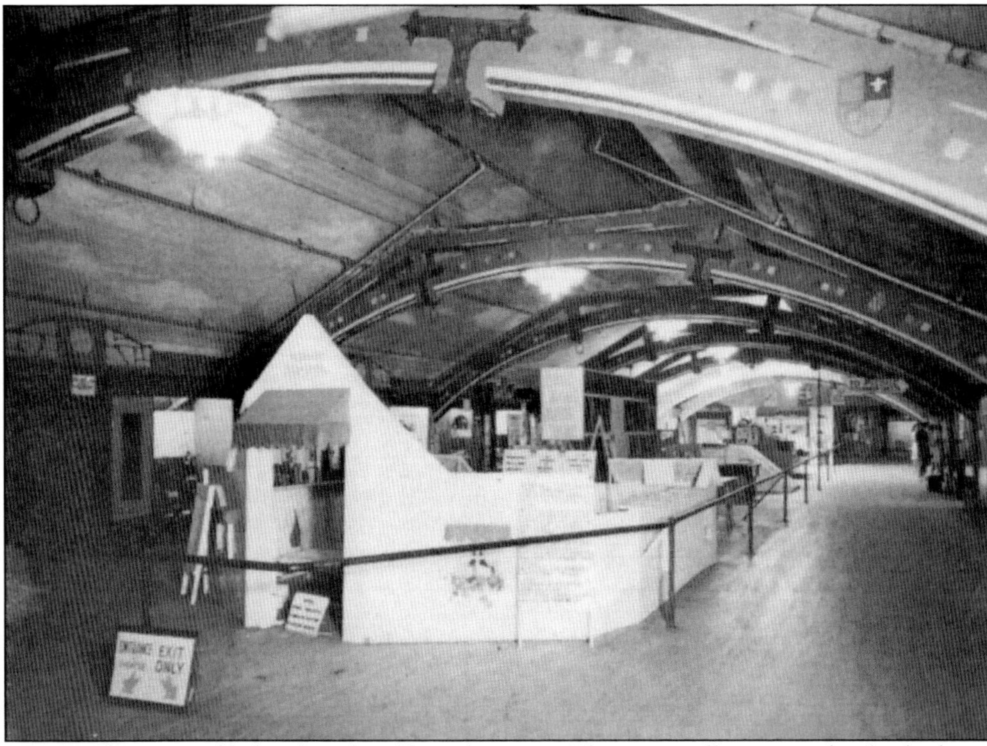

Another floor was added within the old pavilion area. This is a small nursery school, which was built to hold the attention of youngsters while their parents took in a stage show, dancing, or a movie. This practice was not unheard of from the 1920s through the 1950s, as many people had more trust in others concerning their children at that time than is common today.

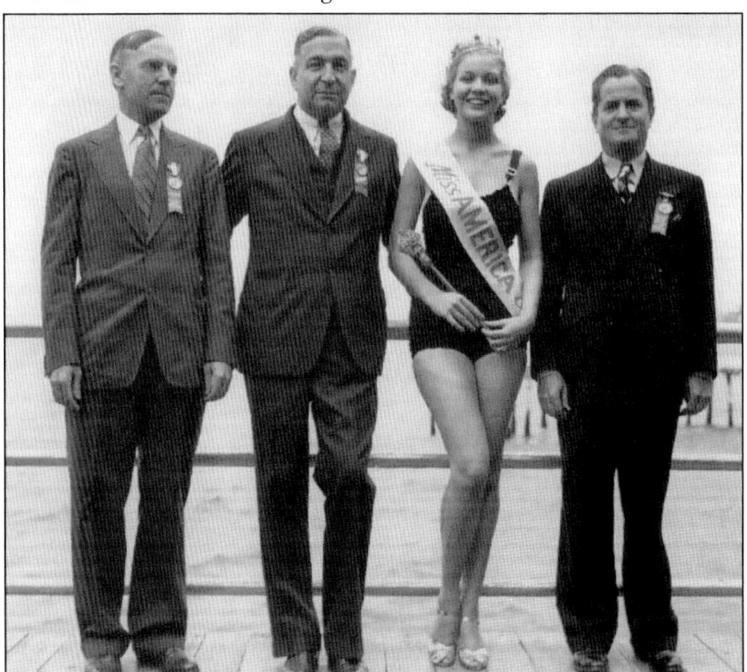

The Miss America Pageant was held in Steel Pier's Marine Ballroom from 1935 to 1939. After a couple of false starts interspersed with the Depression, Gravatt and other civic-minded individuals took it to task to revive the custom for an entire week, culminating with the crowning of Miss America. Gravatt (left) poses with officials and Miss America 1938, Marilyn Meseke.

The last Steel Pier crowning of Miss America in September 1939 found the pageant in heavy competition with the Ink Spots, one of the hottest vocal groups in the country. As the first African American musical headliners on the pier, the "Spots" were one of the few to crossover to white audiences with many hits and appearances.

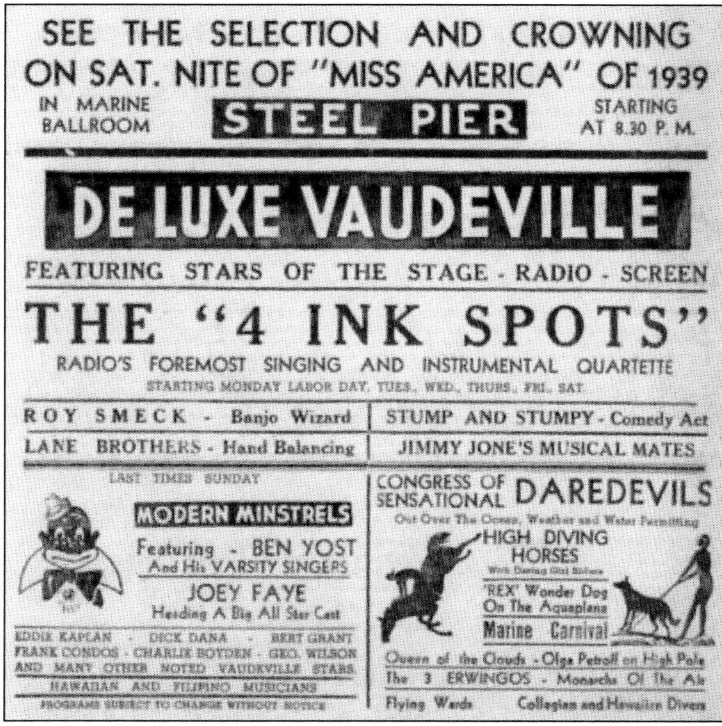

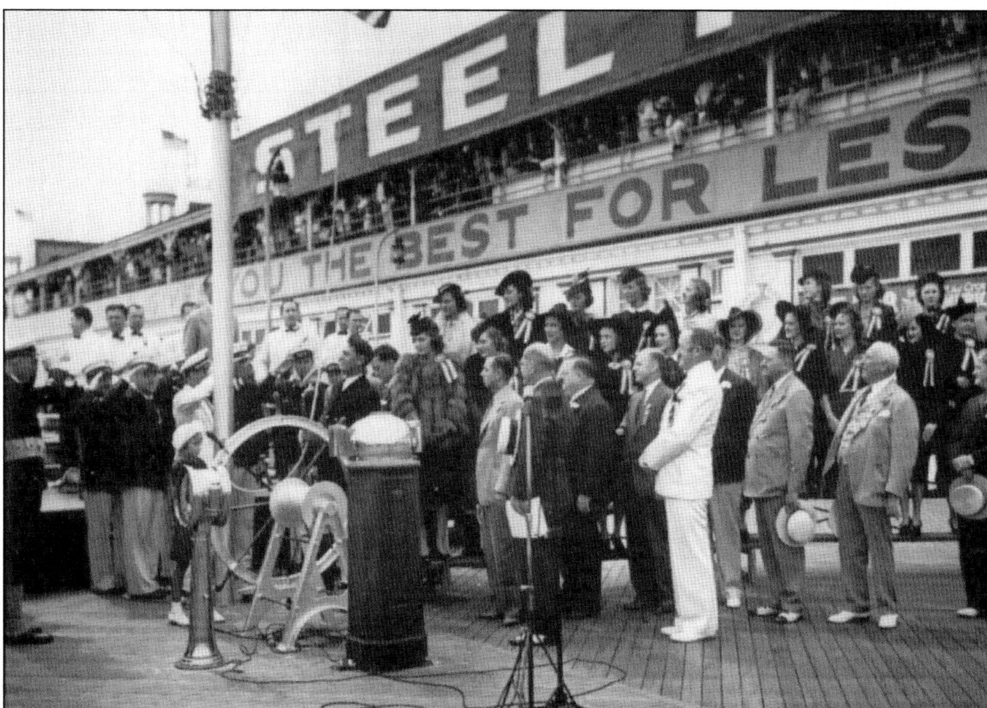

Miss America contestants of 1938 watch a flag-raising ceremony on the north side of the pier. The week before the actual crowning was filled up promptly with talent shows, Mardi Gras balls, a large parade down the boardwalk, and a championship six-mile ocean swim.

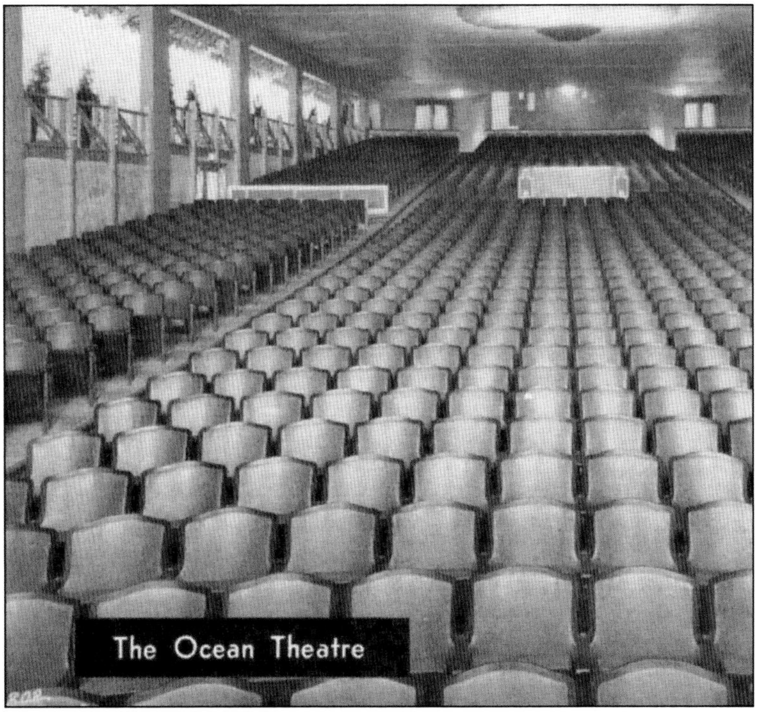

Gravatt built the new Ocean Hall (later Ocean) theater in 1929 exclusively for motion pictures. Its big gala opening was on May 29 with an engagement of the all-talking *Bulldog Drummond* starring Ronald Colman. The modern theater, which held 1,400 people on one floor, was upgraded to Cinerama and 3-D specifications and renamed the Midway in 1954.

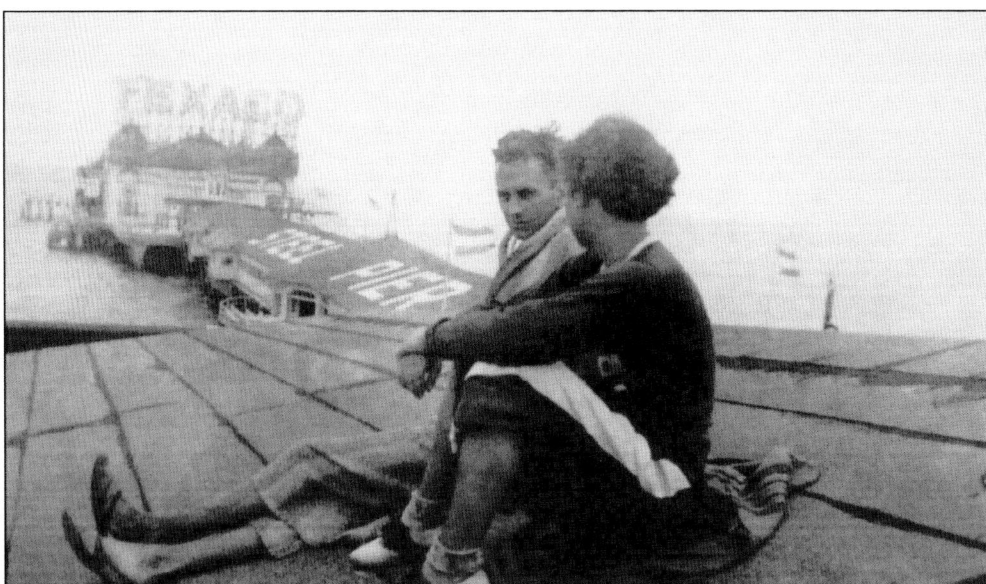

Promotional advertising abounded from companies willing to pay hefty sums. This 1930s view displays two pier workers relaxing on the Ocean theater's roof with the Marine Ballroom in the background. The giant Texaco gasoline sign was added on during the early part of that decade and remained brightly illuminated for all to see.

Four

Let Us Entertain You

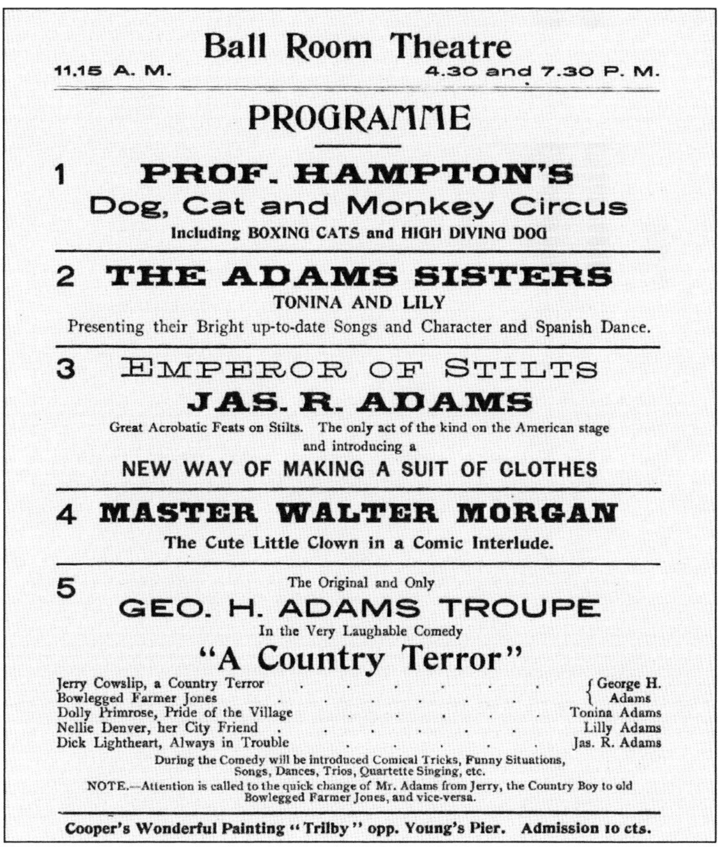

Ball Room Theatre

11.15 A. M. 4.30 and 7.30 P. M.

PROGRAMME

1 PROF. HAMPTON'S
Dog, Cat and Monkey Circus
Including BOXING CATS and HIGH DIVING DOG

2 THE ADAMS SISTERS
TONINA AND LILY
Presenting their Bright up-to-date Songs and Character and Spanish Dance.

3 EMPEROR OF STILTS
JAS. R. ADAMS
Great Acrobatic Feats on Stilts. The only act of the kind on the American stage and introducing a
NEW WAY OF MAKING A SUIT OF CLOTHES

4 MASTER WALTER MORGAN
The Cute Little Clown in a Comic Interlude.

5 The Original and Only
GEO. H. ADAMS TROUPE
In the Very Laughable Comedy
"A Country Terror"

Jerry Cowslip, a Country Terror . . . . George H. Adams
Bowlegged Farmer Jones . . . . George H. Adams
Dolly Primrose, Pride of the Village . . . . . Tonina Adams
Nellie Denver, her City Friend . . . . Lilly Adams
Dick Lightheart, Always in Trouble . . . . . . Jas. R. Adams

During the Comedy will be introduced Comical Tricks, Funny Situations, Songs, Dances, Trios, Quartette Singing, etc.

NOTE.—Attention is called to the quick change of Mr. Adams from Jerry, the Country Boy to old Bowlegged Farmer Jones, and vice-versa.

Cooper's Wonderful Painting "Trilby" opp. Young's Pier. Admission 10 cts.

Entertainers have always been a major part of Steel Pier since it opened. This 1899 vaudeville program showcases a potpourri of animals, singers, acrobatics, comics, and even a one-act comedy. From the 1930s onwards, the majority of entertainers trod the boards in the middle Music Hall theater. In fact, up until 1975, Steel Pier was the very last place in the United States, except maybe Las Vegas, where a continuous daily vaudeville show with a headliner could be experienced.

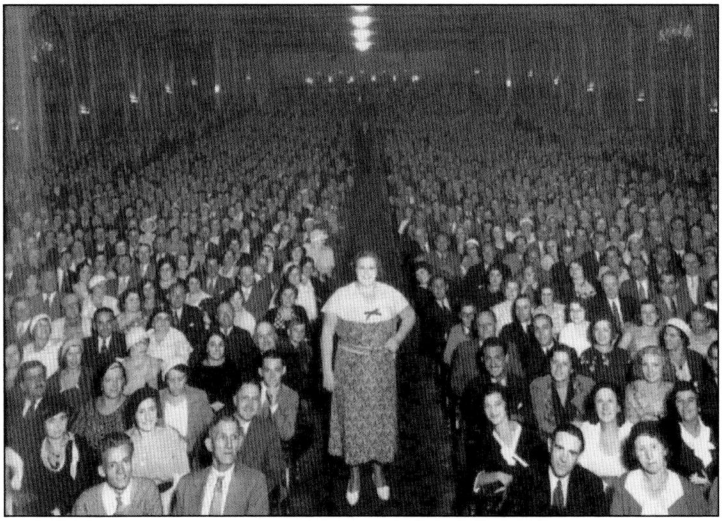

Singer Kate Smith stands in the aisle of the Music Hall in 1932 with a full crowd of over 2,000 people. Smith, known as the "First Lady of Radio," began broadcasting a year earlier and became a major star. Her voice was an operatic contralto, and she probably became most famous for singing Irving Berlin's "God Bless America"—the first time in 1939.

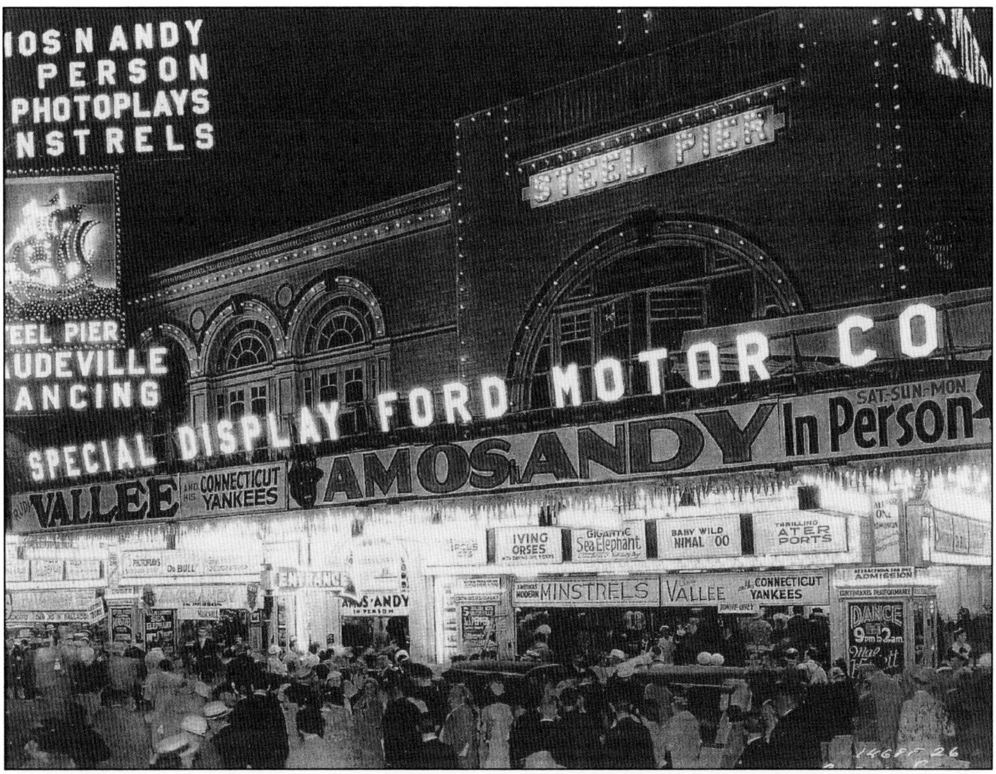

This image was captured during Labor Day weekend in 1933. Radio's biggest superstars, Amos 'n' Andy, performed and broke the one-day Steel Pier record of 39,000 customers. Freeman Gosden and Charles Correll, both white men, developed a daily serial in 1926, featuring the trials and tribulations of two black men in Harlem that became radio's biggest hit. Gosden and Correll appeared in the then-accepted form of blackface, as bandleader Rudy Vallee and played for dancers in the packed Marine Ballroom.

A young Milton Berle performs with Baby Rose Marie on the stage of the Music Hall in 1933. Berle, of course, went on to become one of the top comics of all time, and Rose Marie became best known, in addition to her singing and nightclub engagements, as Sally Rogers on the classic 1960s *Dick Van Dyke Show* on TV. (Courtesy of Dick Shine.)

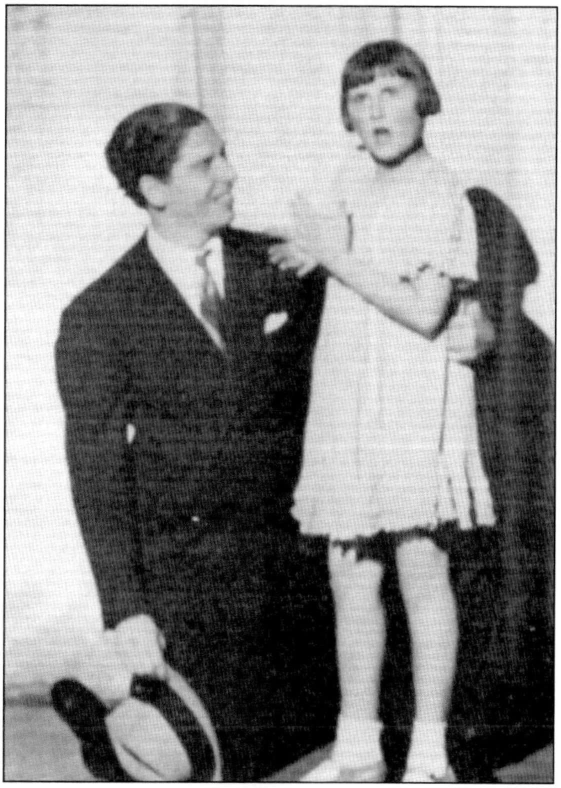

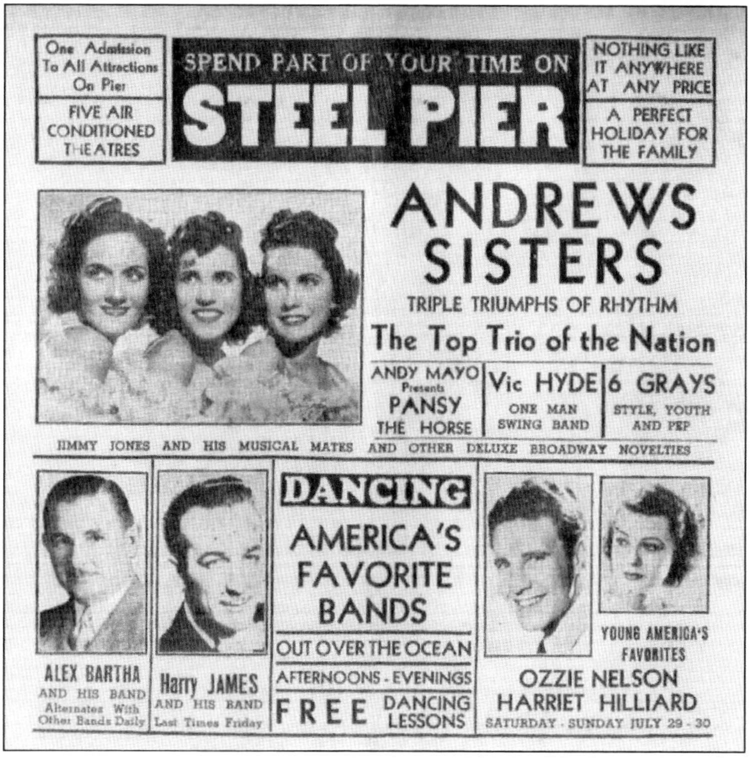

The Andrews Sisters appeared first in July 1939 and nine times thereafter. A big favorite with audiences, the sisters had many harmonic hits throughout the following decade. Also featured were TV's Ozzie and Harriet Nelson, then just a bandleader and his singer. The great trumpet man Harry James played, as did house bandleader Alex Bartha, a regular in the ballroom through the 1950s.

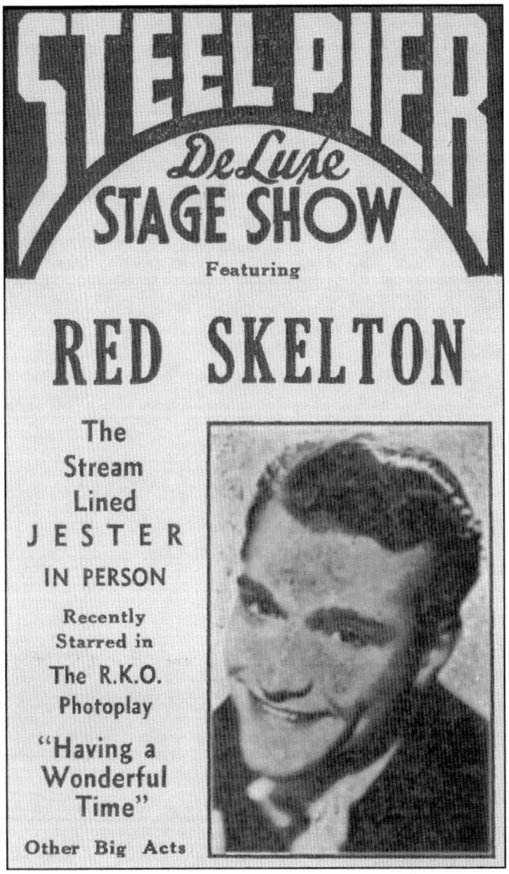

Red Skelton, a true and original clown, headlined in July 1938 just as he began to climb the show business ladder to became a major radio, movie, and TV star. This was not Skelton's first time in Atlantic City. He was a comic emcee a few years before during the Depression dance marathons that were held at Million Dollar Pier.

No, Hitler did not visit Steel Pier, but Moe Howard of the Three Stooges did many times. From the decking outside the Music Hall in July 1938, Moe heils his vaudeville pal George Mann. There is also a rare color home movie of the Stooges and Mann from this same day on YouTube. The Stooges appeared six times at the pier, as late as 1960.

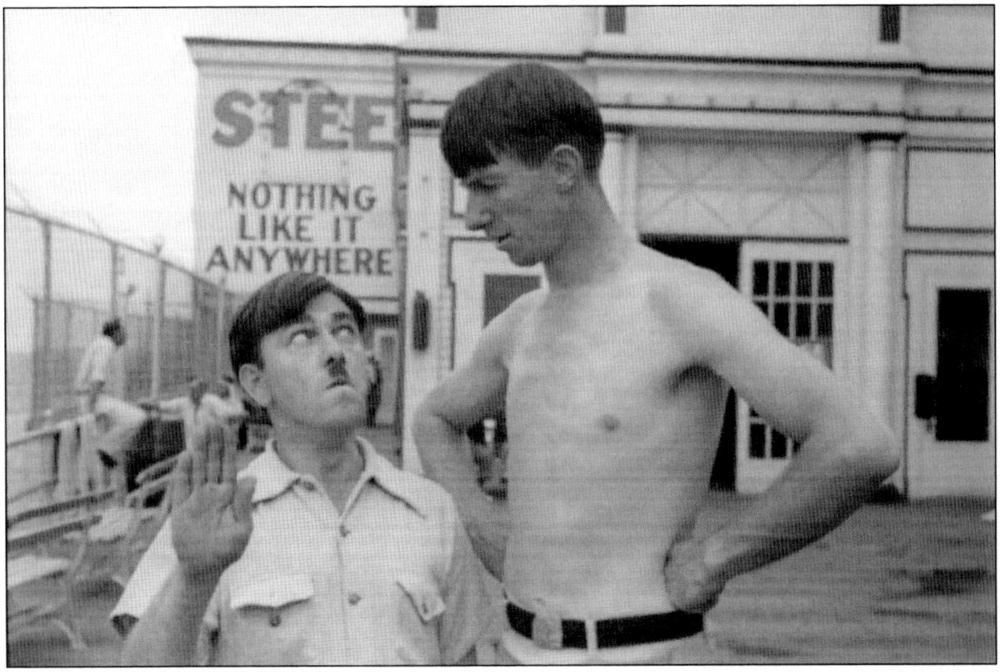

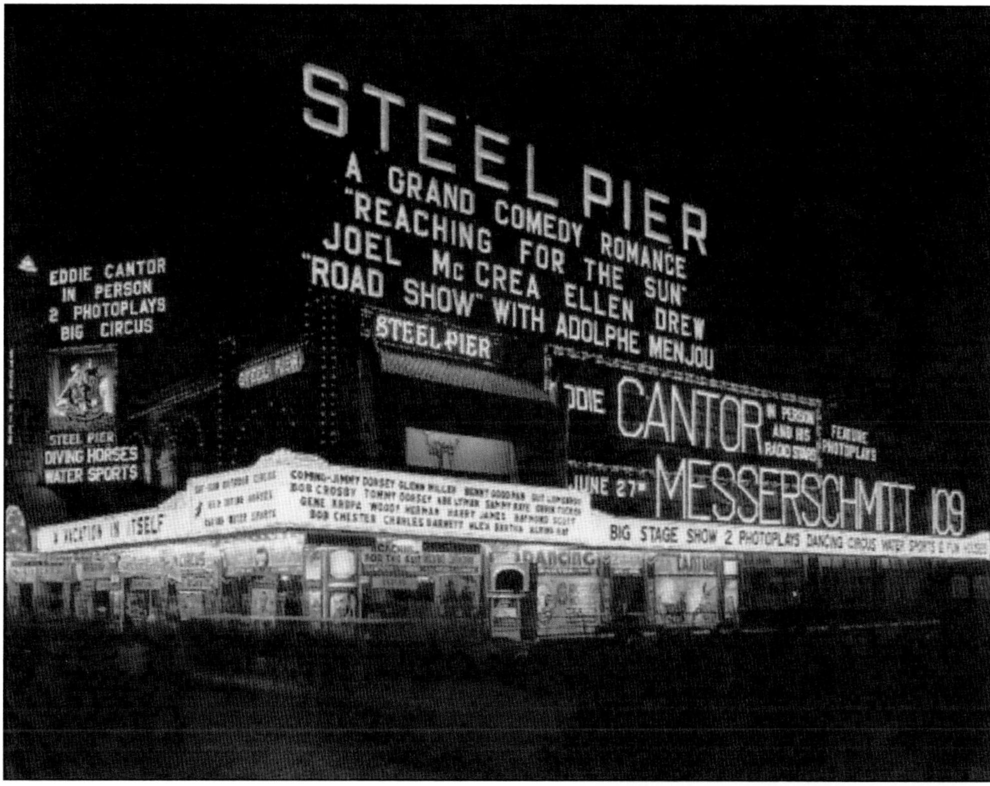

Eddie Cantor, a showbiz legend, entertained in June 1941. A comic and a singer, Cantor was a frequent visitor to Atlantic City but only appeared one other time on Steel Pier, in 1930. Even though this picture was taken six months before the United States entered World War II, a German Messerschmitt shot down over England was on display.

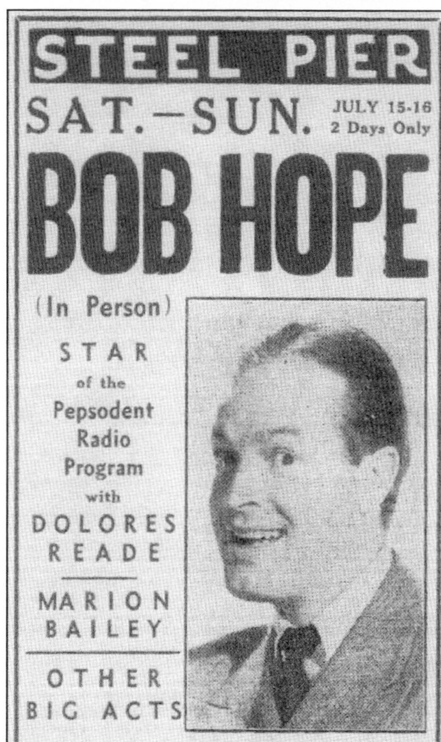

Legend Bob Hope stopped by at the beginning of his long radio and movie career in both 1939 and 1940. Hope had not yet hit the icon status he would receive during World War II when he made countless appearances entertaining armed forces around the globe. Dolores Reade was his wife in real life, and their marriage lasted for an incredible 69 years.

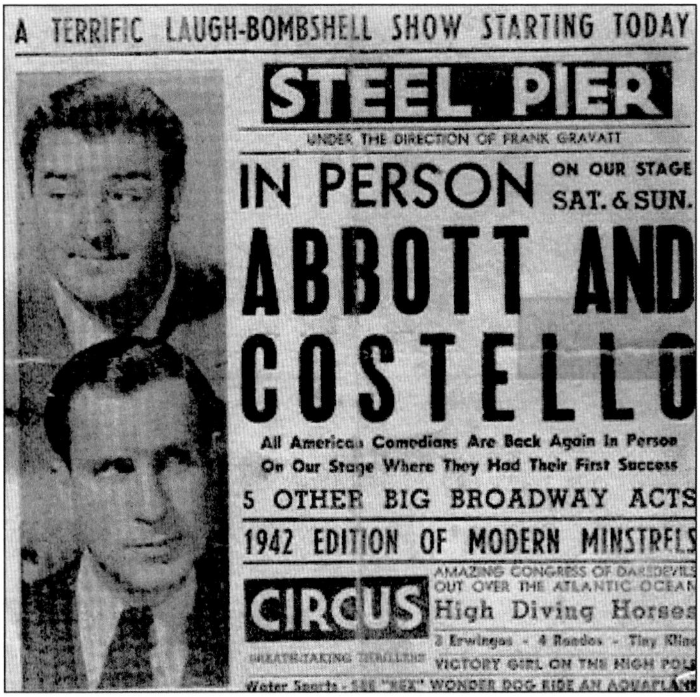

Bud Abbott and Lou Costello, the premier movie comedy team of the 1940s, became partners in a New York burlesque house and were brought to Steel Pier in 1936 to present their bits in the Casino minstrel show. Abbott and Costello never wore blackface; instead, they brought down the house with their famous "Who's on First?" routine, among others. When the boys hit it big a few years later, they never forgot the pier and returned regularly.

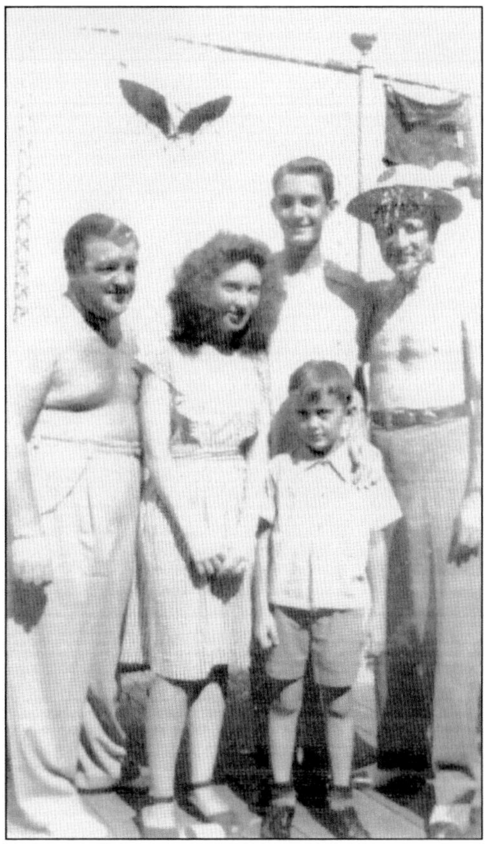

Abbott and Costello, sans shirts, meet fans in September 1942. Down to earth and never with bodyguards or an entourage, these guys were, hard as it may be to believe, the top stars in Hollywood and on radio at that time. Always happy to meet their audience, they were present on the pier a year earlier at the world premiere of their movie *Hold That Ghost.*

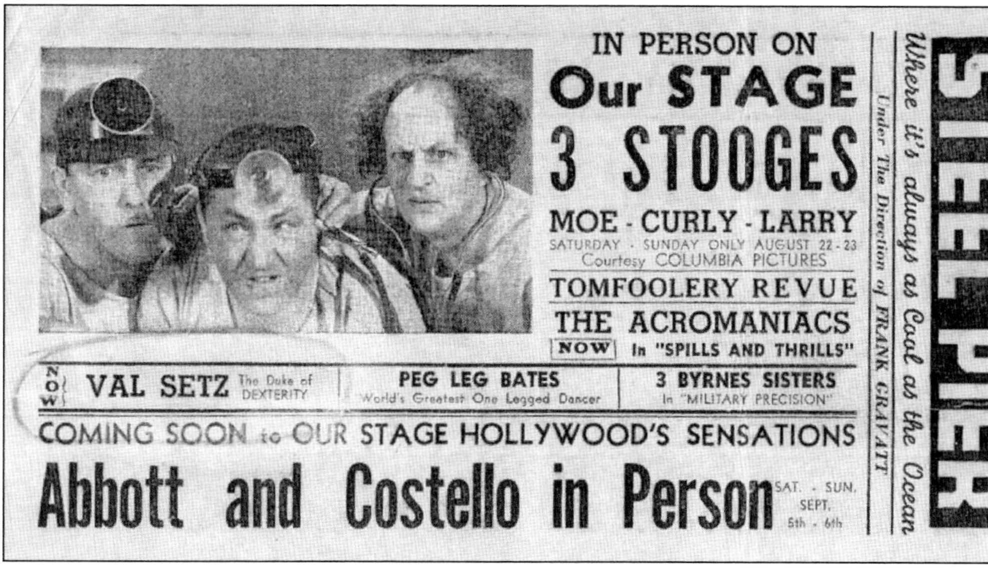

In 1942, the Three Stooges returned for more Music Hall shenanigans. On the bill was famed tap dancer Clayton "Peg Leg" Bates, named so because he had only one leg. The headliner was supported with an entire vaudeville program complete with singers, jugglers, dancers, and comedians that played at least five shows continuously throughout the day and night. When it rained, Steel Pier was jammed with more people than usual, which meant more performances.

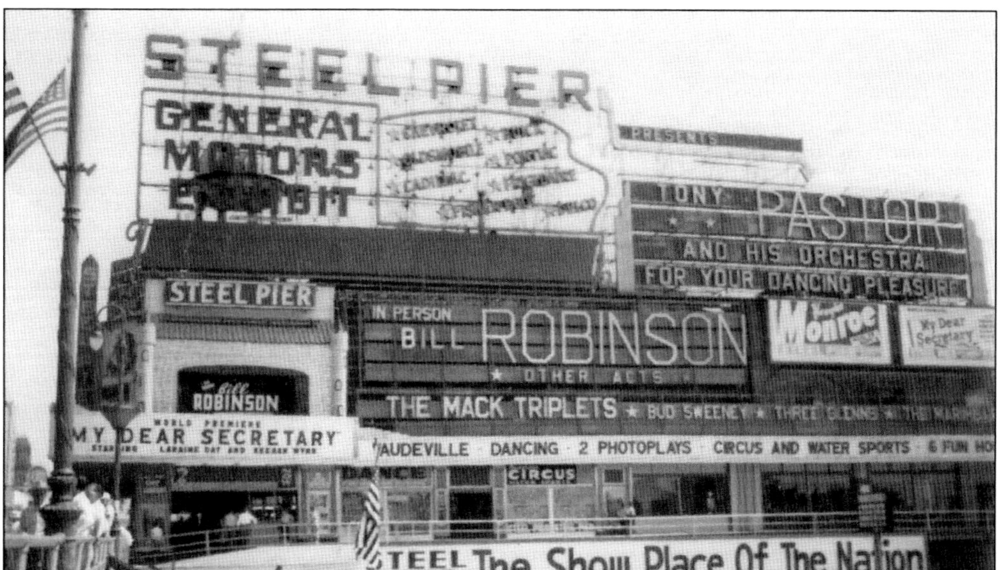

The fabulous Bill "Bojangles" Robinson appeared in August 1948 along with the Tony Pastor band. Considered the greatest tap dancer who ever lived, Robinson was one of the few African American headliners on the pier during this era. He was 70 during his stay and died the following year. Pastor also featured the two Clooney sisters; Rosemary went on to become a major star a few years later.

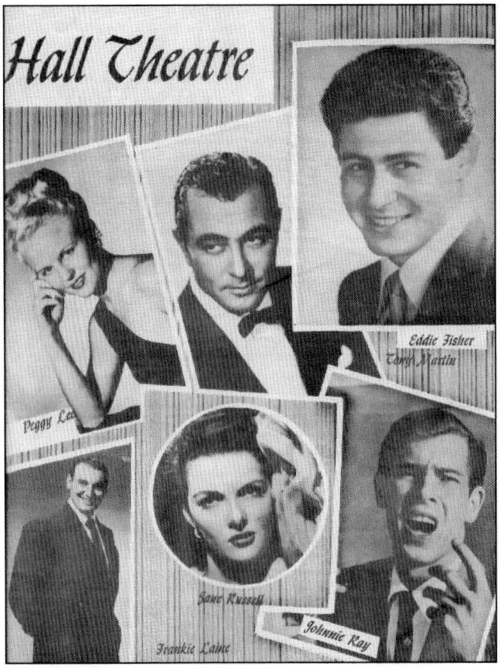

Some of the entertainers of the early 1950s were the pop singers of the day. Playing the Music Hall of Steel Pier for a week in the summer was just as prestigious as playing the Copacabana or Paramount Theatre in New York and was highly regarded as such. It meant one had made it to the top. The acts featured here are representative of the favorite top headliners before the rock-and-roll era.

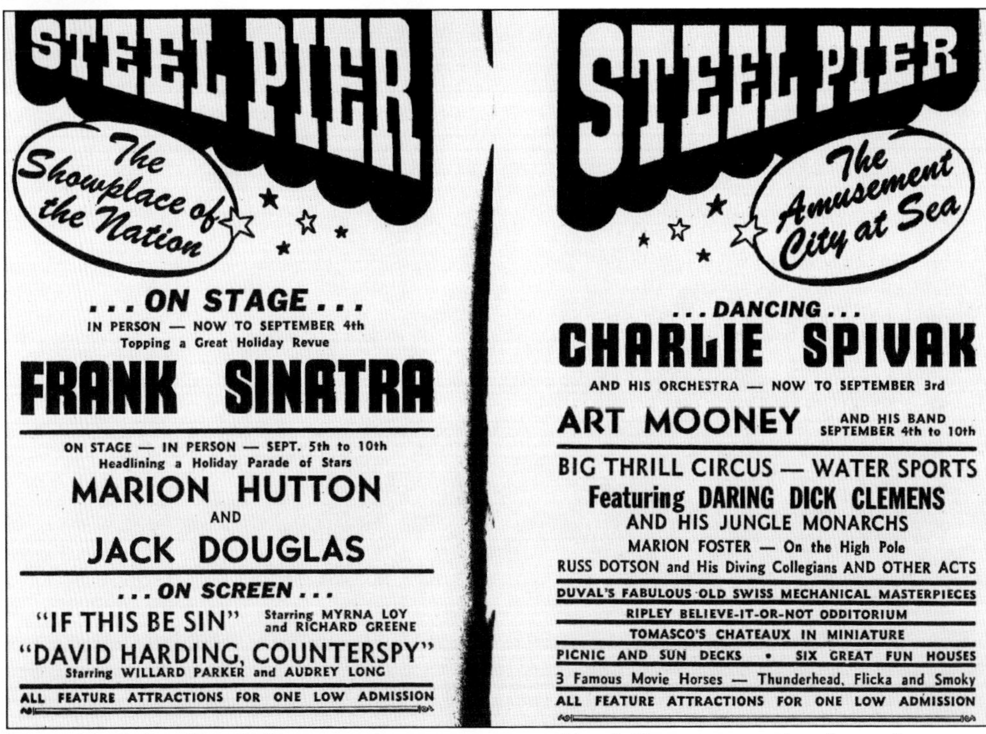

This ad for Labor Day 1950 was surely an engagement Frank Sinatra wanted to forget. It was not that he did not love Steel Pier or Atlantic City; it was just that the mobs of fans on the pier were turning over so fast, he played double the shows and threw his voice out. It was impossible for Sinatra to even take a lunch break. What makes this more interesting was that Sinatra's career was starting to slide to the bottom (temporarily) at this time, but in New Jersey, no one noticed.

Singers Johnnie Ray and Tony Bennett are mentioned in the advertisement from 1953. Ray had a unique style of crying while he sang and was a huge sensation in the early 1950s, while Bennett still enjoys a long and productive career in 2016, the longevity of which may never be equaled. Also on this bill is comic Henny Youngman, who appeared on the pier 10 different times.

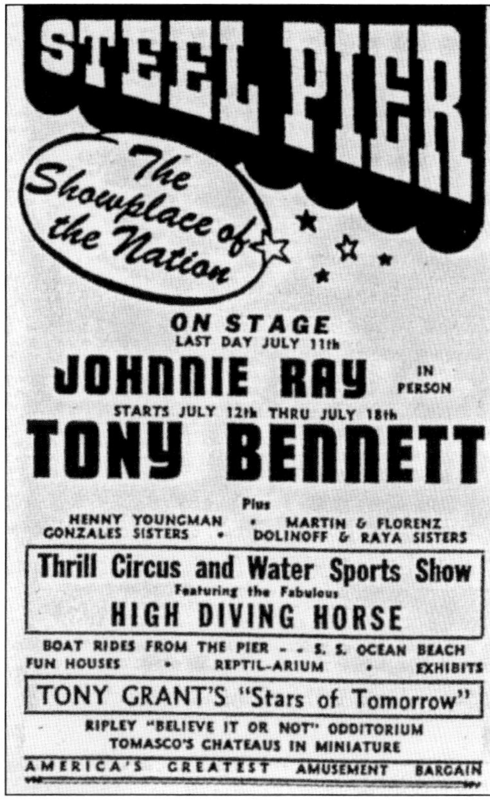

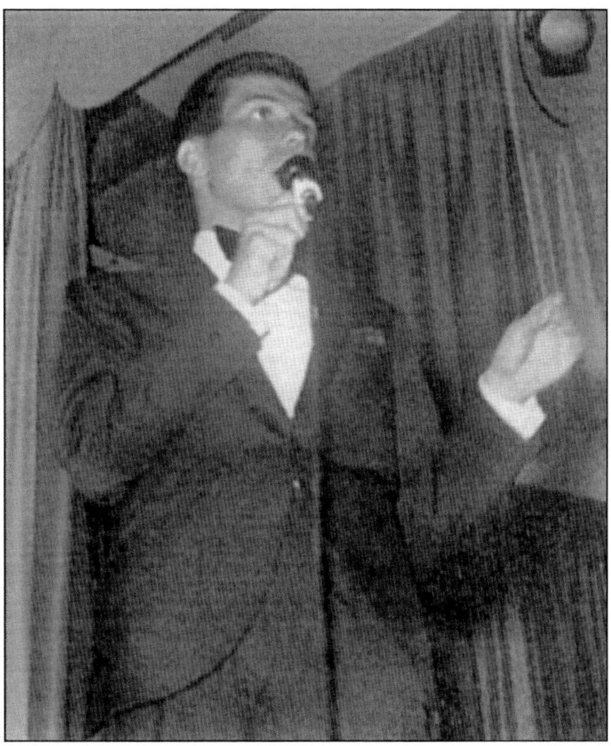

Like father, like son: Frank Sinatra Jr. is pictured performing in 1967. Sinatra Jr. performed on the pier five times—once in 1966 when Stevie Wonder was the Music Hall headliner. Living in the shadow of his legendary father was hard on Sinatra Jr., even though his voice could stand on its own. (Courtesy of Jim Gray.)

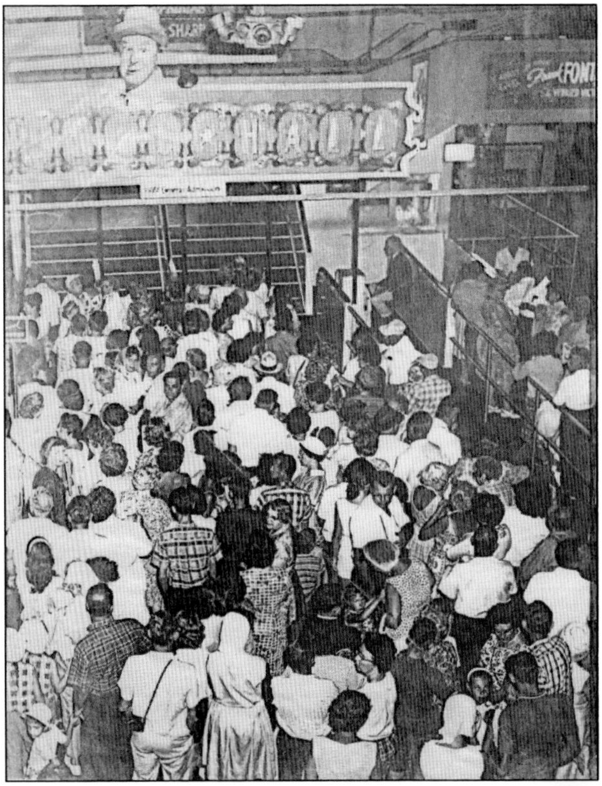

Large crowds line up at the entrance of the Music Hall in 1963 to see a performance by comic and singer Frank Fontaine. A baritone by trade, Fontaine developed a character named Crazy Guggenheim on the well-known *Jackie Gleason Show* on television. When this picture was taken, Fontaine was "hot," as he had the number one album in the country.

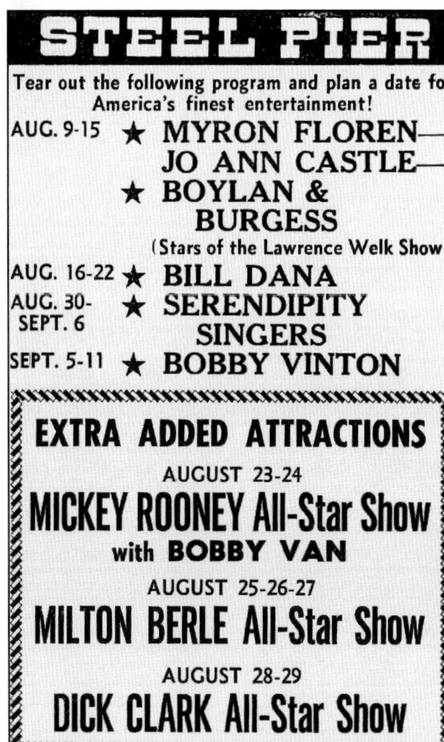

A 1964 Music Hall schedule shows the variety of big-name performers that summer. Besides comics Milton Berle and Bill Dana, featured entertainers include pop singer Bobby Vinton, stars of *The Lawrence Welk Show*, motion picture legend Mickey Rooney, and Dick Clark's rock-and-roll revue.

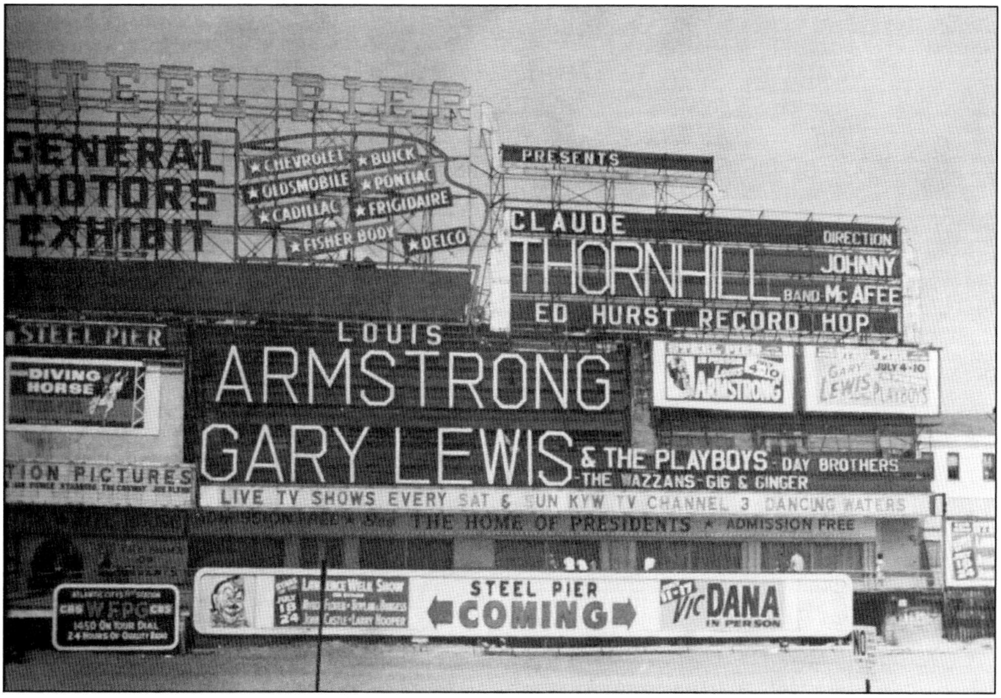

The marquee from July 4, 1965, demonstrates the uniqueness of Steel Pier. Where else could one find the renowned Louis Armstrong sharing a bill with rock band Gary Lewis and the Playboys and the Claude Thornhill orchestra? Unfortunately, Thornhill had passed away just a few days before this engagement, and his band was led by Johnny McAfee.

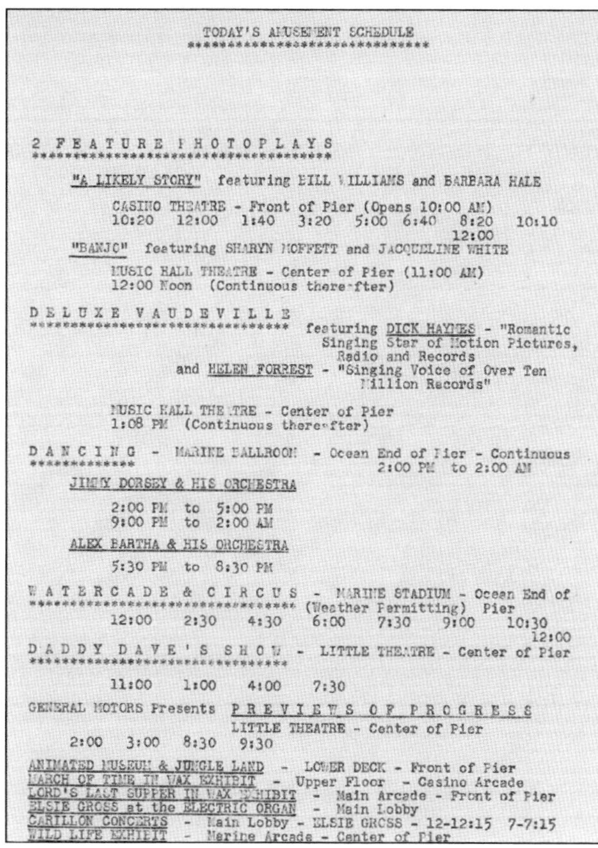

TODAY'S AMUSEMENT SCHEDULE

2 FEATURE PHOTOPLAYS

"A LIKELY STORY" featuring BILL WILLIAMS and BARBARA HALE

CASINO THEATRE - Front of Pier (Opens 10:00 AM)
10:20 12:00 1:40 3:20 5:00 6:40 8:20 10:10 12:00

"BANJO" featuring SHARYN MOFFETT and JACQUELINE WHITE

MUSIC HALL THEATRE - Center of Pier (11:00 AM)
12:00 Noon (Continuous thereafter)

DELUXE VAUDEVILLE featuring DICK HAYMES - "Romantic Singing Star of Motion Pictures, Radio and Records
and HELEN FORREST - "Singing Voice of Over Ten Million Records"

MUSIC HALL THEATRE - Center of Pier
1:08 PM (Continuous thereafter)

DANCING - MARINE BALLROOM - Ocean End of Pier - Continuous 2:00 PM to 2:00 AM

JIMMY DORSEY & HIS ORCHESTRA

2:00 PM to 5:00 PM
9:00 PM to 2:00 AM

ALEX BARTHA & HIS ORCHESTRA

5:30 PM to 8:30 PM

WATERCADE & CIRCUS - MARINE STADIUM - Ocean End of Pier (Weather Permitting)
12:00 2:30 4:30 6:00 7:30 9:00 10:30 12:00

DADDY DAVE'S SHOW - LITTLE THEATRE - Center of Pier

11:00 1:00 4:00 7:30

GENERAL MOTORS Presents PREVIEWS OF PROGRESS
LITTLE THEATRE - Center of Pier
2:00 3:00 8:30 9:30

ANIMATED MUSEUM & JUNGLE LAND - LOWER DECK - Front of Pier
MARCH OF TIME IN WAX EXHIBIT - Upper Floor - Casino Arcade
LORD'S LAST SUPPER IN WAX EXHIBIT - Main Arcade - Front of Pier
ELSIE GROSS at the ELECTRIC ORGAN - Main Lobby
CARILLON CONCERTS - Main Lobby - ELSIE GROSS - 12-12:15 7-7:15
WILD LIFE EXHIBIT - Marine Arcade - Center of Pier

A schedule from July 4, 1947, displays how movies, vaudeville, dancing, and other activities could be planned without duplication. Singers Dick Haymes and Helen Forrest are in the Music Hall, while the Jimmy Dorsey band plays in the Marine Ballroom. Surprisingly, the famed Diving Horse was not on the pier but would return in 1953.

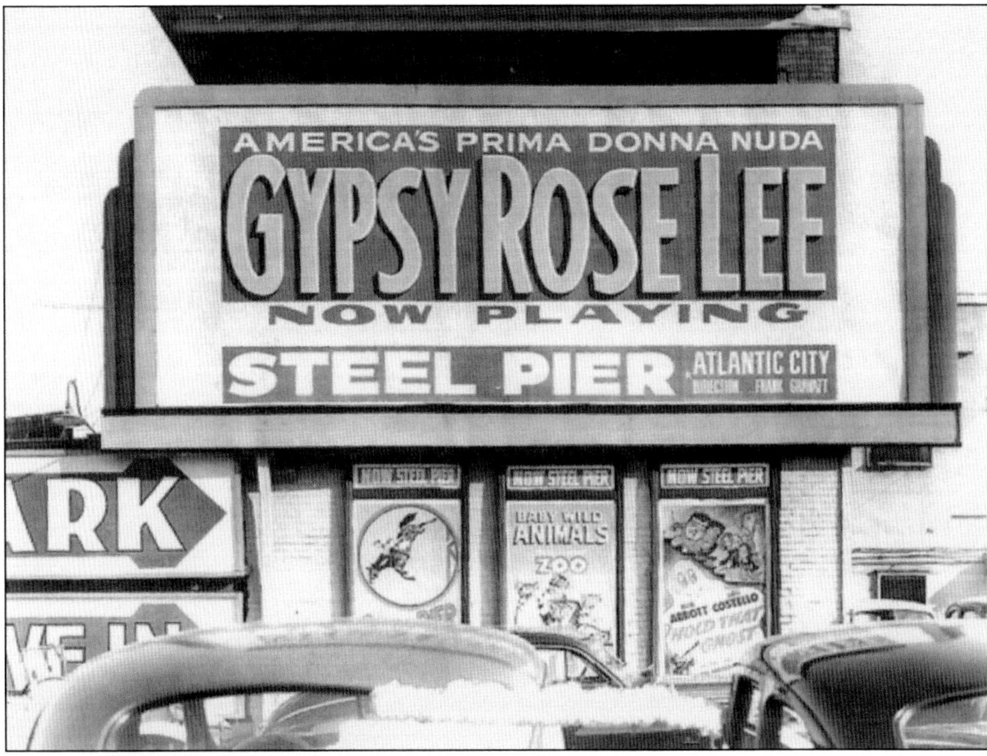

A billboard from 1941 announces stripper Gypsy Rose Lee, whose autobiographical story was turned into a hit musical starring Ethel Merman. Lee was a major star in burlesque and movies and never truly exposed herself onstage because burlesque was never really about nudity; it was about risqué comedy sketches and bump and grind and was, by modern standards, just a little naughty.

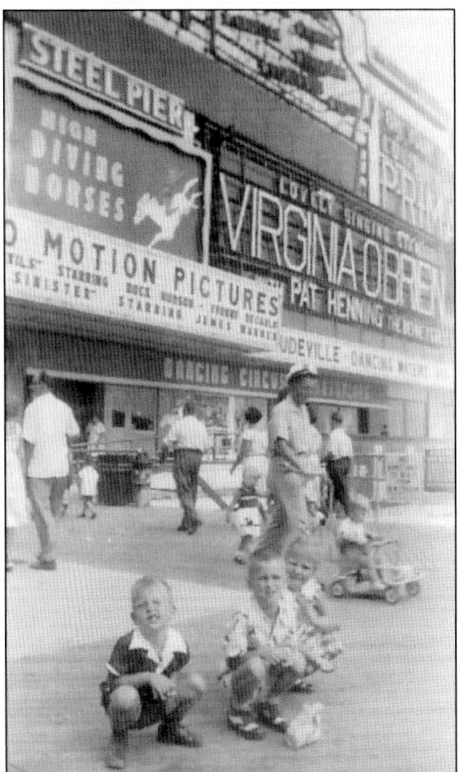

Sometimes, the main attraction was a known movie star or a character actor from the movies. In 1953, it was Virginia O'Brien, an attractive woman who is featured in supporting comedic roles in MGM musicals like *Lady Be Good*, *Ziegfeld Follies*, *The Harvey Girls*, and *Thousands Cheer*. Her gimmick was singing in a deadpan manner without any emotion.

Five

SWING AND SWAY

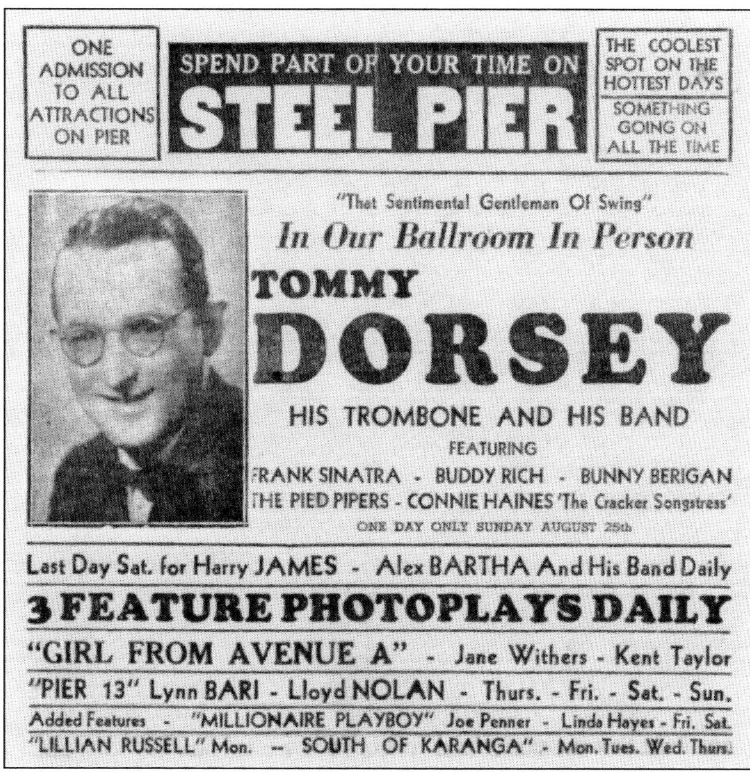

Tommy Dorsey and his orchestra played in Steel Pier's Marine Ballroom 14 times, but his best roster was in August 1940, when he had an all-star band that included legendary drummer Buddy Rich as well as legendary trumpeter Bunny Berigan. Plus, his boy singer was someone named Sinatra.

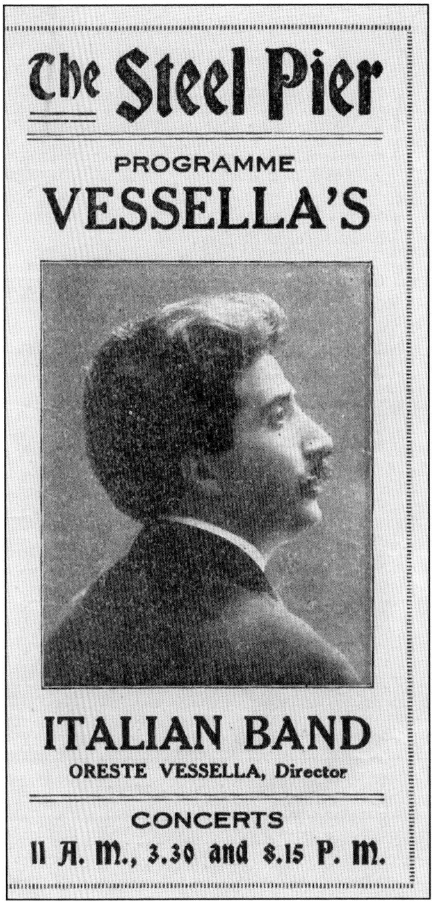

Oreste Vessella led a band on Steel Pier most years from 1902 until 1927. Usually playing light classical or Italian melodies, Vessella was a big hit with the ladies who enjoyed the maestro's unruly thick hair while he conducted. Along with Martini's band, Lehman's orchestra, and Goldman's and Creatore's bands, Vessella catered to the refined patrons and held his position the longest.

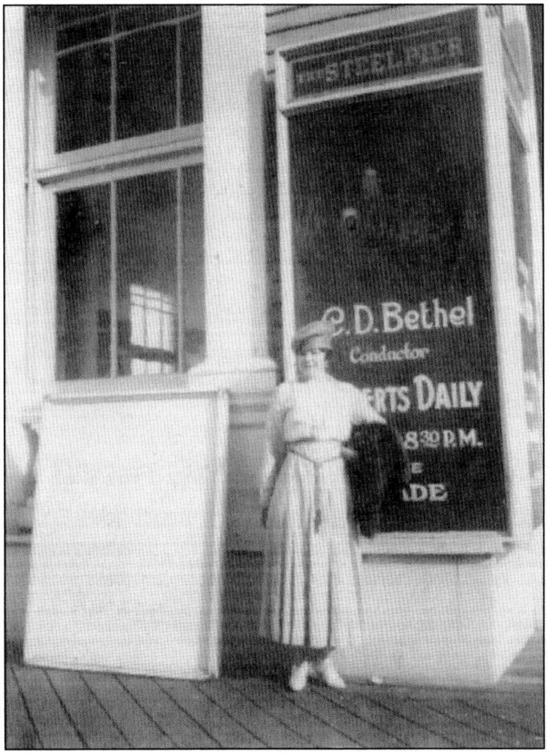

This is an early picture of a display poster announcing concerts by Bethel's band. Music was an integral part of the pier, especially in its first 30 years. It was not until Frank Gravatt bought the pier in 1925 that the concert orchestras began to dissipate in favor of popular dance bands.

Frank Gravatt signed the celebrated "March King" John Philip Sousa to play the pier every summer from 1926 through 1931. Sousa died on May 6, 1932, at the age of 77, but his name and compositions live on as the most familiar patriotic marches in the United States. This ad from 1931 touts Sousa's last appearance.

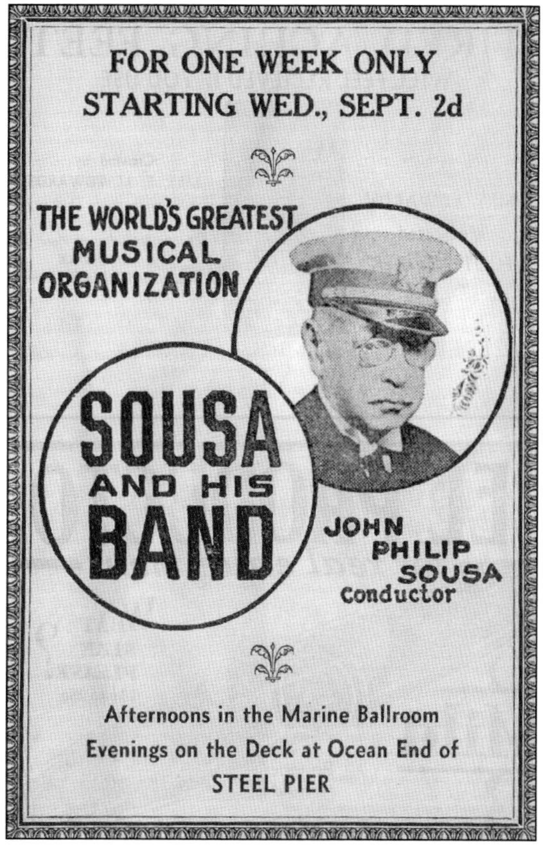

Sousa stands in the Music Hall in this 1927 picture. The rounded, old open-air pavilion beams can be seen still existing in the back of the theater and would remain until a renovation would hide them for good. Sousa was so popular that his marching band played in both the Music Hall and the Marine Ballroom.

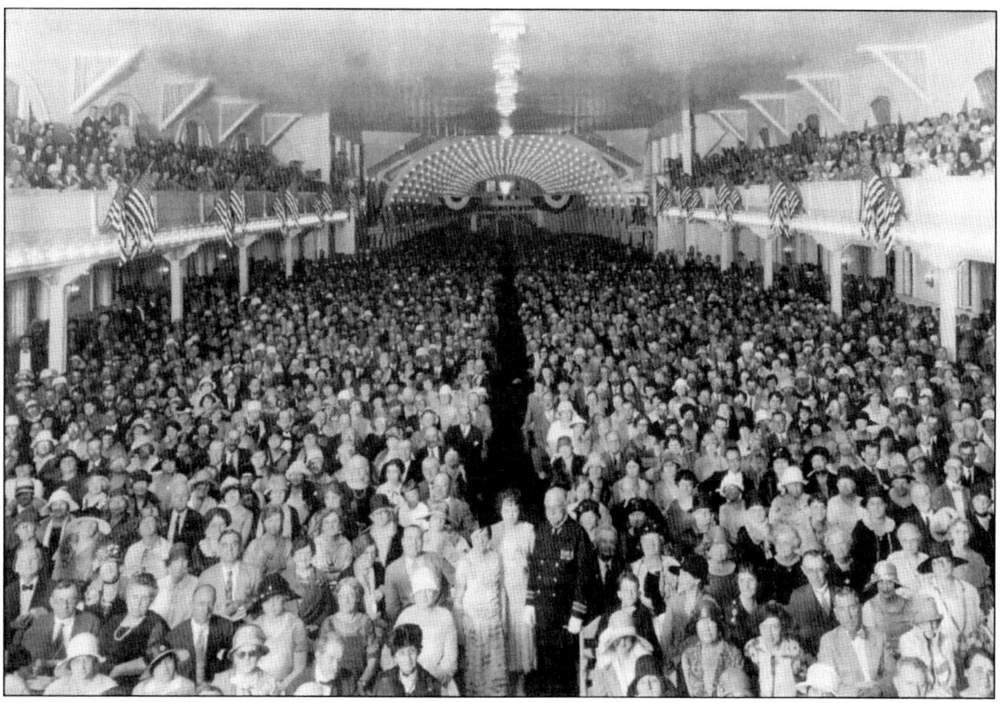

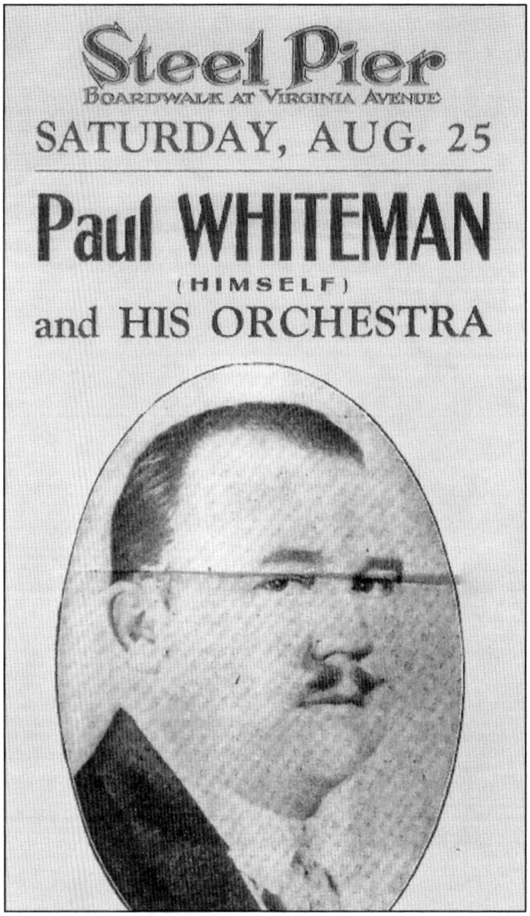

Paul Whiteman, the so-called "King of Jazz," was no doubt the most well-known dance-orchestra bandleader of the 1920s, with 28 number one records. A young Bing Crosby started his career with Whiteman as one of the singing Rhythm Boys. This 1928 ad assures that, yes, Whiteman himself would definitely be on the bandstand—as would a then unknown Crosby.

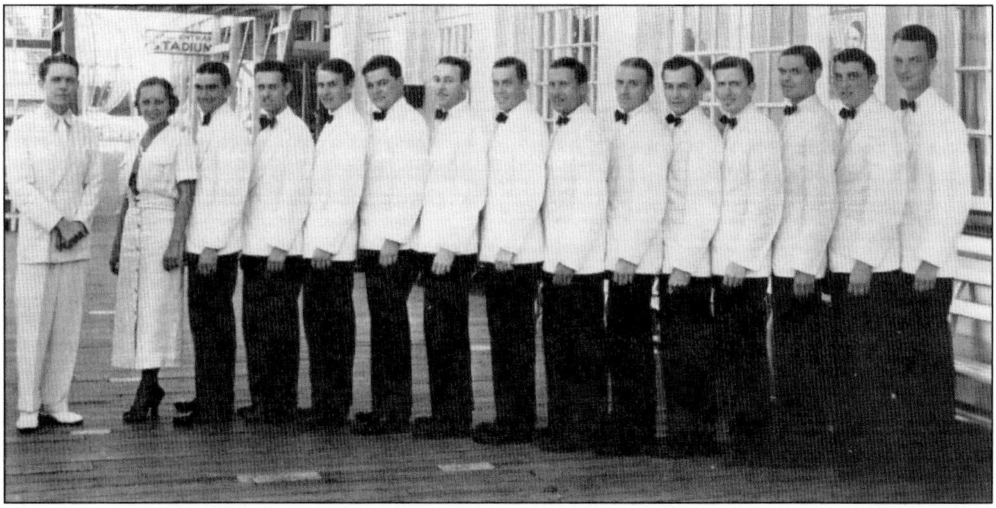

Members of the Joe Haymes band stand outside the Marine Ballroom in August 1934 in their splendid white jackets. Haymes had an excellent band and, while not known today, had a number of hits in the early 1930s. When Tommy and Jimmy Dorsey split up their band in 1935, Tommy took over the Haymes band as leader.

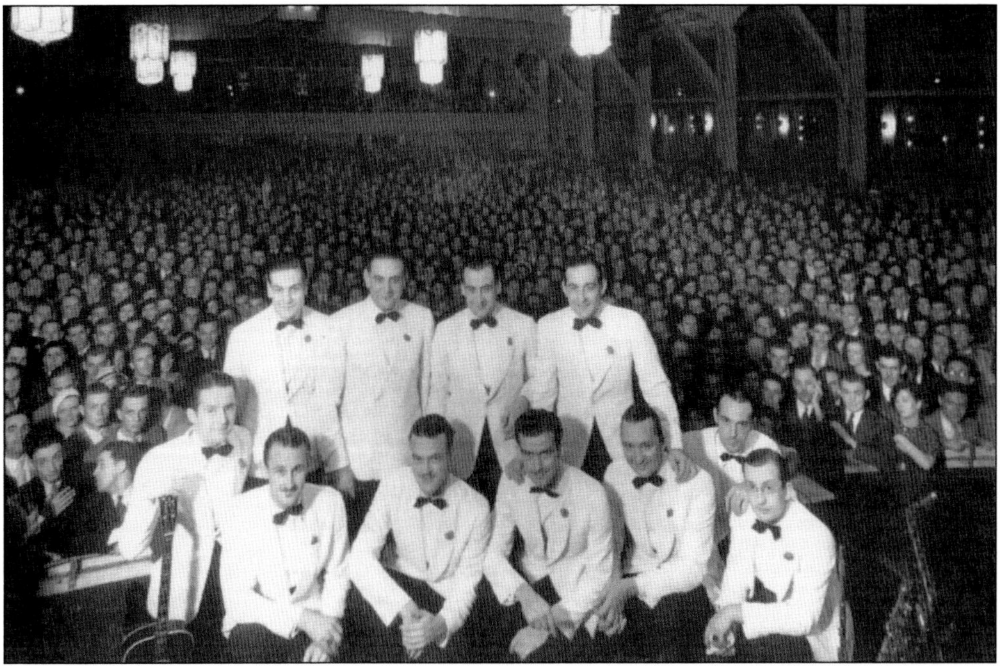

Guy Lombardo's orchestra was known as the "Sweetest Music This Side of Heaven" and played Steel Pier 12 times. It was not a swing band at all; nevertheless, Lombardo's band was perhaps one of the most popular bands ever because of its sweet, no-jazz sound. The band once played Harlem's Savoy Ballroom, the home of swing, to a record-setting crowd. Lombardo (second row, second from left) stands with his brothers, from left to right, Victor, Carmen, and Lebert on the stage of an overflowing Marine Ballroom.

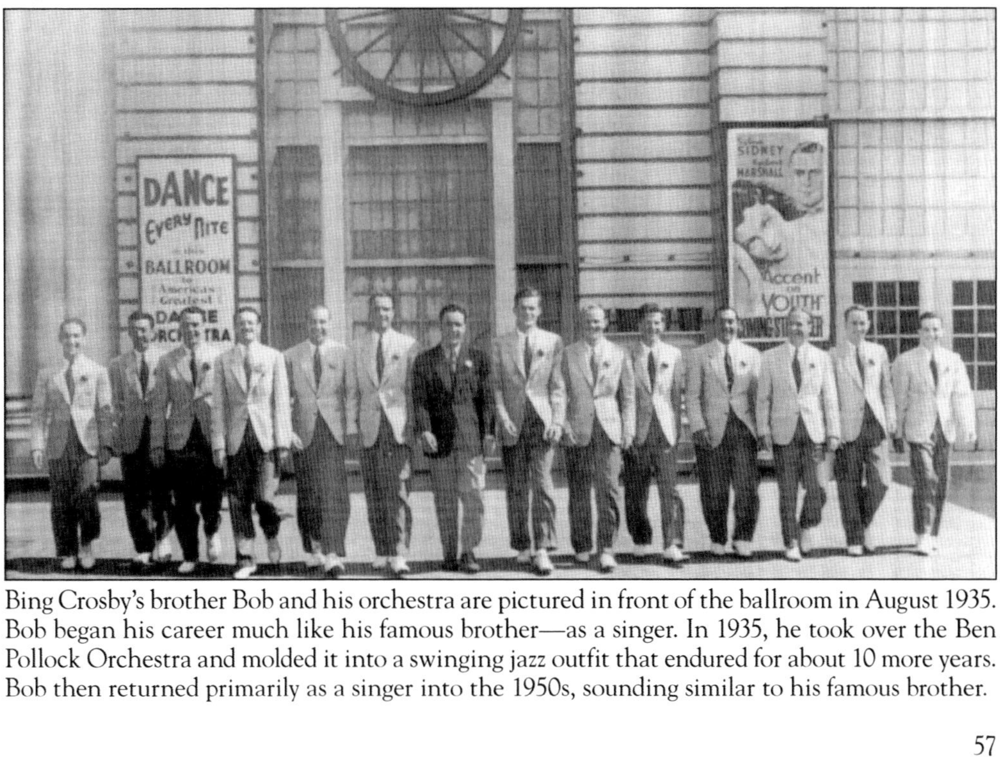

Bing Crosby's brother Bob and his orchestra are pictured in front of the ballroom in August 1935. Bob began his career much like his famous brother—as a singer. In 1935, he took over the Ben Pollock Orchestra and molded it into a swinging jazz outfit that endured for about 10 more years. Bob then returned primarily as a singer into the 1950s, sounding similar to his famous brother.

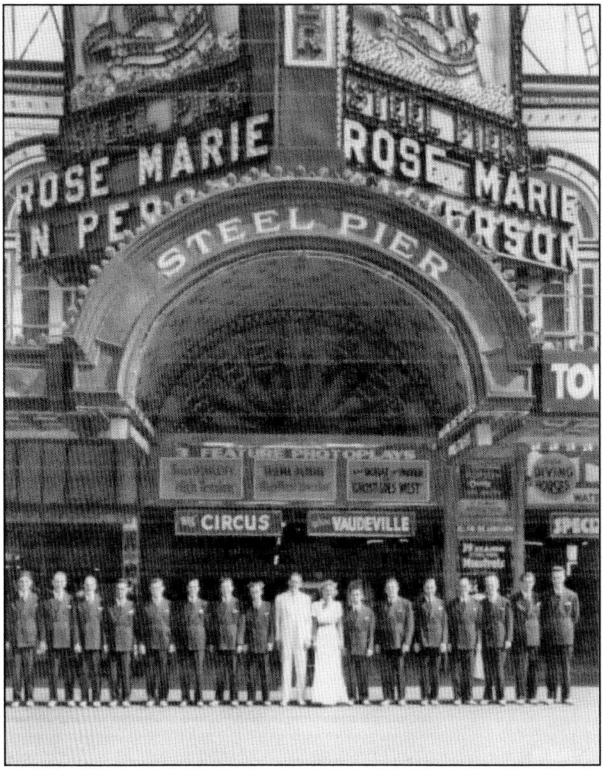

Tommy Dorsey and his band stand in front of the entrance in July 1936. Dorsey's band was an immediate hit after he took over the remains of the Joe Haymes band. During the next 10 years, he recorded 17 number one hits.

When Gene Krupa split with Benny Goodman in early 1938, he formed his own band and decided to make its debut over Easter weekend on Steel Pier. Major music magazines *Down Beat*, *Metronome*, *Billboard*, and *Variety* all covered the event amongst a large and adoring public. Pictured is the band before its first performance on the ballroom stage.

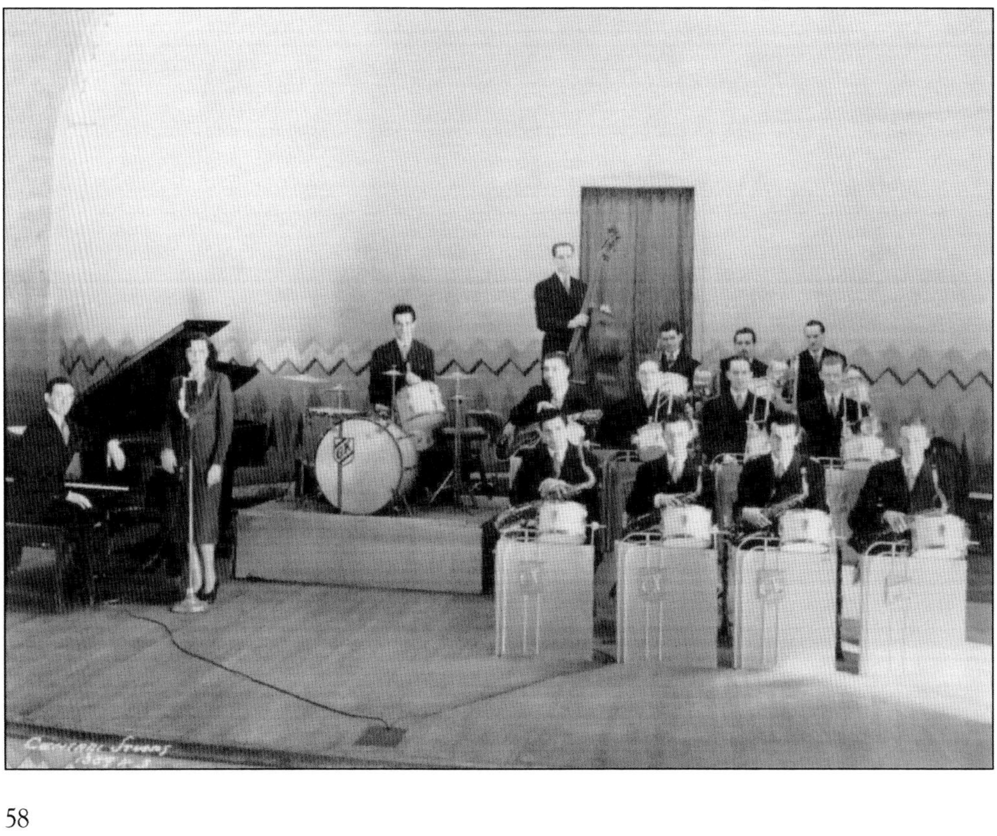

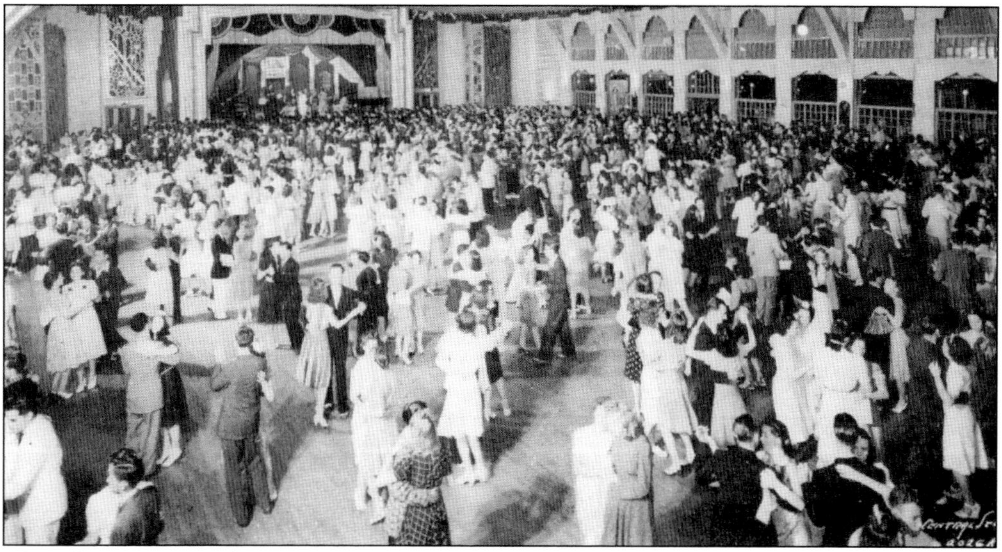

The Alex Bartha Orchestra provides dancing entertainment to the large crowd in the Marine Ballroom. Bartha was a local musician who led the house band from 1932 until 1946 and then sporadically into the 1950s. Atlantic City native Ziggy Elman was plucked from the band to become the featured trumpeter with Benny Goodman and later had a career of his own.

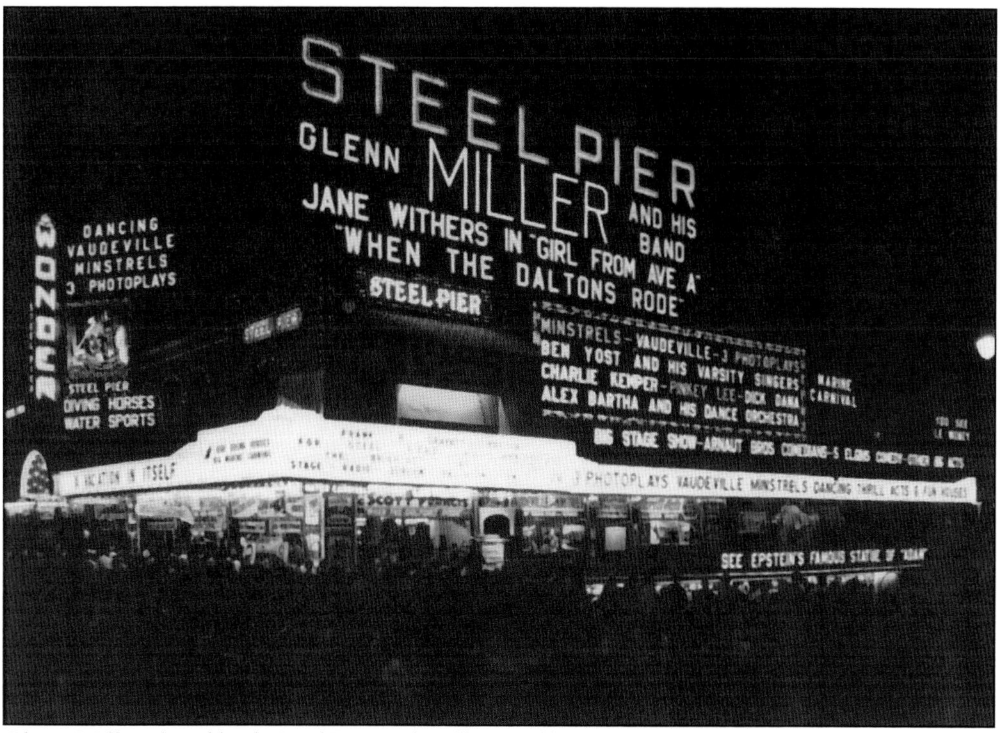

Glenn Miller played both Steel Pier and Million Dollar Pier, the latter twice during the summer of 1942 before he enlisted in the Army Air Forces. Miller's band was voted the top band in America in 1940, 1941, and 1942 in the annual *Billboard* College Music Poll and could swing and also play sweet romantic ballads, owing its popularity to its distinctive clarinet on top of saxophones sound.

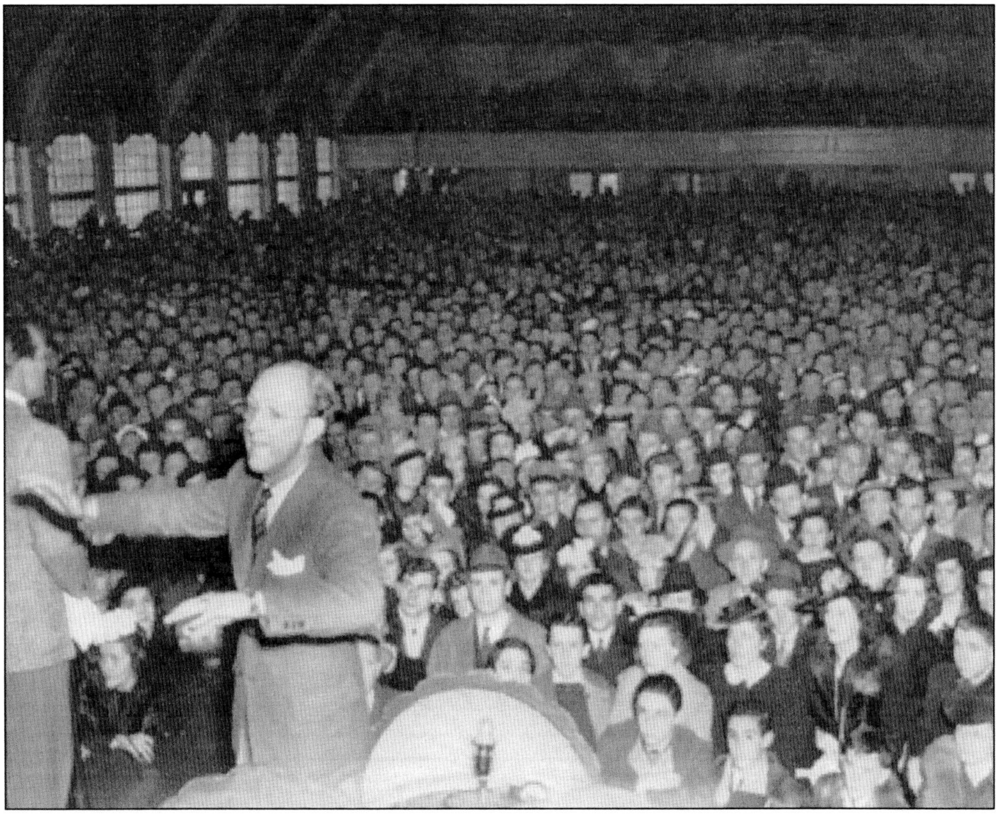

Kay Kyser leads the band onstage in front of a large audience. Many times, the crowds would just stand in front of their favorite bands in awe and watch their heroes play. Swing and dance orchestras were really the rock stars of the 1930s and 1940s, and real fans knew the names of every player and even their solos.

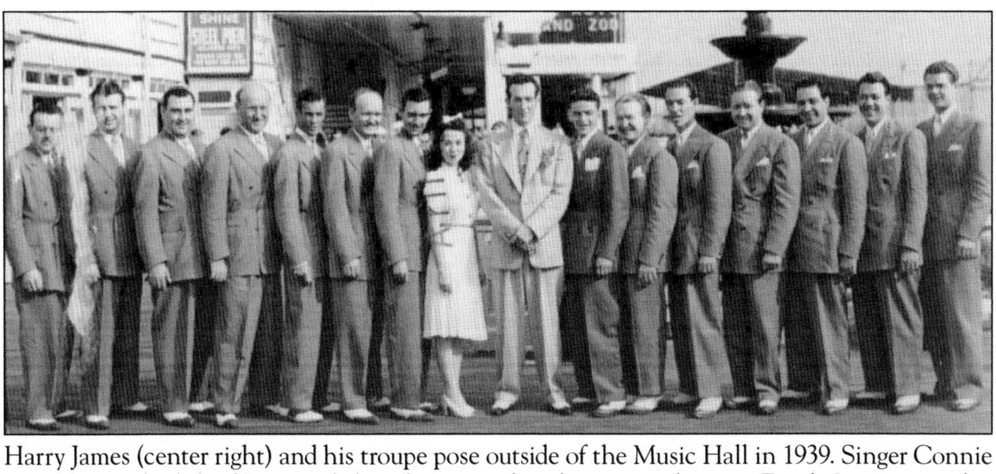

Harry James (center right) and his troupe pose outside of the Music Hall in 1939. Singer Connie Haines is to the left of James, while a skinny, and at the time unknown, Frank Sinatra is to his right. James had heard Sinatra sing at a North Jersey roadside spot and hired him. A year later, Sinatra debuted with Tommy Dorsey, and the rest is history.

Benny Goodman looks out into the crowd in 1938. Gene Krupa had already left and was replaced on drums by Dave Tough. Harry James, seen as the tallest man in the back row, would soon leave to form his own unit. Goodman played the pier 14 times.

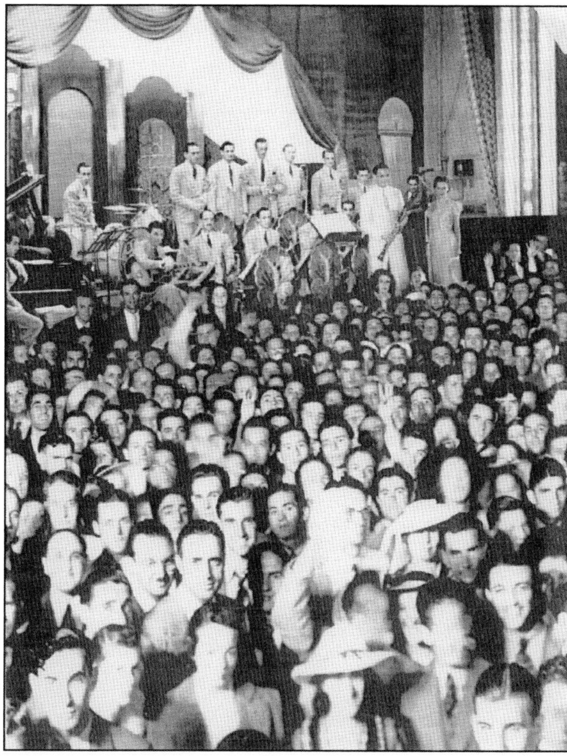

Van Alexander and his crew pose in front of the pier in July 1939. Alexander was primarily an arranger who led his own band for a few years before embarking on a successful career scoring movies and television shows. He died on July 19, 2015, at age 100.

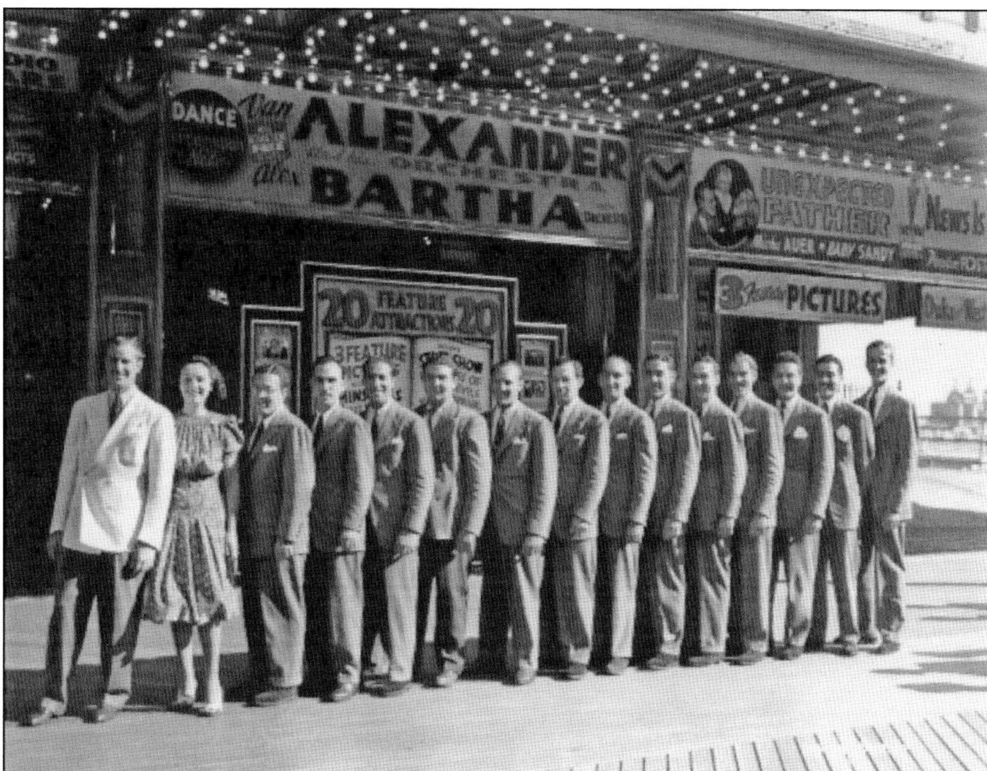

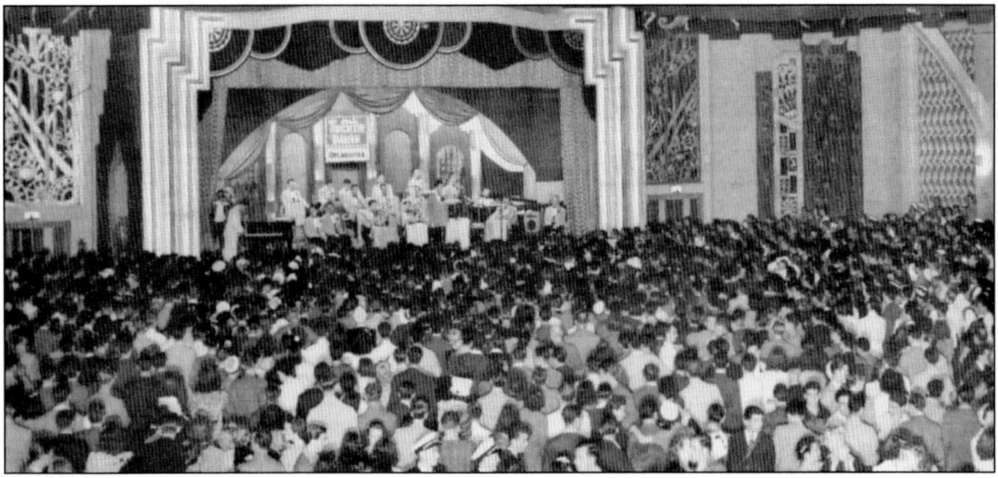

Orrin Tucker and his band play to a thoroughly crowded ballroom. The cavernous building could hold many thousands, including a seated area on the side and a small balcony located in the back. With only the sea air ventilating through its open windows, the bandstand could get very hot due to stage lighting. On a hot afternoon, many a musician would usually lose a few pounds.

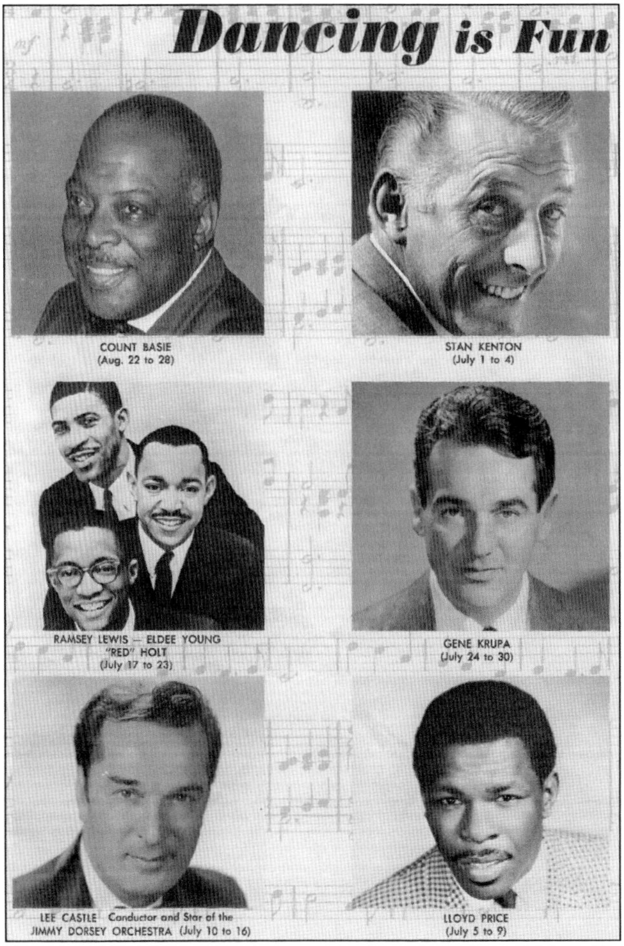

Big band leaders from 1966 include Count Basie, Stan Kenton, and Gene Krupa. The great drummer played on the pier a record 22 times, more than any other dance-bandleader. African American bands finally broke the color line in 1964 when Duke Ellington stepped up to the microphone and announced his first number.

Six

You Will Believe a Horse Can Dive

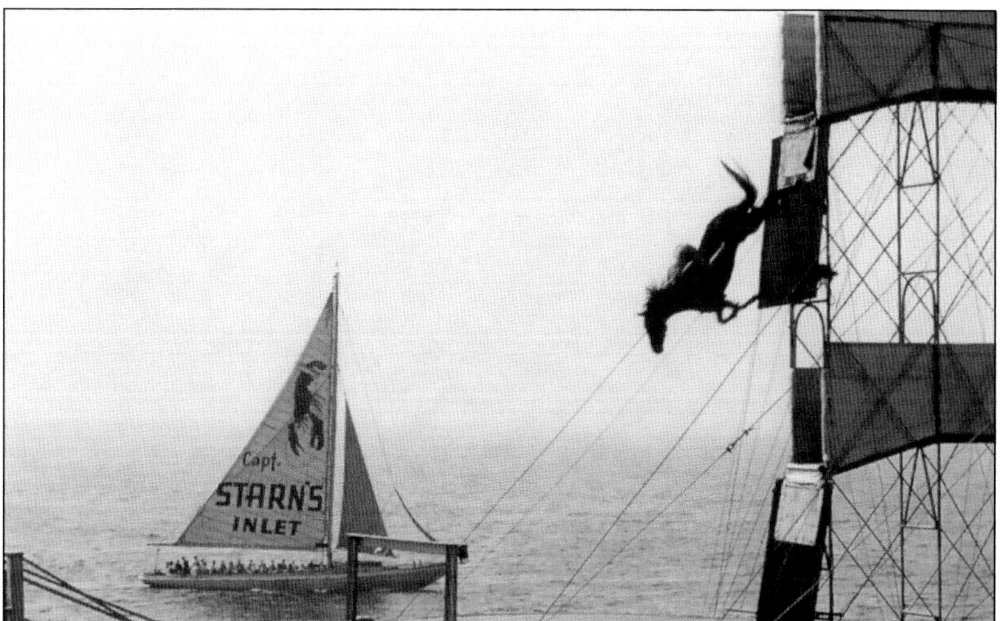

The classic photograph of the famous Diving Horse is the image most think of when remembering the Atlantic City of pre-casino days. In this picture, the horse and its rider have just pushed off as passengers on a crowded sailboat look on in awe. Capt. Starn's was a well-known seafood restaurant that existed for about 35 years in the inlet area.

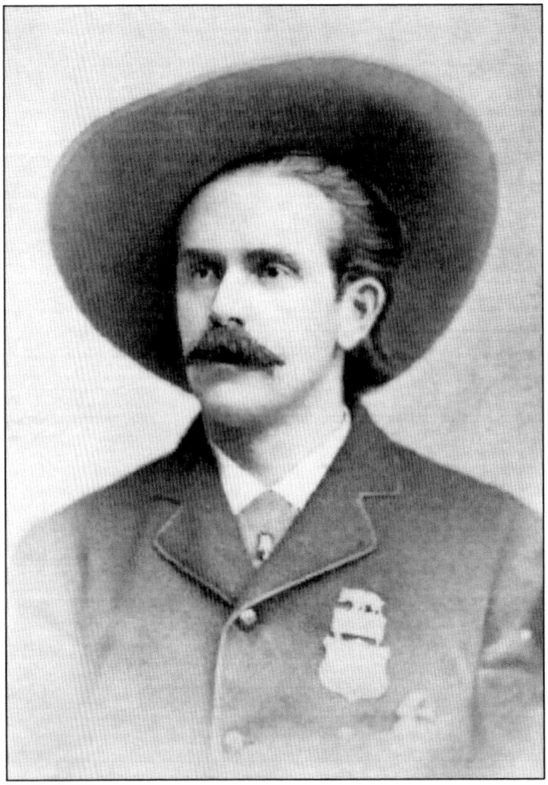

W.P. "Doc" Carver was the originator of the Diving Horse act. Born in Winslow, Illinois, on May 7, 1851, Carver became friends with Buffalo Bill Cody and Wild Bill Hickock as he set records in shooting exhibitions in the United States and Europe. When his horse dove into water from a 40-foot-high washed-out bridge at the Platte River in Nebraska, Carver came up with an idea that became a sensation. He died August 31, 1927, and never saw his creation on Steel Pier.

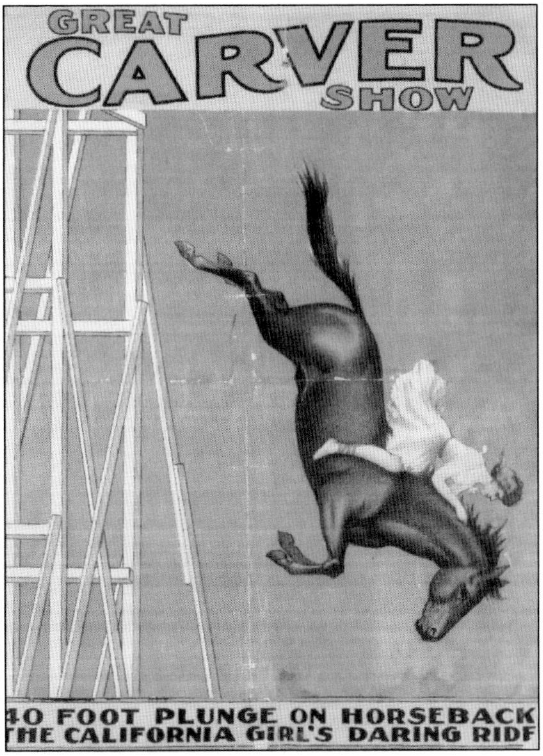

Doc Carver did not perfect his act until 1905 and began displaying it at state fairs and carnivals. Originally, the horse would dive from a rickety structure into a dug-out water-filled hole or even sometimes into the ocean itself. But after a few mishaps and injuries to both the horse and diver, the diving apparatus was modified for safety, and the horse would dive into a specified tub made especially for the act.

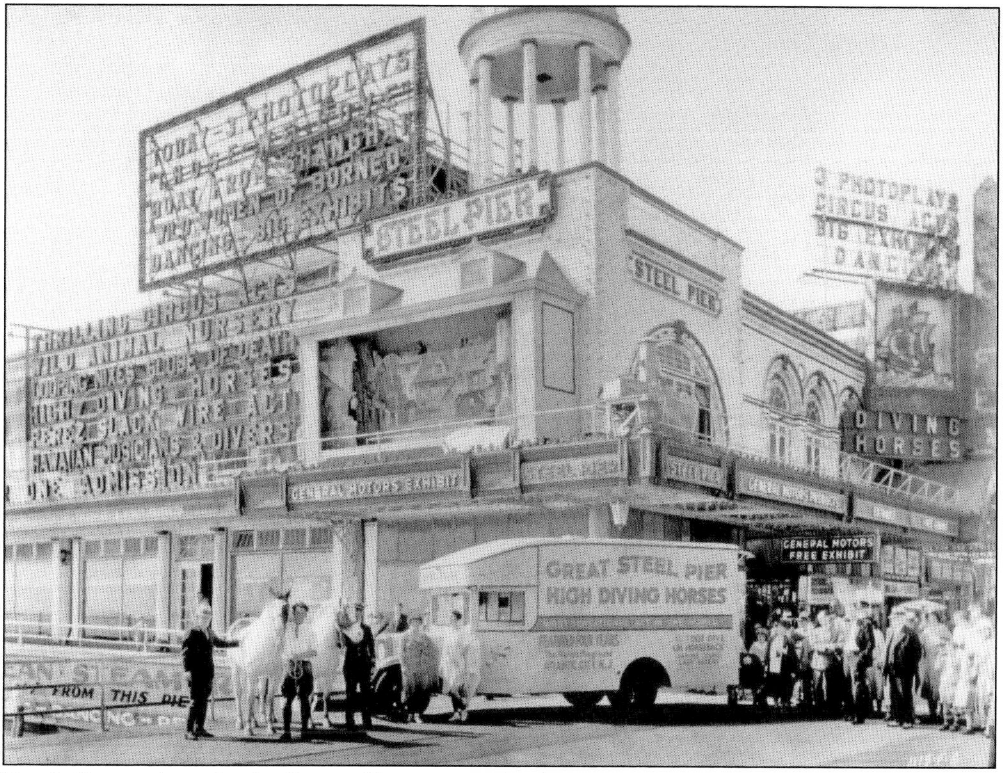

Frank Gravatt brought the Diving Horse act to Steel Pier in 1929 on the recommendation of his booking agent George Hamid, the man responsible for many of the pier's exotic acts and, later, the diving-horse act's owner. Gravatt spent $35,000 to expand the back end of the pier into a vast seating and stage area that would hold thousands. This picture of the front of the pier in 1931 shows the vehicle used to transport the horses as well as the General Motors exhibit.

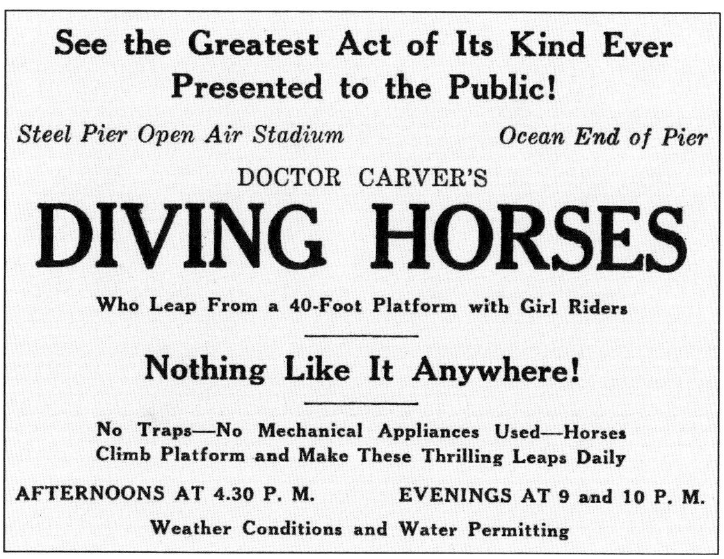

Pictured here is an early advertisement from 1929. The act took place multiple times each day, except when the weather was inclement. Large lights were erected on top of the ballroom, illuminating the Water Circus area for nighttime performances.

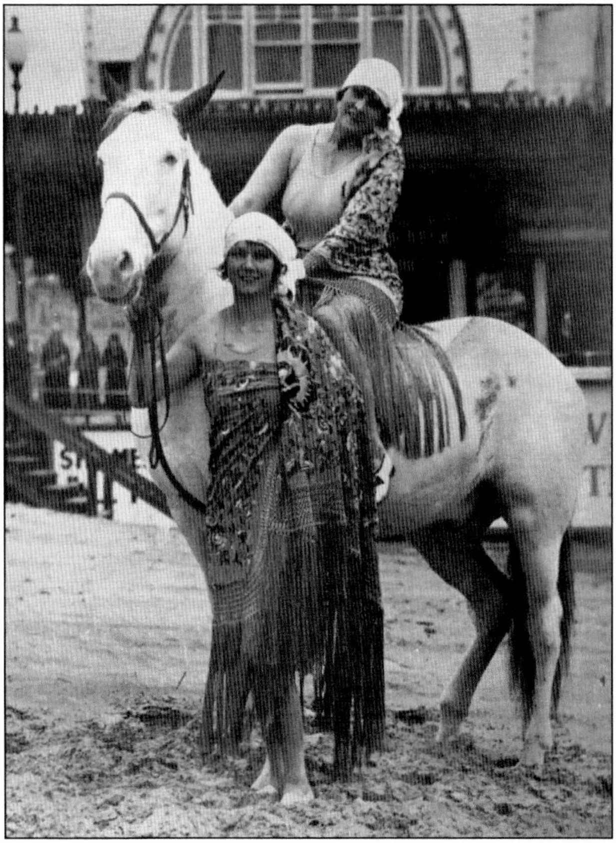

Sonora (Webster) Carver leads the horse Lightning on the beach on the side of the pier as sister Arnette Webster rides. Sonora answered an ad in 1924 calling for riders, married Doc's son Al Carver in 1928, and called up sister Arnette to join her a year later. No helmets were worn then, and Sonora lost her sight in 1931 when she hit the water with open eyes. She became permanently blind but dove with the horses for 11 years thereafter. The movie *Wild Hearts Can't Be Broken* is based on her life.

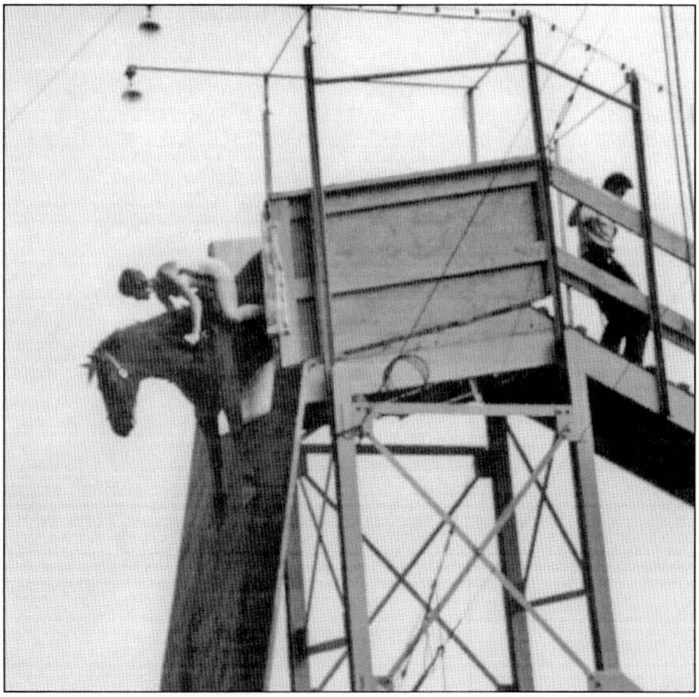

This horse is ready to dive as its legs hang over the apron. The hind legs will then push off, and with the rider's head tucked into the shoulder of the horse, the dive will be complete. Notice the handler walking down the ramp, as his job was finished. No pushing and no trap doors—just the horse, the diver, and patience.

Diver Ann Miles is seen on the horse from a rare angle—above. The drop was 40 feet into a huge 12-foot-deep padded tank filled with water. Miles, who rode from 1958 to 1966 and was a model and movie stand-in, performs (uncredited) the very creepy "spider walk" on the staircase in *The Exorcist*. (Courtesy of Ann Miles.)

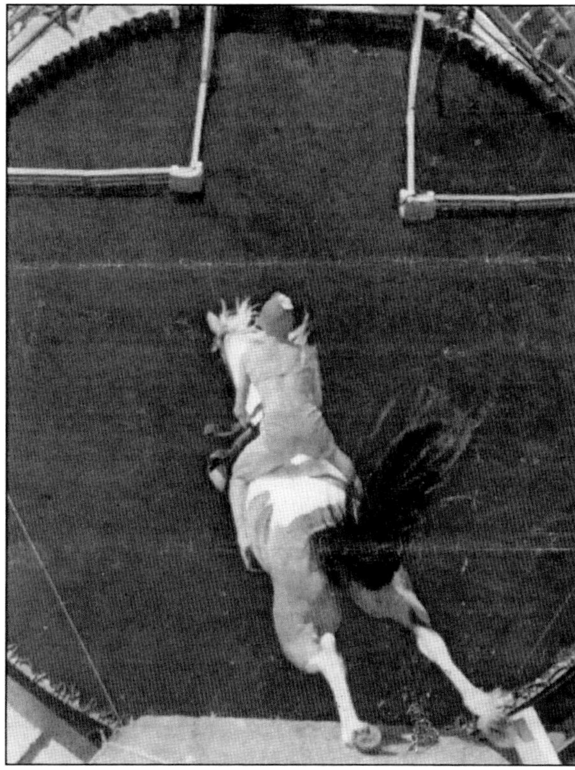

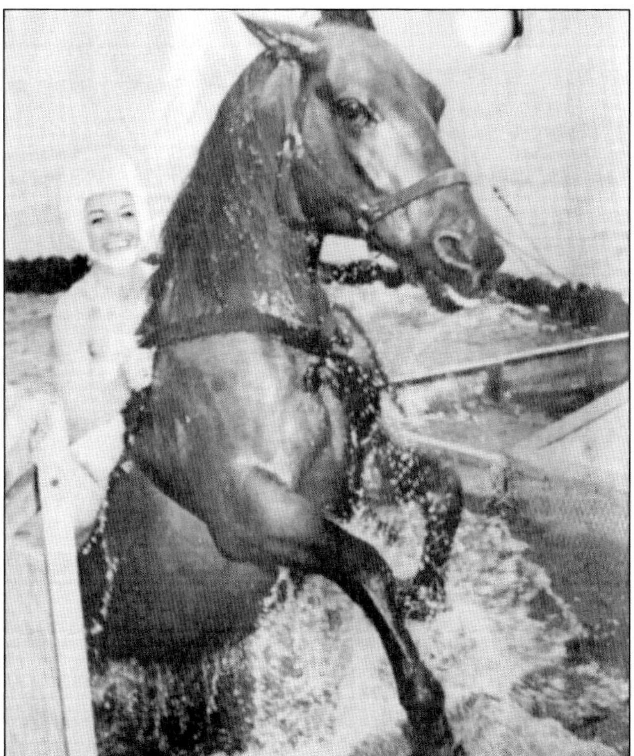

Diver Marion Hackney emerges after her dive with Dimah, which is Hamid spelled backwards. Hackney was a rider from 1952 through 1965 and wore a crash helmet for protection, as did most divers. Her father, Joe Hackney, was a high diver in the Water Circus and once dove 150 feet from a blimp into the ocean. Marion died in 1978 at age 44.

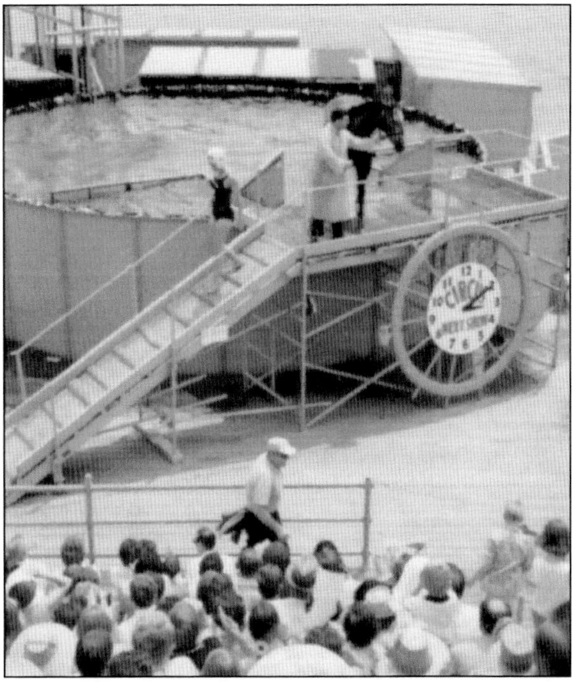

The pool area is seen here in the late 1960s. Due to storms, the back-end stage area of Steel Pier was reconfigured many times. Sometimes, the Diving Horse would be seen diving straight on and other years in silhouette, depending on where the apparatus was placed. For a few years, an elevator was even used in place of a ramp, but due to public outcry, the ramp returned.

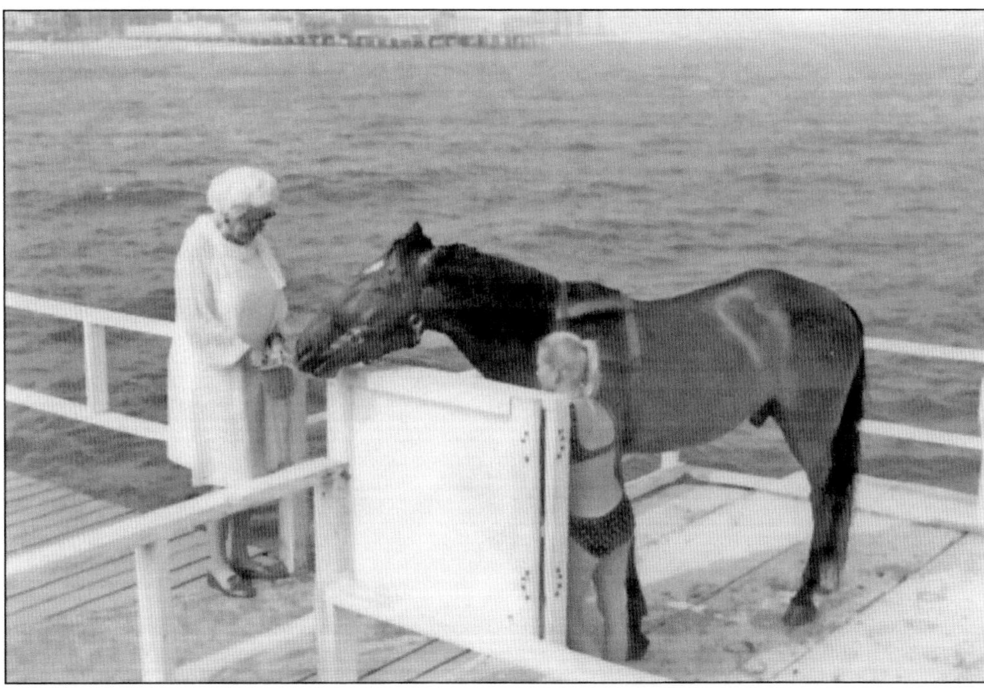

The horses always had an eye out for the woman who rewarded them with a carrot after their dive. Lorena Carver, Doc Carver's daughter, trained and owned the horses that performed not only on Steel Pier, but also in Florida during the winter. Lorena was the act's first female rider, from 1905 to 1930, and averaged one broken bone per year. It took about three years to fully train the horses to perform and most loved the water. This picture is from the mid-1970s. Lorena died in 1981 at age 95.

The audience for the Diving Horse and Water Circus always faced out to sea in the large grandstand, but in 1970, it was reversed, due to the fire that destroyed the entire ocean end, including the Marine Ballroom. The rider seen here is probably Terrie McDevitt, who was a teenager when she joined the act.

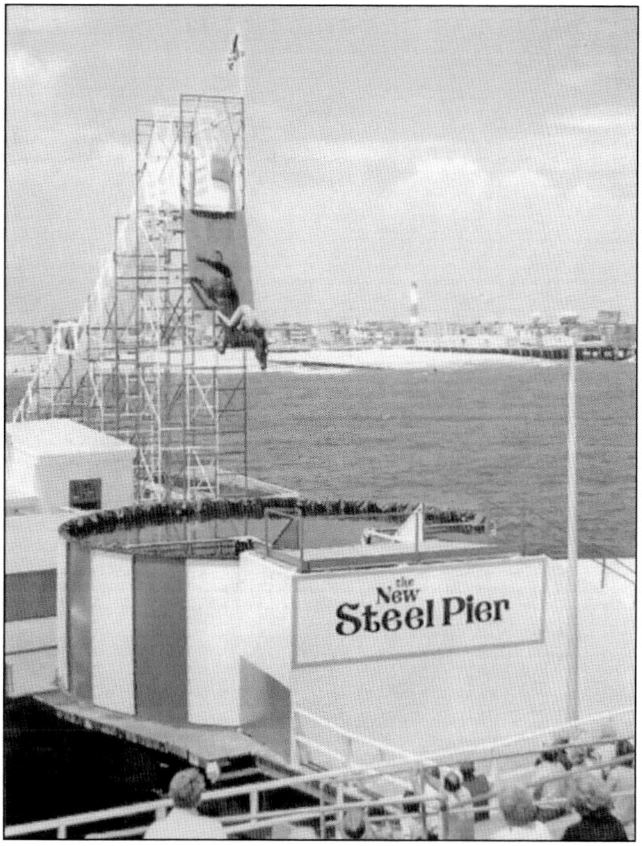

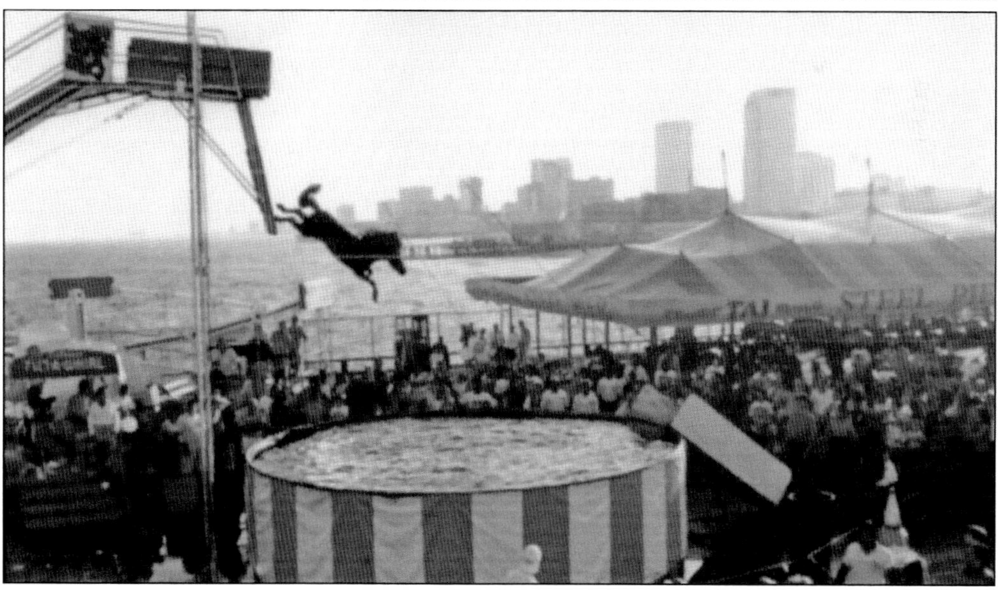

When Steel Pier was rebuilt and opened in 1993, the attempt to continue the Diving Horse legacy was symbolized with a small donkey plunging 30 feet without a rider. However, the times had changed, and the act was not looked upon favorably. It was the last hurrah of an amazing and controversial spectacle that was an integral part of the Steel Pier story.

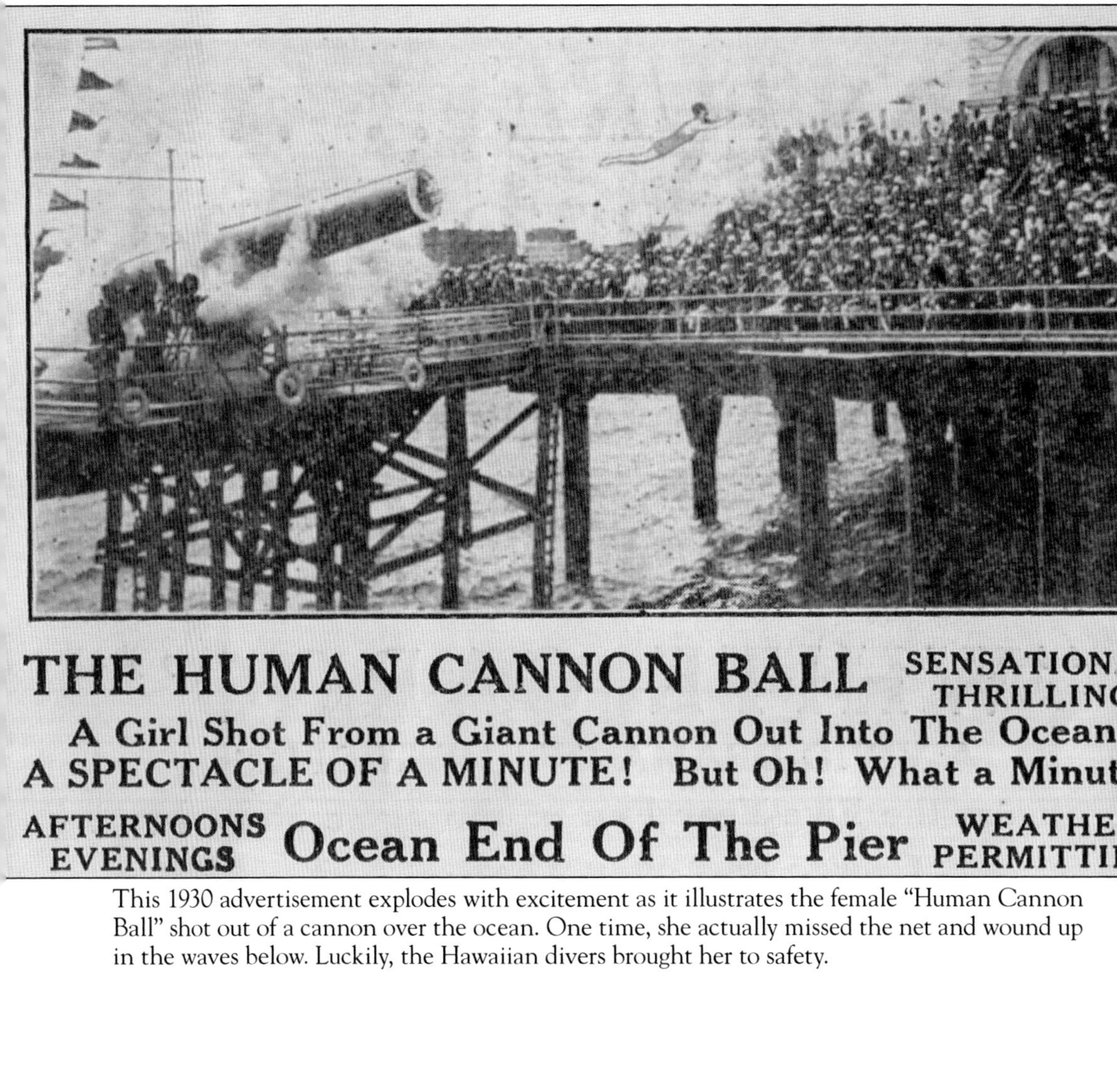

This 1930 advertisement explodes with excitement as it illustrates the female "Human Cannon Ball" shot out of a cannon over the ocean. One time, she actually missed the net and wound up in the waves below. Luckily, the Hawaiian divers brought her to safety.

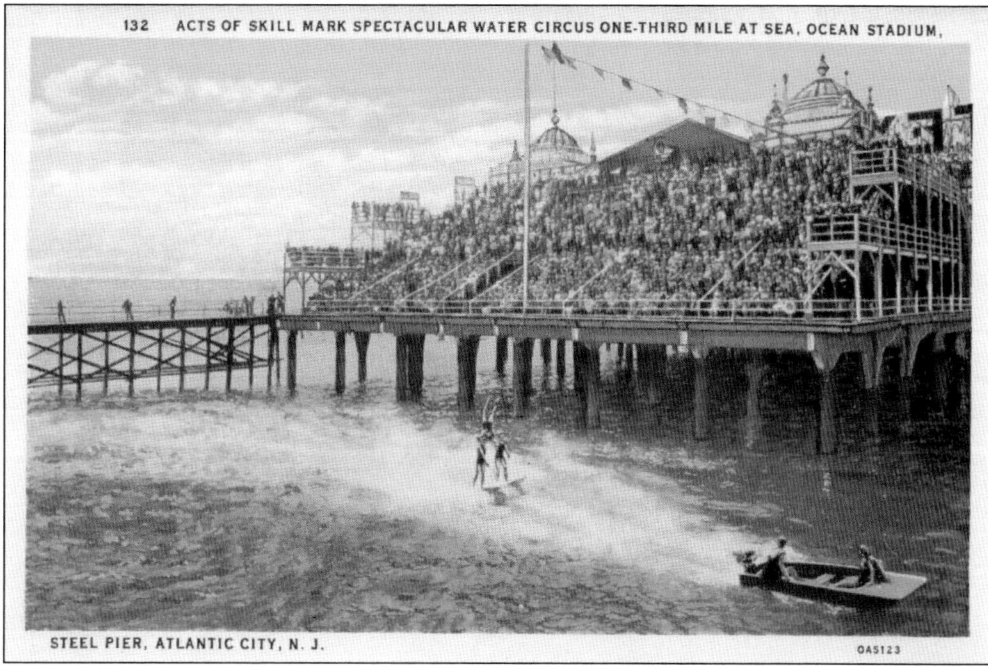

The Ocean Stadium, seating thousands, was separated from the stage of the Water Circus and Diving Horse by the water, utilized as the performance area for speedboats and water-skiers. This postcard displays the multitude of people who would fill the seating area several times per day.

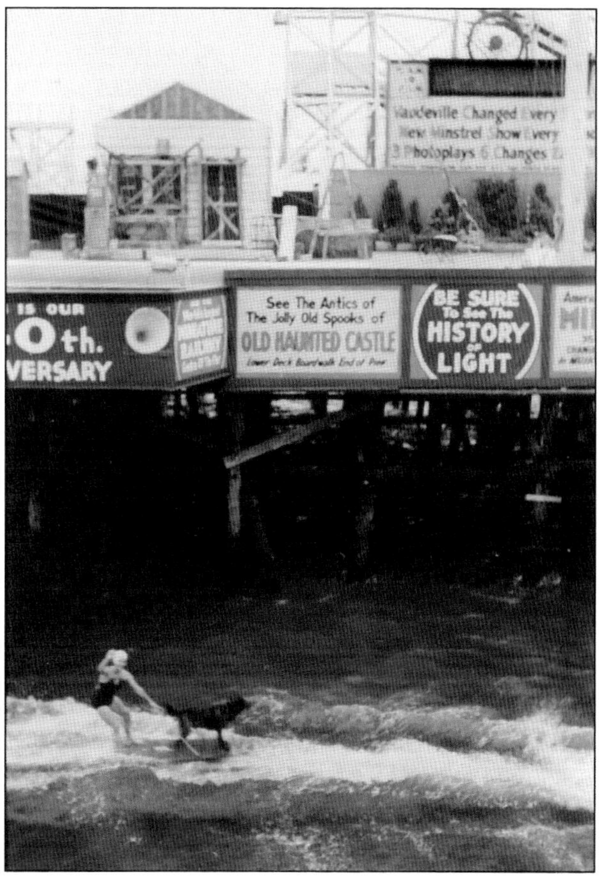

One of the most famous acts in the Water Circus was that of Rex the Wonder Dog. Rex was a found shepherd-mix dog who took to the water, especially behind a speedboat or an aquaplane. Rex enjoyed his time in the show from 1934 to 1942 and always received a big hand from the crowd. This picture was taken from the stadium seating in 1937.

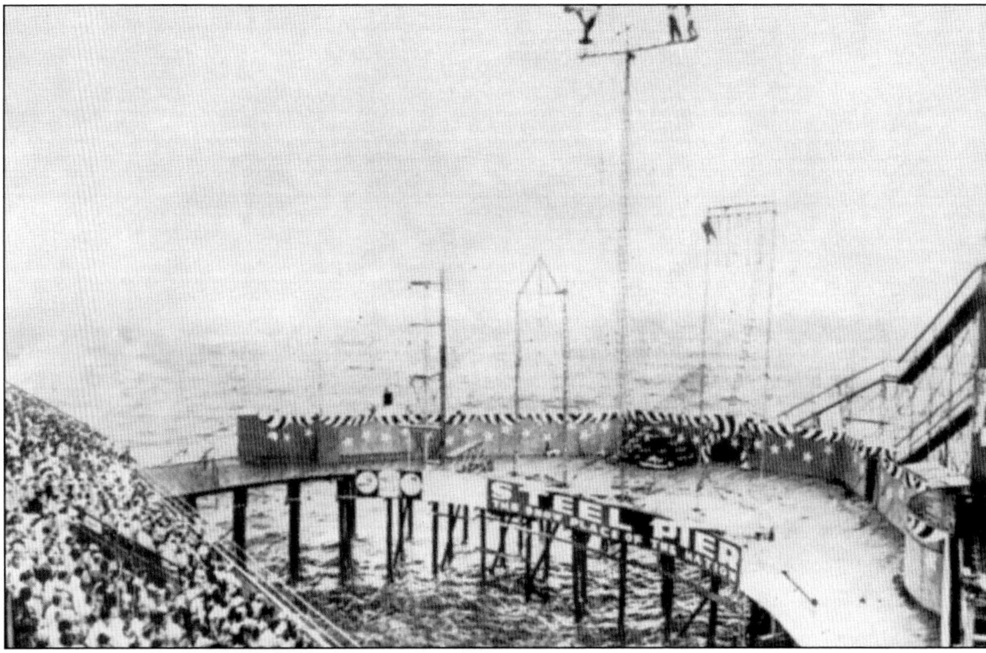

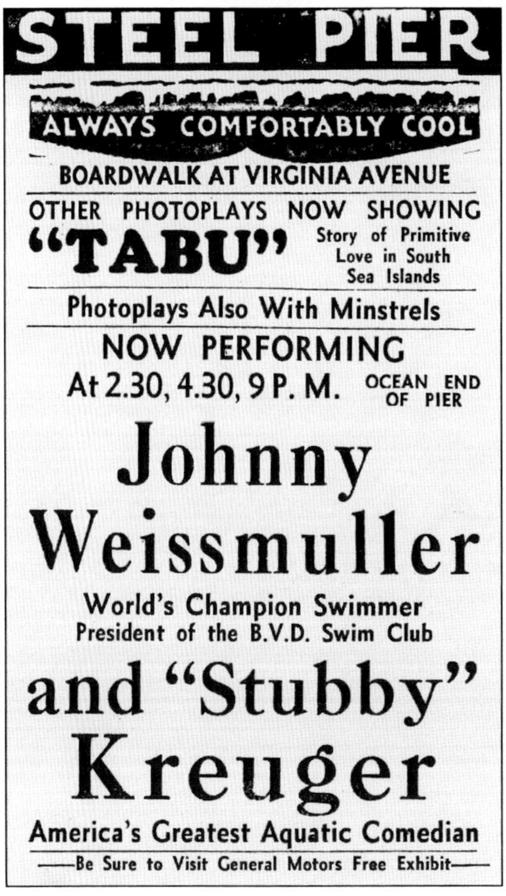

This view looking down at the Water Circus area from the ocean displays how enormous the outside seating area was and how the stage was configured in the 1960s. Because of many storms, especially a horrendous one in 1953, the stage area tore away and was rebuilt. The open area utilized during the speedboat days was replaced with an enclosed diving area. An addition to the Marine Ballroom can be seen on the building's right side.

This 1931 ad headlines Olympic gold medalist swimmer Johnny Weissmuller just before he headed to Hollywood to play Tarzan in 12 motion pictures. On Steel Pier, Weissmuller was just one of a long line of excellent athletes who would dive into the ocean with remarkable precision.

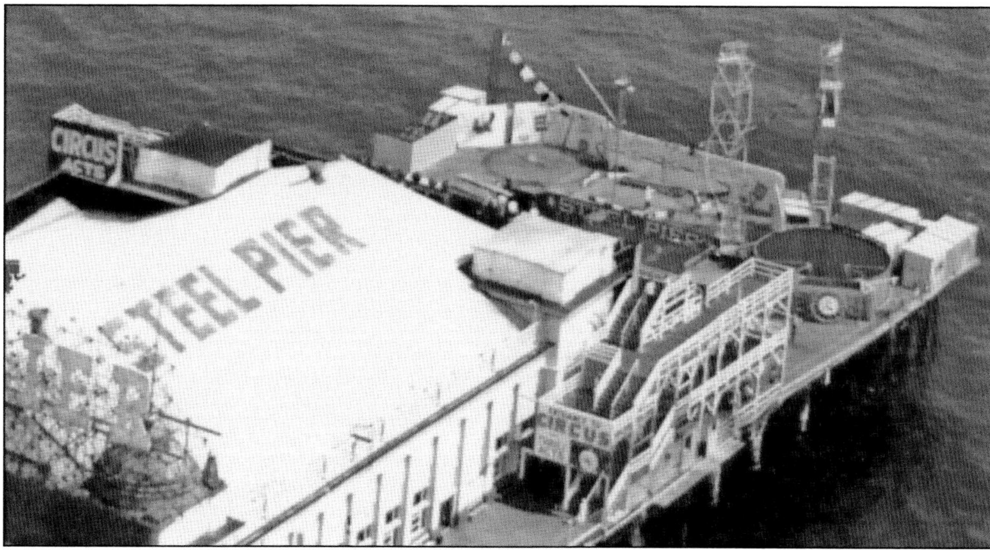

Pictured here is the Water Circus stage in the 1960s, as seen behind the Marine Ballroom. The Diving Horse tank and elevator can be seen on the right while a performing structure for aerialists can be seen to its left. This was the farthest end of the pier and was almost a half mile out over the ocean.

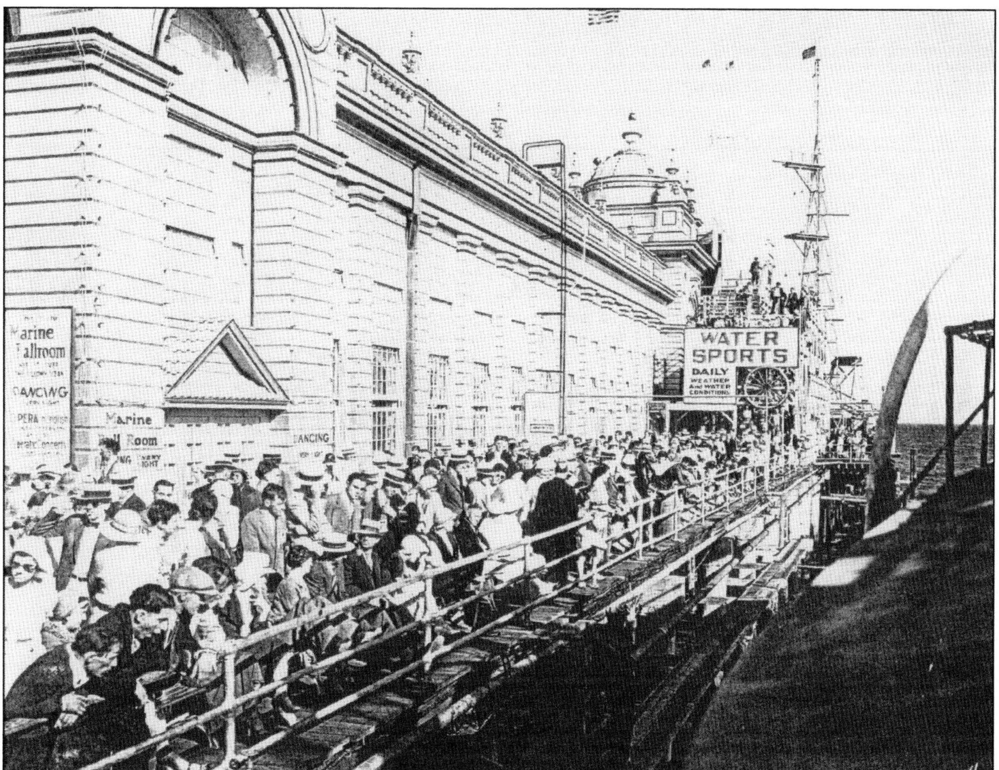

An excited and large crowd mingles on the side of the Marine Ballroom just in front of the entrance to the Water Circus. Since the circus was right behind the ballroom, many bands that played in the ballroom had to get used to the sudden demise of the crowd once the water show began.

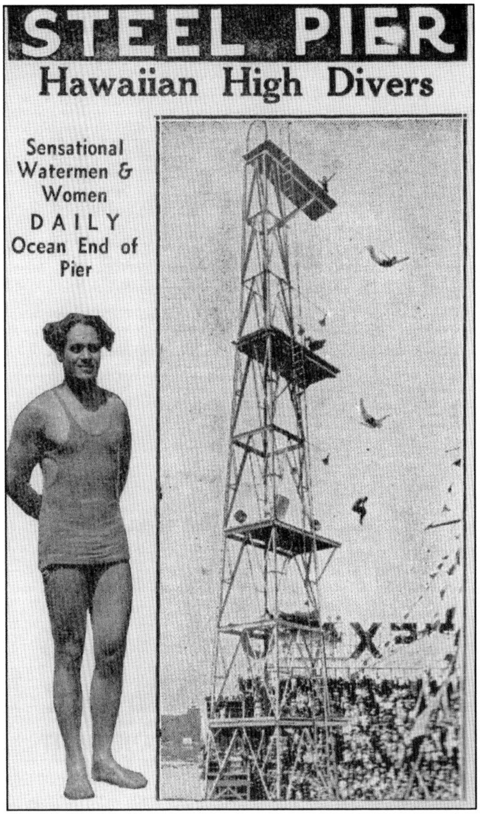

The Hawaiian High Divers actually began on Steel Pier a year before the Ocean Stadium was built. The Hawaiians were a major attraction from 1928 through 1940, and crowds would witness spectacular dives into the ocean from a 100-foot-tall tower.

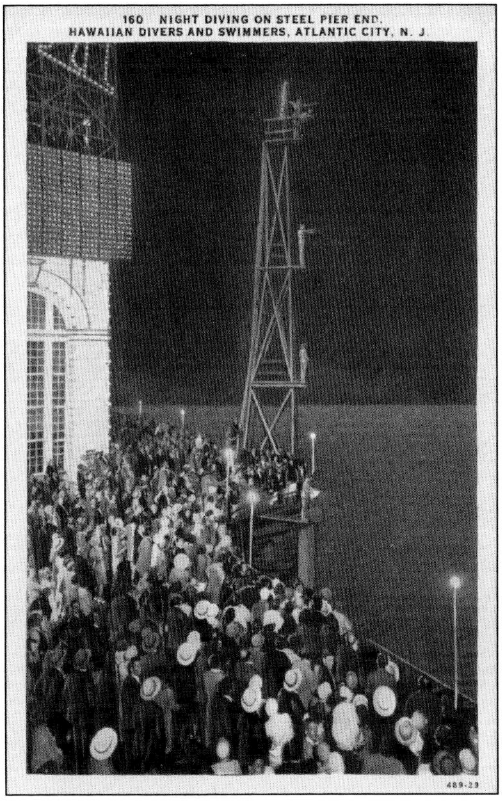

Because the pier was open until at least midnight daily into the 1930s, night performances were common. This postcard from 1928 shows the tower on the side of the Marine Ballroom before the building of the Ocean Stadium. This was a dangerous act because the stage lights that were available did not produce much guidance for the Hawaiian divers into the blackness of the ocean.

This 1931 act promoting the Death Globe explains the amazing act of CeDora, who rode her motorcycle inside a small iron sphere at high speeds. Many of the acts in the Water Circus were of this thrilling nature, and audiences were not used to seeing such daredevil acts. George Hamid is credited for finding these amazing feats from around the world.

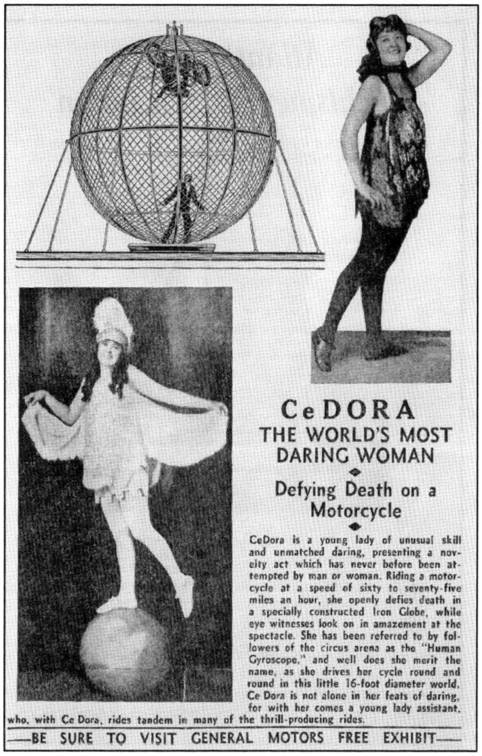

A trapeze act is in motion in the early 1930s. Memorable circus acts included, at various times, dancing bears, elephants, seals, porpoises, and dogs. Clowns were also present and performed comedic dives into the ocean. The final bit of business was regularly the Diving Horse.

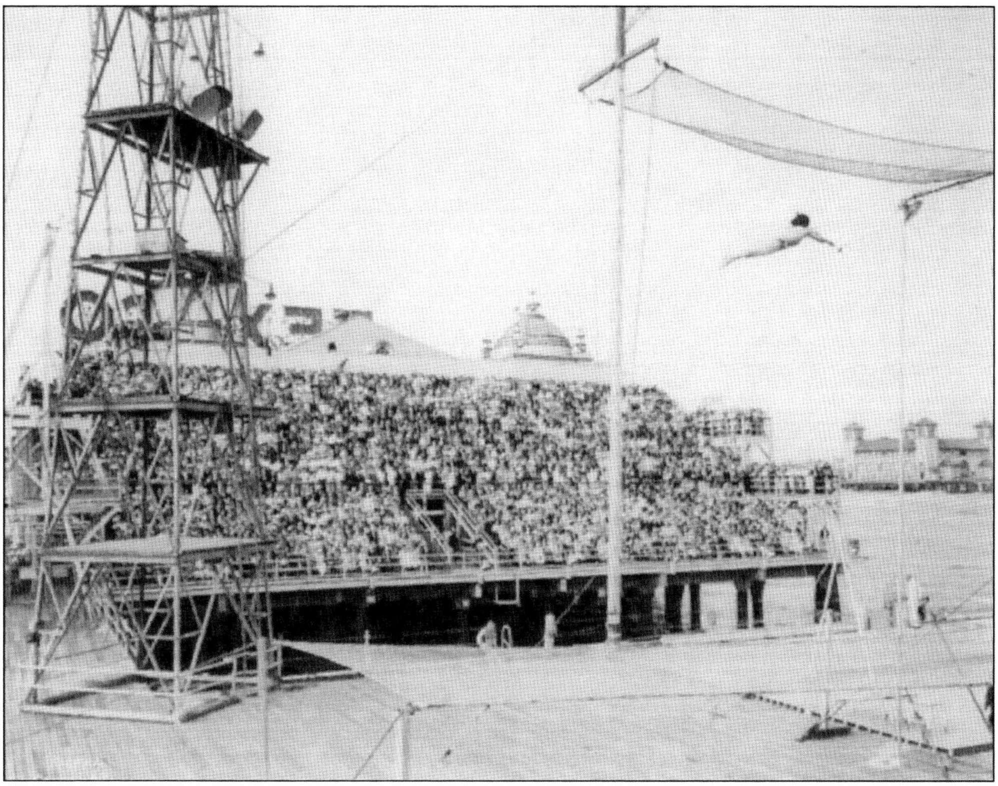

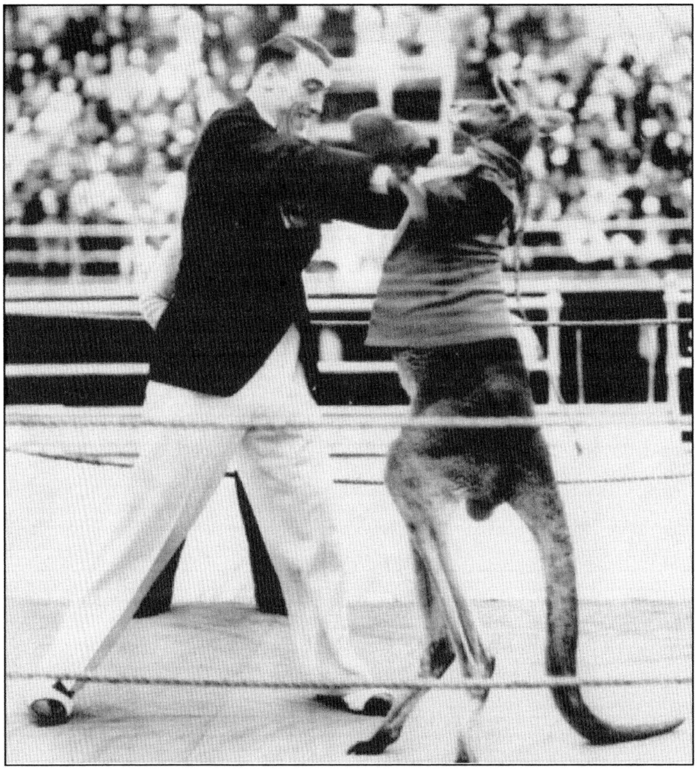

Anything could happen on Steel Pier—from boxing cats to a boxing kangaroo. Primo Carnera, the heavyweight champ who knocked out Jack Sharkey in 1933, decided he did not get enough punishment in New York. Sohe sparred with a kangaroo in a ring on the Water Circus stage to a draw.

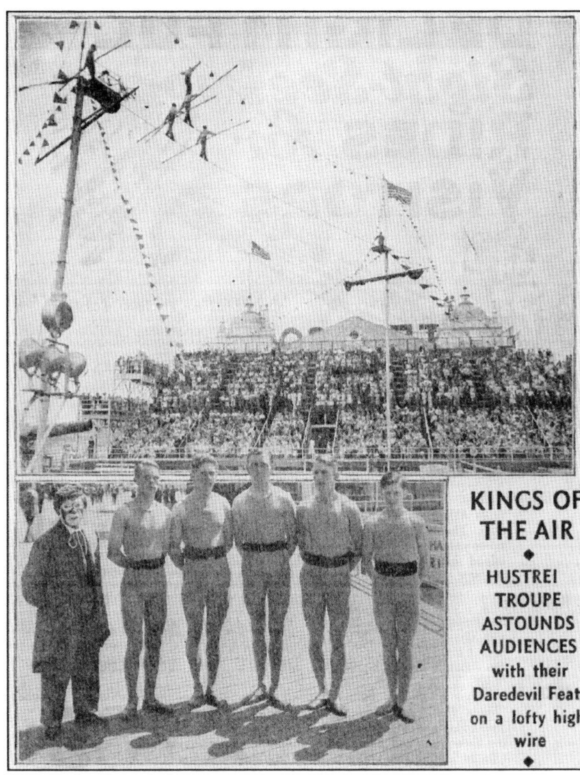

Tightrope artists from Germany, like the Hustrei Troupe and the Flying Wallendas, were a sensation. Performing inside a tent was one thing, but balancing 100 feet over the ocean was something else. No other pier in Atlantic City could offer the unique and dazzling entertainment provided by Steel Pier.

Goliath arrived in 1934 and stayed for two years. Weighing in at 6,000 pounds, he was the world's largest known sea elephant. Goliath did not have to do much—just exist and eat a particular type of fish that would arrive from Cincinnati. And if this particular fish from Cincinnati did not arrive for him, Goliath just would not eat.

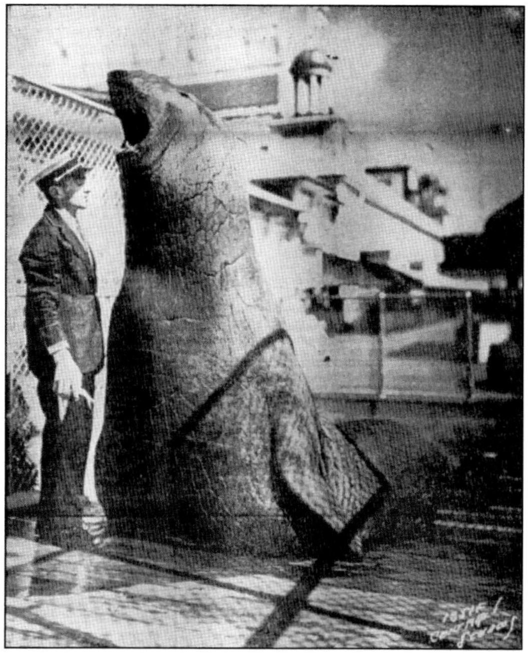

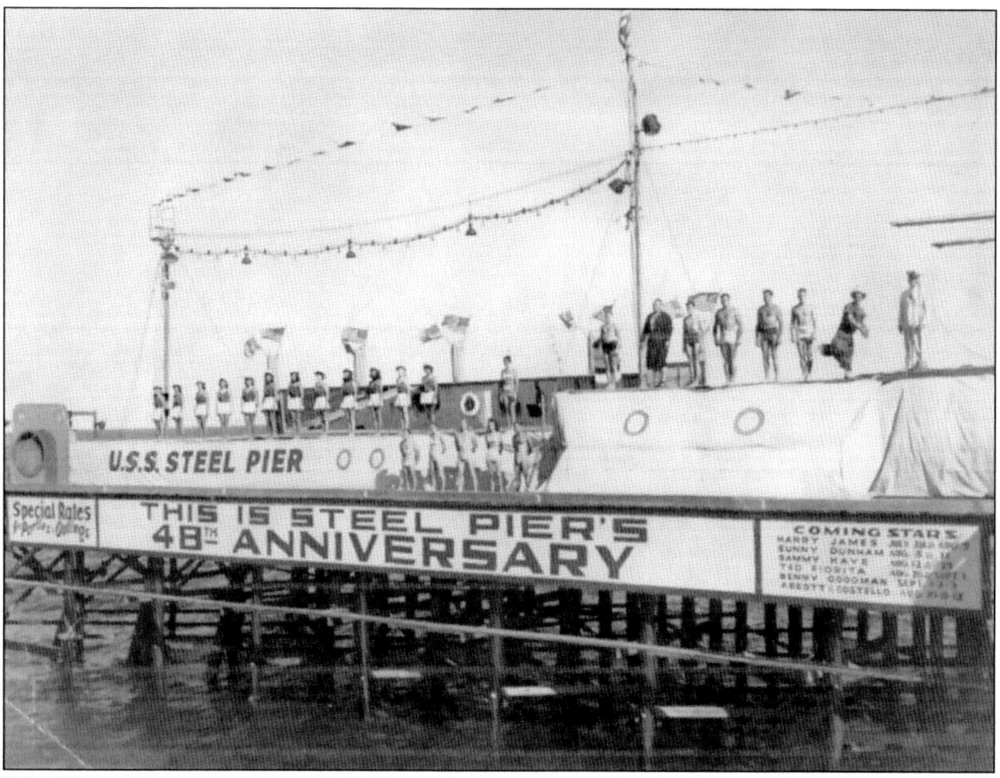

The Water Circus company of 1945 stands at a patriotic finale. Due to the war effort, many celebrities and bands were not able to visit the pier. The big boardwalk hotels had become hospitals and training centers for the armed forces, and the city was overwhelmed with military personnel. Drills and calisthenics were frequently seen in motion on the beach.

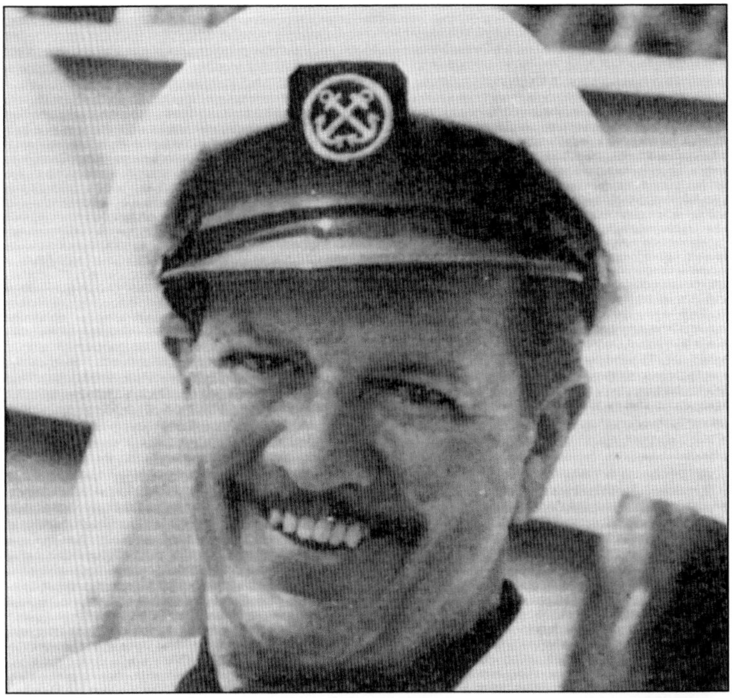

The affable Jack Montez was the Water Circus emcee from 1936 until 1965 and always wore his familiar captain's headgear when announcing, "Ladies and gentlemen, prepare yourselves for the thrill of a lifetime!" Another familiar emcee was Gene Hart, who had various jobs on the pier as a young boy and later became the voice of the National Hockey League's Philadelphia Flyers.

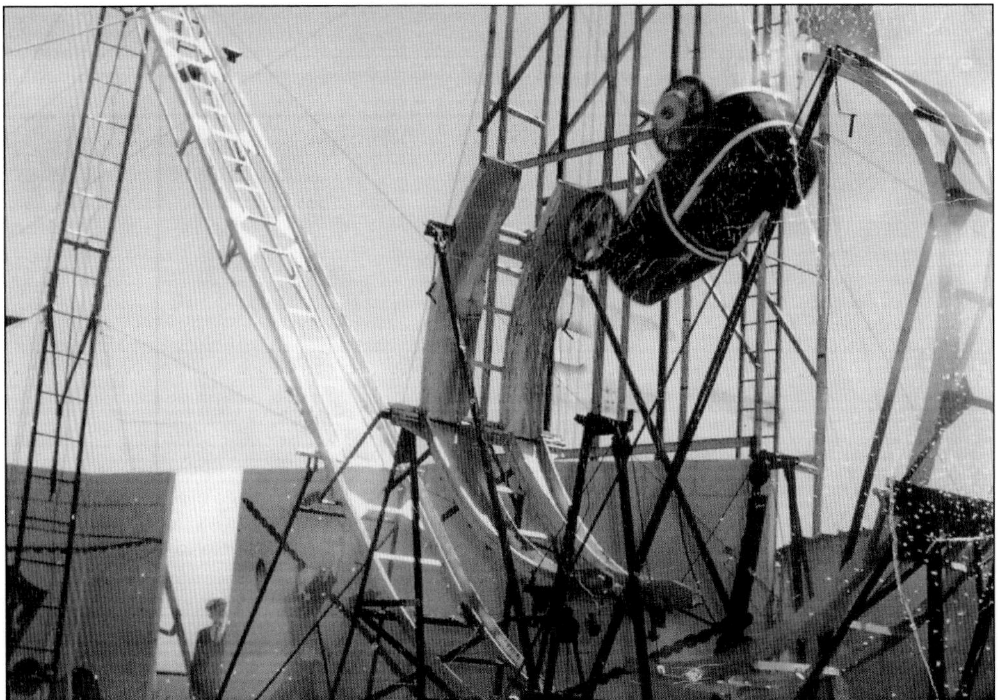

Rich "Cannonball" Carty is pictured in action in his rocket car during the early 1960s. Carty would climb into a small car atop a 50-foot-tall tower and would barrel down a track and then backflip over the water. Carty worked on the pier for many years and did everything from carpentry to security. He passed away June 18, 2015, at age 75.

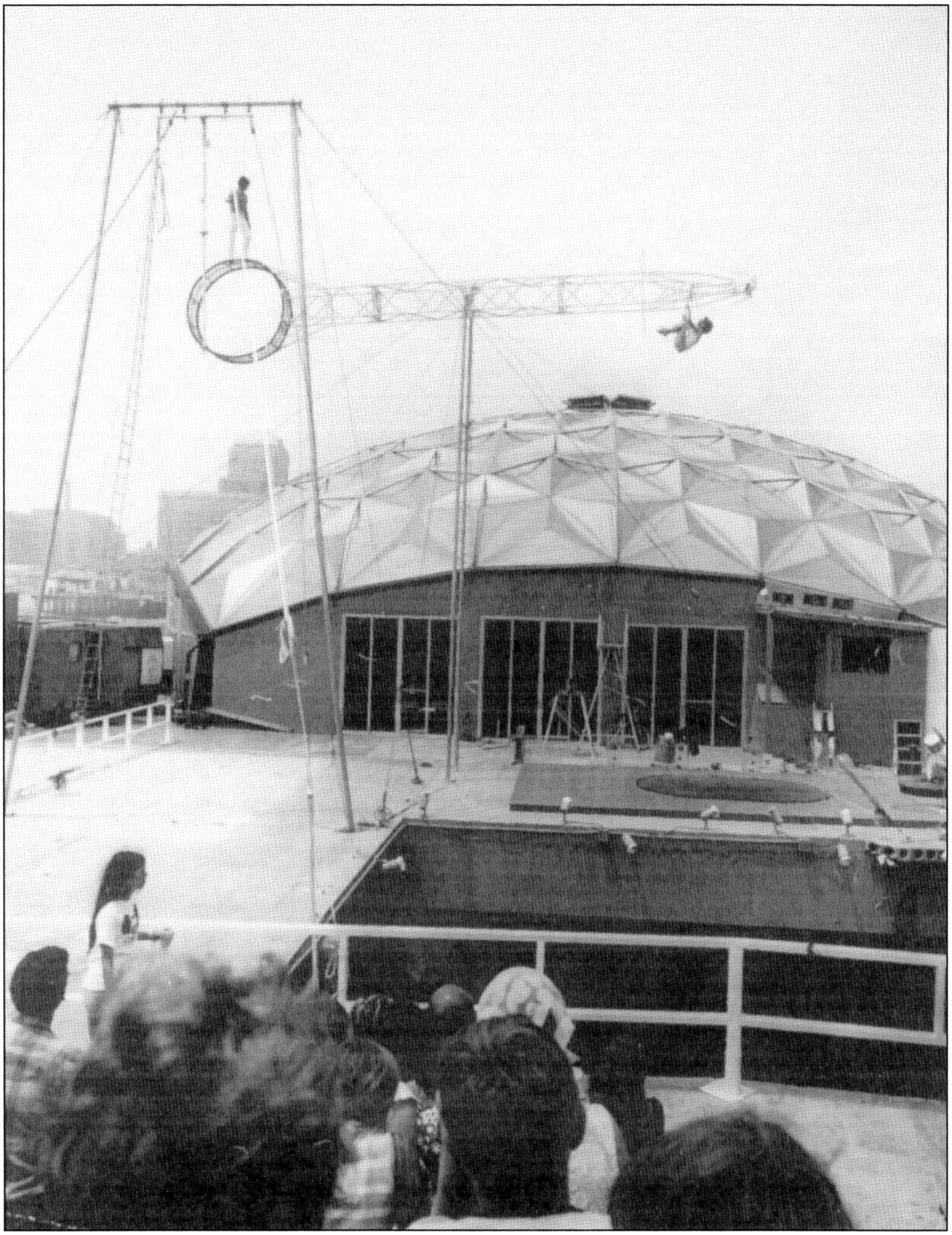

After the ocean end of the pier burned in 1969, it was reconfigured, with a geodesic, gold-colored dome taking the place of the sadly missed Marine Ballroom. The Water Circus continued into the 1970s in the back of the Golden Dome Ballroom and with the grandstand now facing inward towards land. The Water Circus was not as big in the 1970s as it was in its heyday, but exciting acts could still be seen up until the pier closed in 1978.

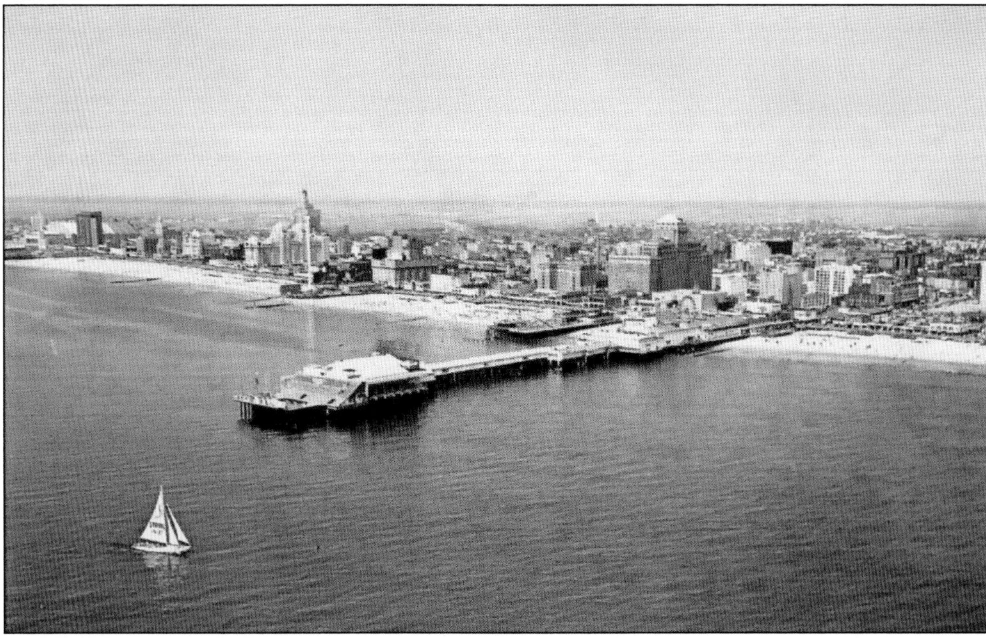

This picture from 1968 shows the entire pier, with the Marine Ballroom and Water Circus area in the foreground. The Ocean Stadium seating faces outward. Left of center is Central Pier's Sky Tower, which offered spectacular views of Atlantic City for many years.

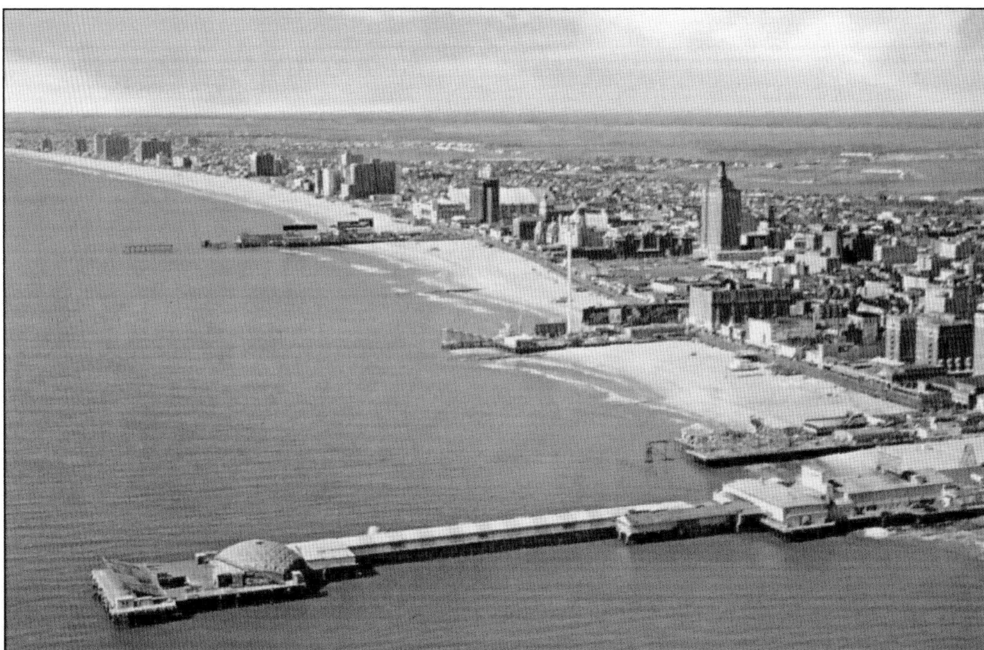

This 1973 image, taken from the same angle, depicts the Golden Dome that replaced the Marine Ballroom. The Water Circus seating now faced inward where the stage was formerly located. The Diving Horse apparatus is on the side of the dome facing the audience rather than its customary spot at the end of the pier.

Seven

Hamid and Son

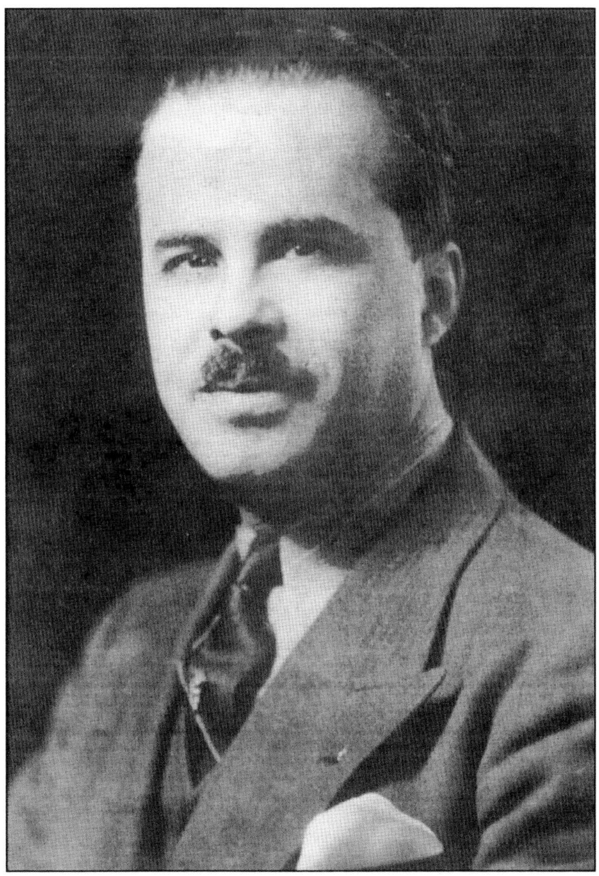

The rags-to-riches story of George A. Hamid—a dirt-poor Lebanese boy with no knowledge of the English language who came to America with a group of tumblers, became a successful carnival booker, and was later owner of Steel Pier—is definitely one for the ages. He learned about the circus and carnivals by touring with Buffalo Bill Cody in 1906 and developed his own company by the 1920s. Hamid worked for Frank Gravatt on Steel Pier, booking many global circus acts, but the two had a falling out. Hamid then leased the Million Dollar Pier in 1938 and waged an all-out war with Gravatt. When Steel Pier was sold by Gravatt in 1945, he thought he kept his rival out of the running but did not know that Hamid had a front man who put in the winning bid. So Hamid got what he wanted, and Gravatt congratulated him. Big into real estate after selling off the pier, Gravatt owned many Atlantic City hotels before passing away on January 28, 1979, at age 89.

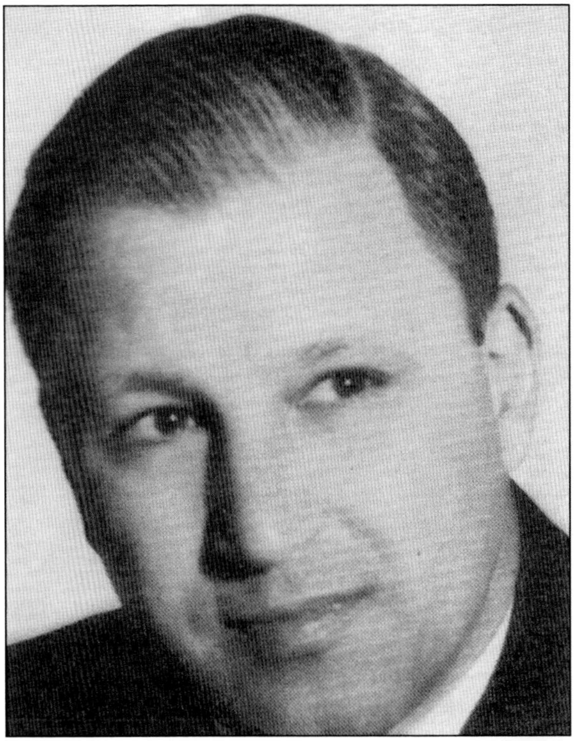

Hamid was fortunate to have a son who followed in his footsteps. George Hamid Jr. attended Princeton University and served in the Navy as a lieutenant commander in the South Pacific. Though he was not as tough a negotiator as his father, Hamid Jr. was instrumental in bringing the hottest rock and soul acts to the pier and recognized trends before they happened.

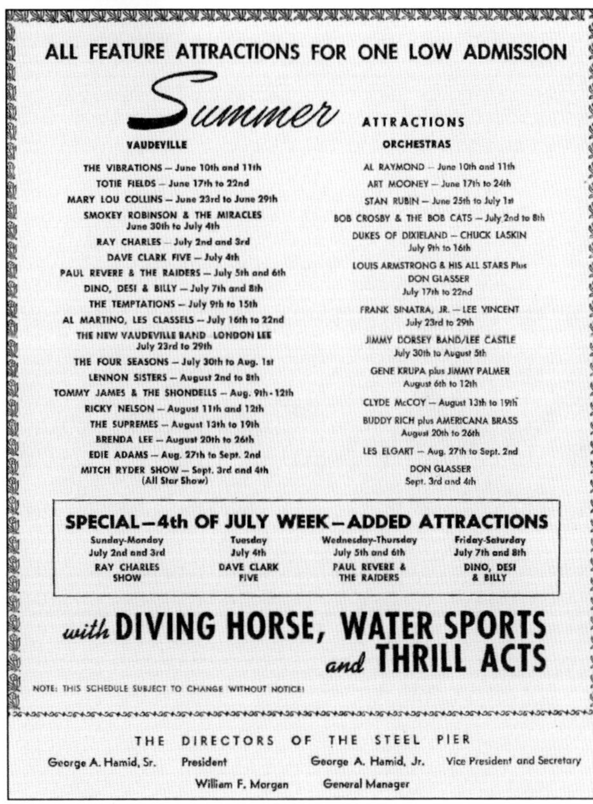

A typical schedule from 1967 during the Hamid years shows that there was something for every member of the family, such as rock and roll for the kids and big bands and dancing for the adults. The takeover from Frank Gravatt was seamless, as far as anyone could tell. The only difference could have been that the Hamids were experienced carnival and state fair people, whereas Gravatt was a real estate man who entered show business.

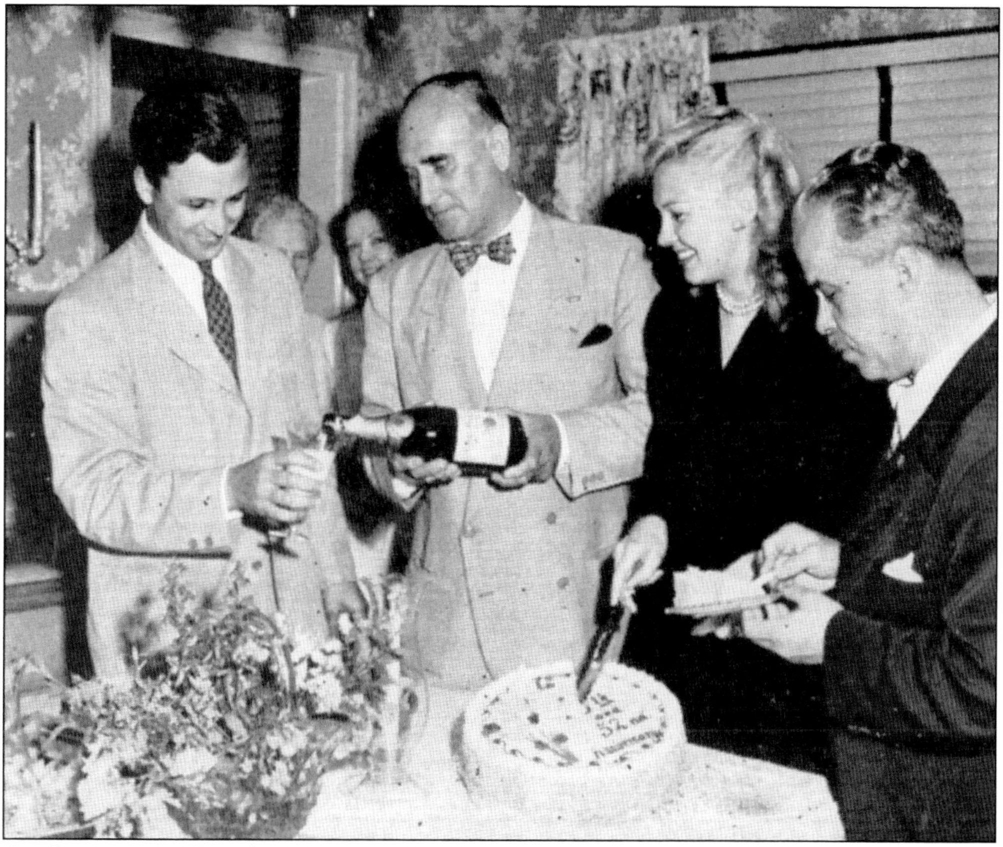

On the occasion of Steel Pier's 52nd anniversary in 1950, George Hamid Jr. (left) celebrates with, from left to right, Home of the Century's architect William Koelle, Miss America 1948 Maria Strohmeier, and George Hamid Sr. in the home's dining room.

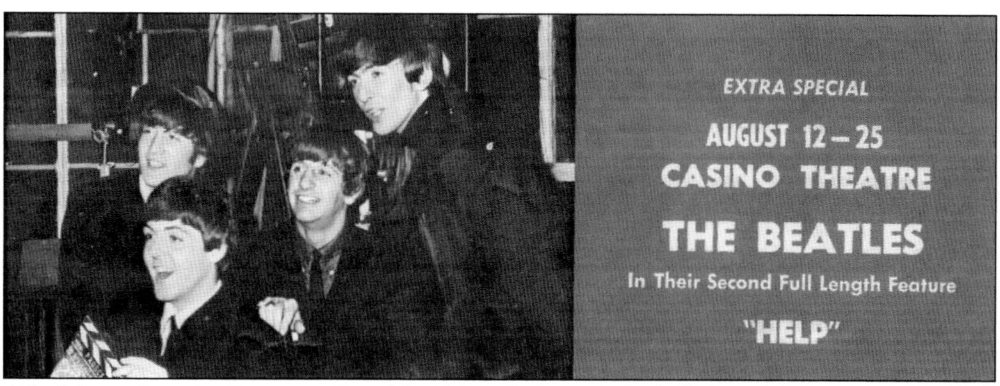

All of the rock-and-roll movies played Steel Pier, beginning with the Beatles' *A Hard Day's Night* in 1964. The Hamids catered to teenagers and embraced rock and Motown groups. Besides the Beatles' films—three movies, including *Let it Be*—others such as *Good Times* (Sonny & Cher), *Head* (the Monkees), and *Mrs. Brown, You've Got a Lovely Daughter* (Herman's Hermits) were all shown.

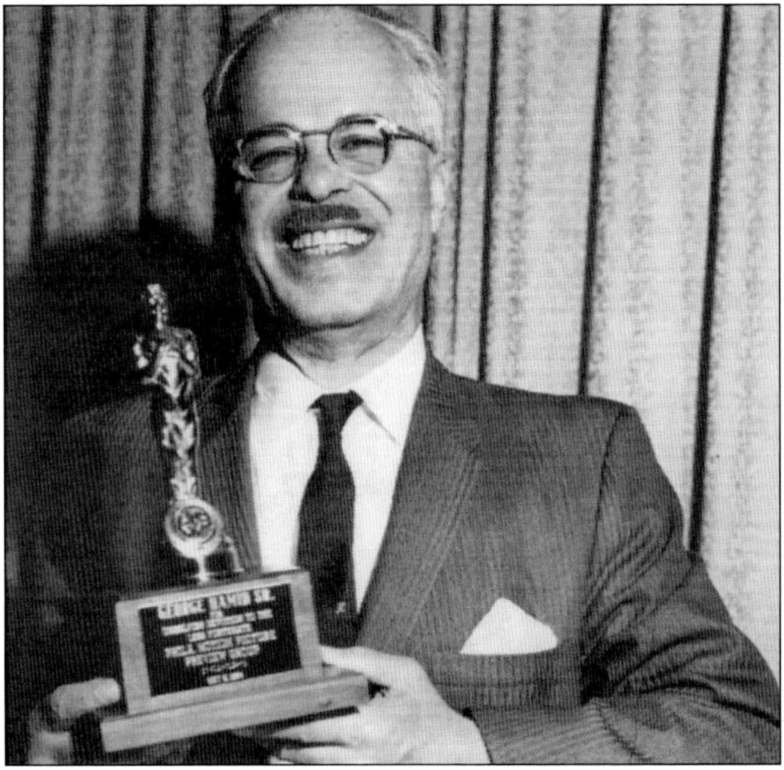

George Hamid was recognized and respected as one of the great showmen of the 20th century. He was a partner in the Hamid-Morton Circus, owned the New Jersey State Fair in Trenton and movie theaters in Atlantic City, and was a civic leader for the improvement of Atlantic City. Unfortunately, he witnessed the beginning of the demise of the city he loved and died of cancer on June 13, 1971, at age 75.

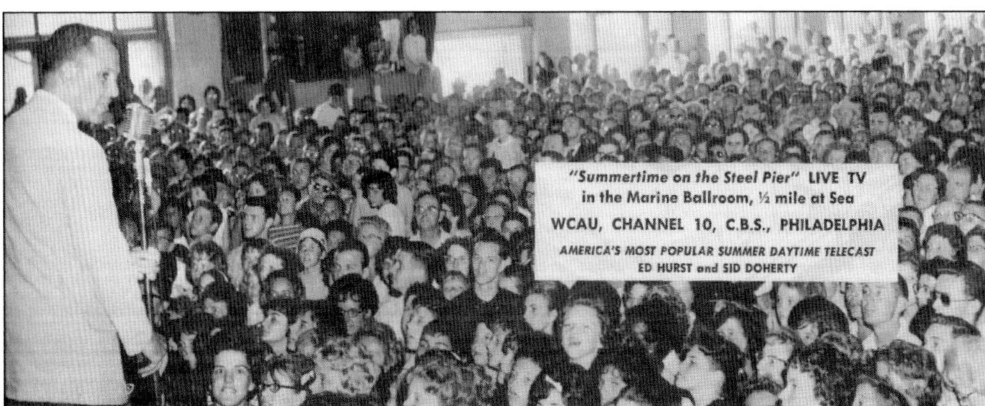

George Hamid Jr. relished announcing the bands to the packed Marine Ballroom, filled with teenagers. He not only booked these bands, musicians, and singers, but also remained close friends with many of them for years. His father was not thrilled with the long-haired bands but knew what the people wanted. Hamid Jr. passed away at age 94 on February 23, 2013.

Eight

Animals, Exhibits, and Kids

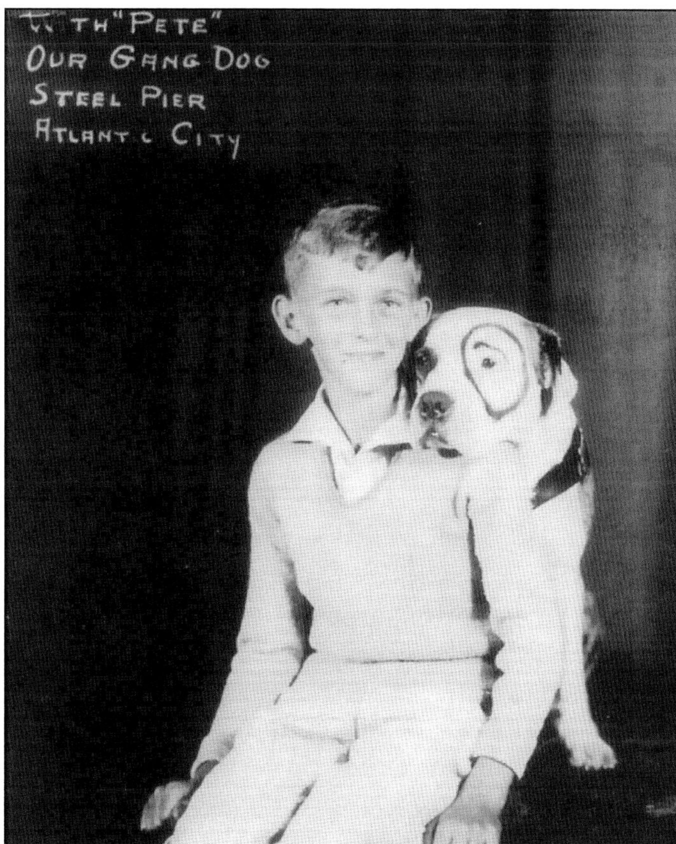

Steel Pier was known for its extraordinary variety. For instance, Petey, the famous dog from the Our Gang films, posed with thousands of boys and girls and adults during his time on the pier, from 1932 to 1938. He usually carried a pipe in his mouth or wore a funny hat with glasses, but here, he is subdued after what was probably a very tiring day.

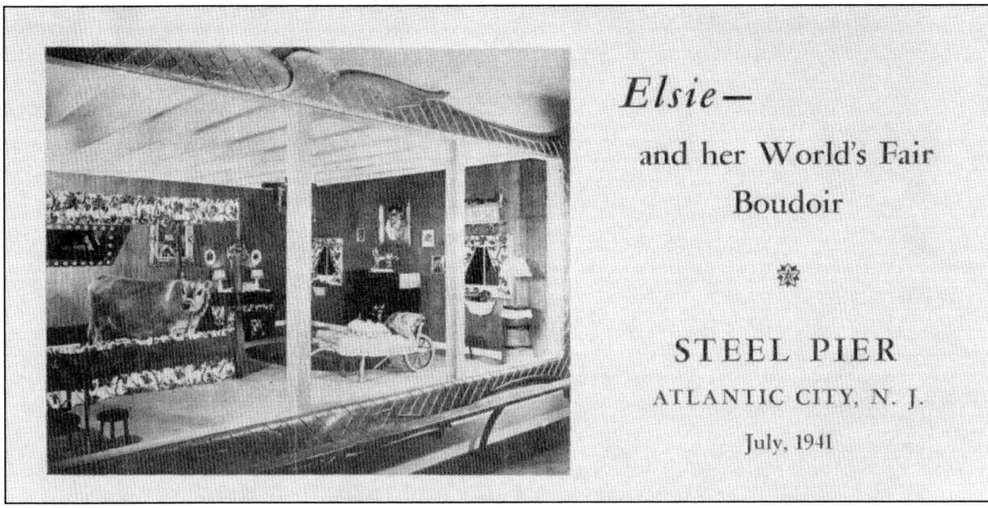

Elsie the cow, Borden Dairy Company's mascot, visited in 1941 with her own living quarters. Exhibited with fresh flowers in her hair and acting like a proper lady, she welcomed thousands that summer and reminded her fans how splendid Borden products were.

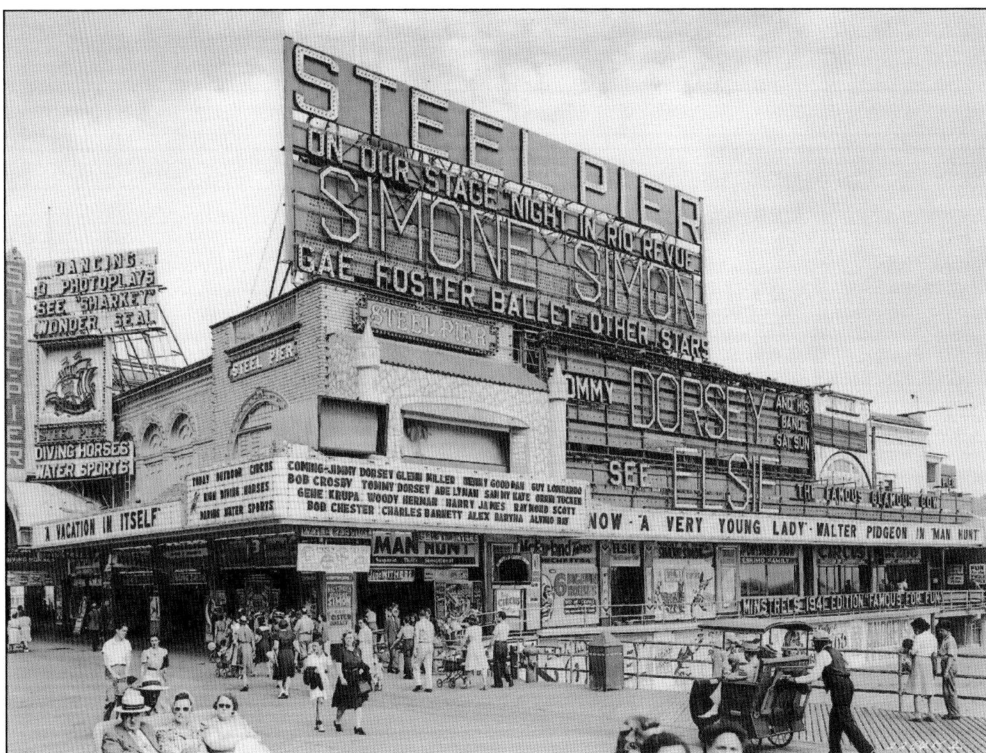

Elsie, whose name appears on the marquee below Tommy Dorsey in this July 1941 photograph, was one of two animal stars. The front marquee announces Sharkey the Wonder Seal, who was trained to play trumpet and also made a cameo appearance in an Abbott and Costello movie.

Minstrels in blackface were a part of Steel Pier until 1943, when they vanished for good. W.C. Fields was very briefly a part of the cast in 1899. This 1905 advertisement promotes the Casino theater, the minstrel shows' 2,000-seat home during their existence.

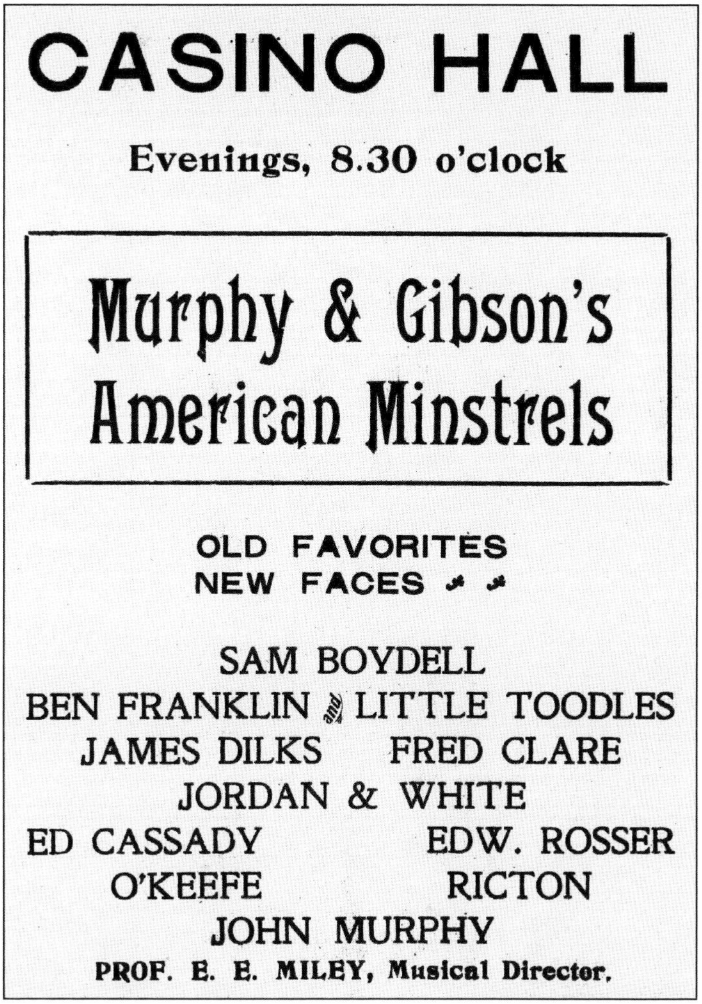

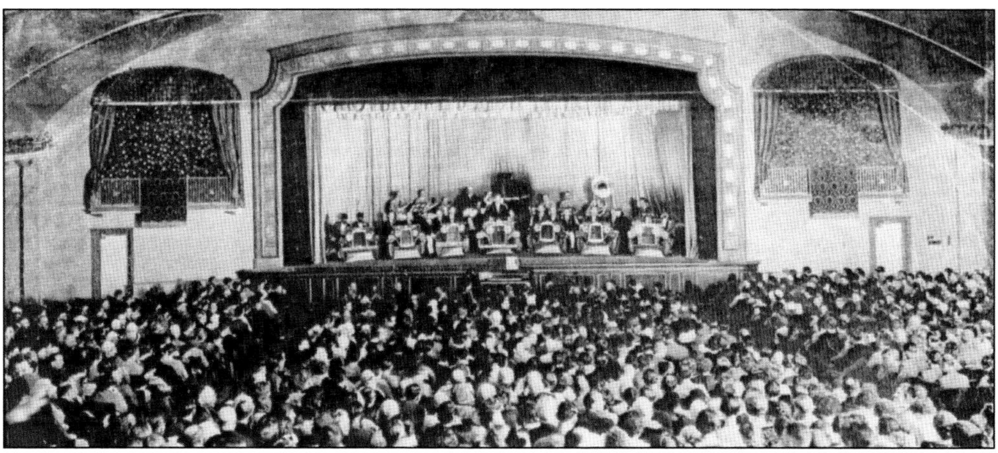

The show is underway in the Casino in 1927. Most of the cast was white, with only the two men on each end in blackface. The theater was located on the second floor of the boardwalk building and was eventually utilized just for movies.

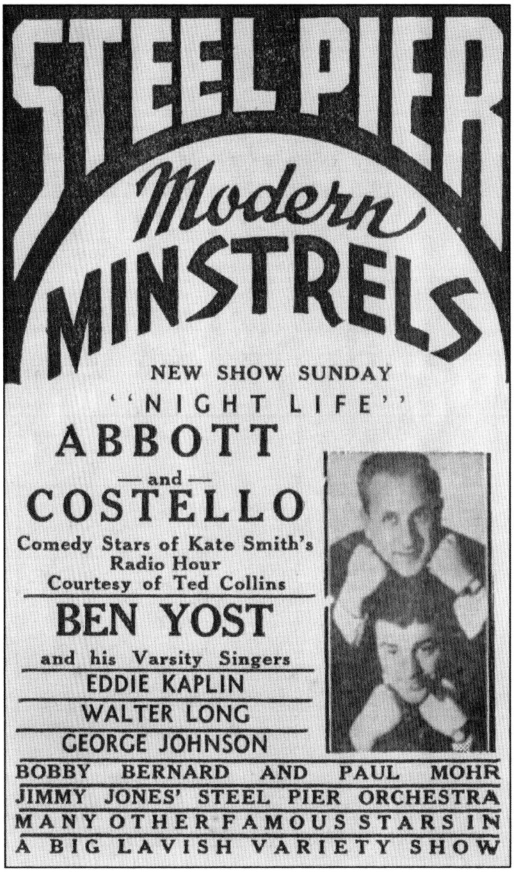

Abbott and Costello are the featured act in the minstrel program from July 1938. They were both natives of New Jersey and familiar with Atlantic City and Steel Pier long before they starred on it. Bud Abbott, the tall straight man, was born in Asbury Park, and Lou Costello, the short comic, was born in Paterson. Costello died on March 3, 1959, at age 52, while Abbott passed on April 24, 1974, at 76.

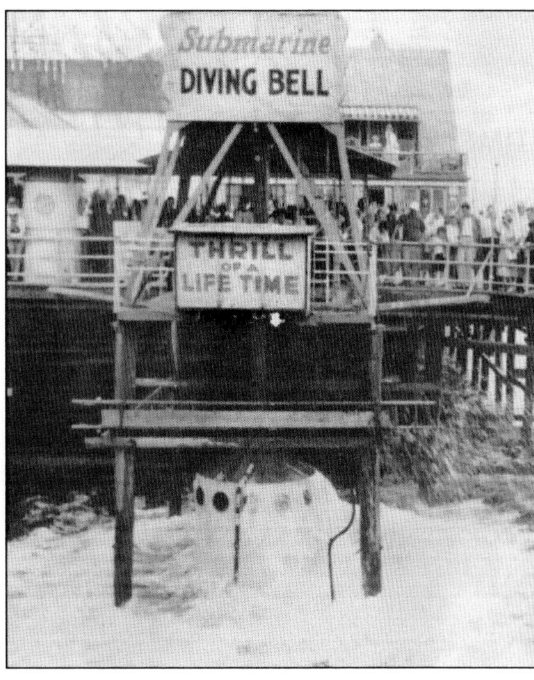

The Diving Bell provided a chance for those brave enough to go underwater and spot rare exotic fish. However, the only reported sightings were of a muddy fog—in other words, nothing. Built in 1942, the bell could hold 15 people and would hit the ocean floor 30 feet below. This picture shows the bell popping to the surface and eliciting many screams from within due to its fast ascent.

The original Diving Bell washed away in the Nor'easter of 1962, but it was rebuilt almost immediately. Utilized on the pier until its demise in 1978, the Diving Bell was rescued before that portion of the pier was demolished. It resides in Gardner's Basin in Atlantic City, one of only a few items still in existence from the pier. Another item that has survived is the Marine Ballroom's neon, 48-star American flag, which hangs in Baltimore's Lexington Market.

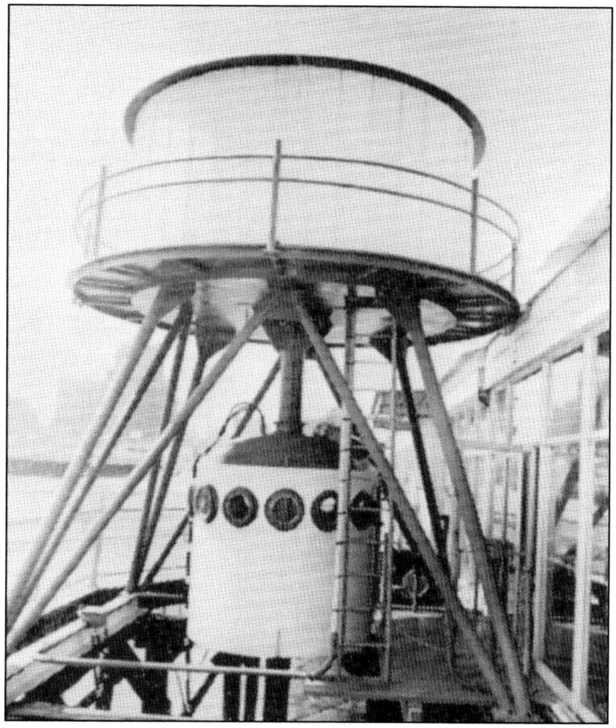

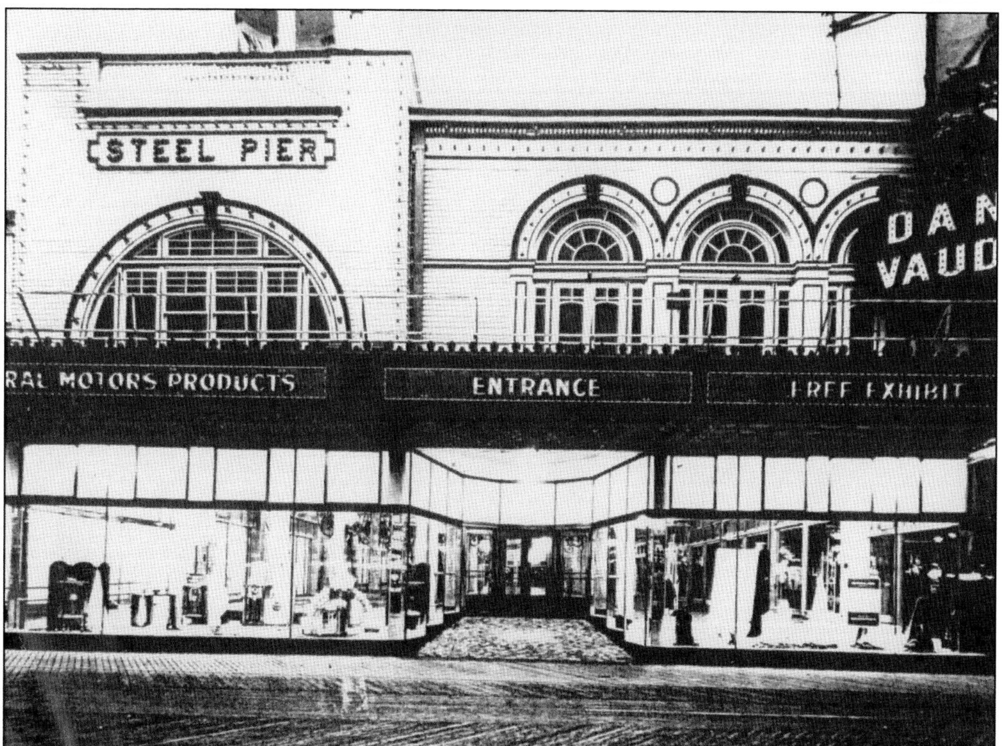

General Motors (GM) began its long association with Steel Pier in 1925. Pictured is the front of the pier with the GM boardwalk space in 1929.

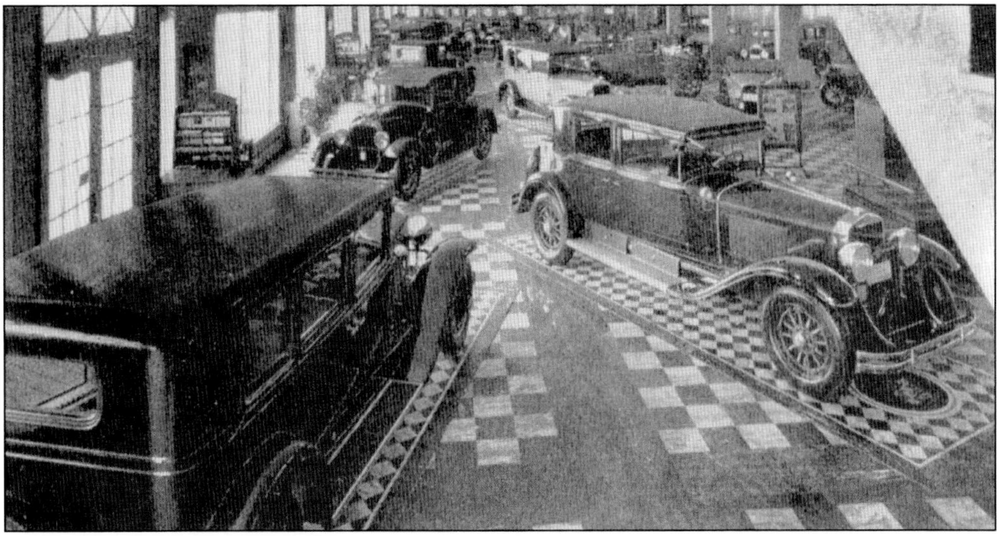

The anticipation from the public was great, as the exhibit presented all of the new models of General Motors cars and products. It was actually a car showroom without the sales. On display here are the 1929 models.

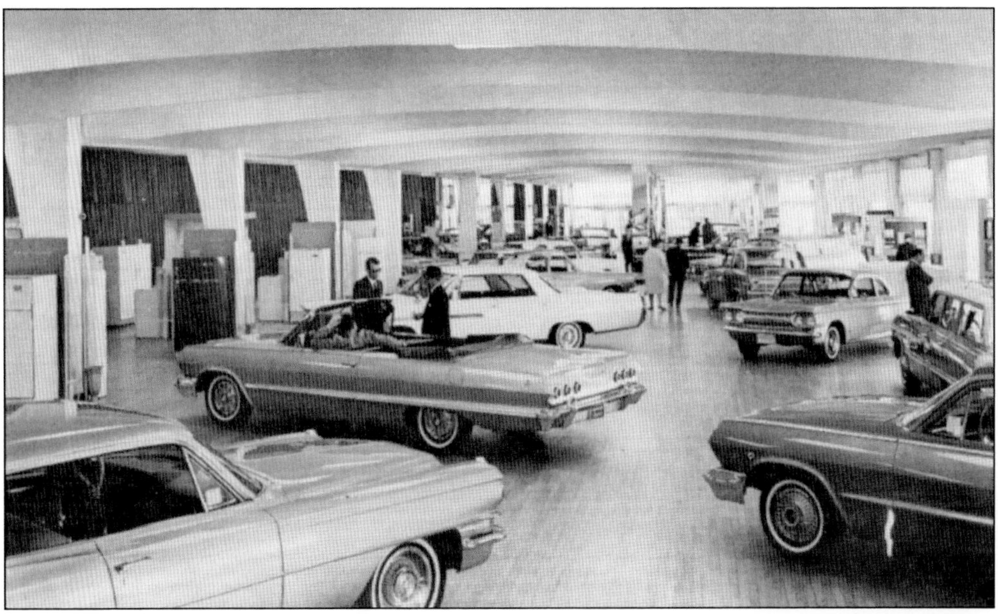

This is the same showroom in 1962. GM was at the pier sporadically from 1925 to 1933. It returned to this space in 1947 and remained there, open year-round, until 1968. By then, attendance in Atlantic City was starting to diminish.

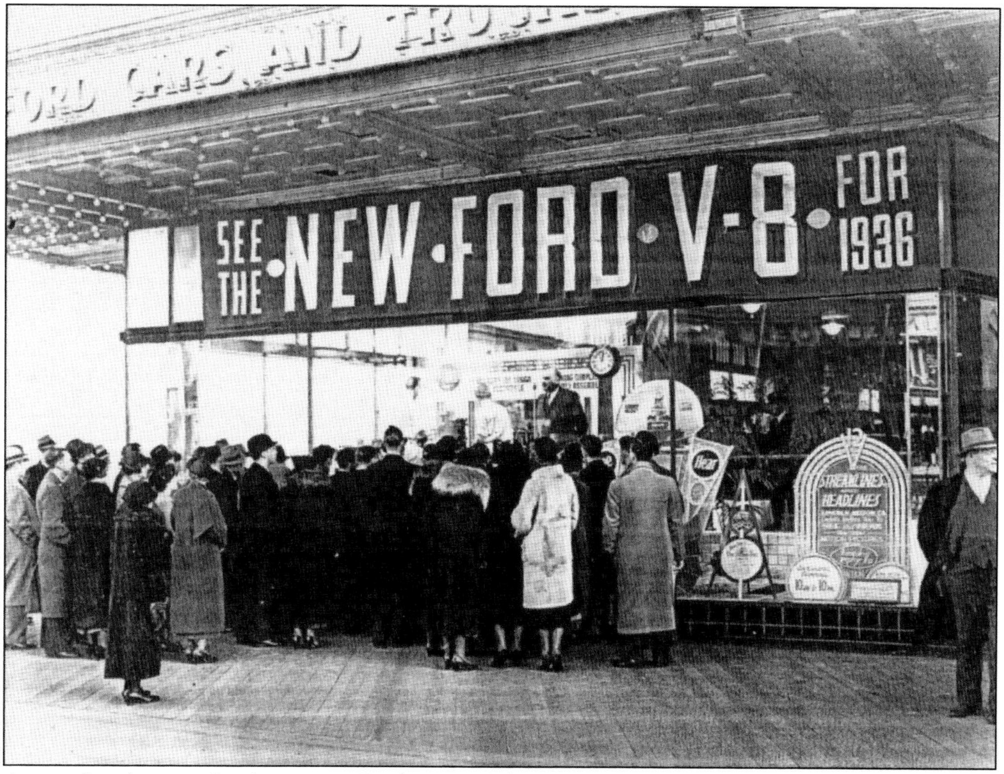

A crowd gathers to check out new Ford automobiles. Ford took over the boardwalk space vacated by General Motors. The contract lasted only a few years, and GM returned in 1947 and remained until 1968.

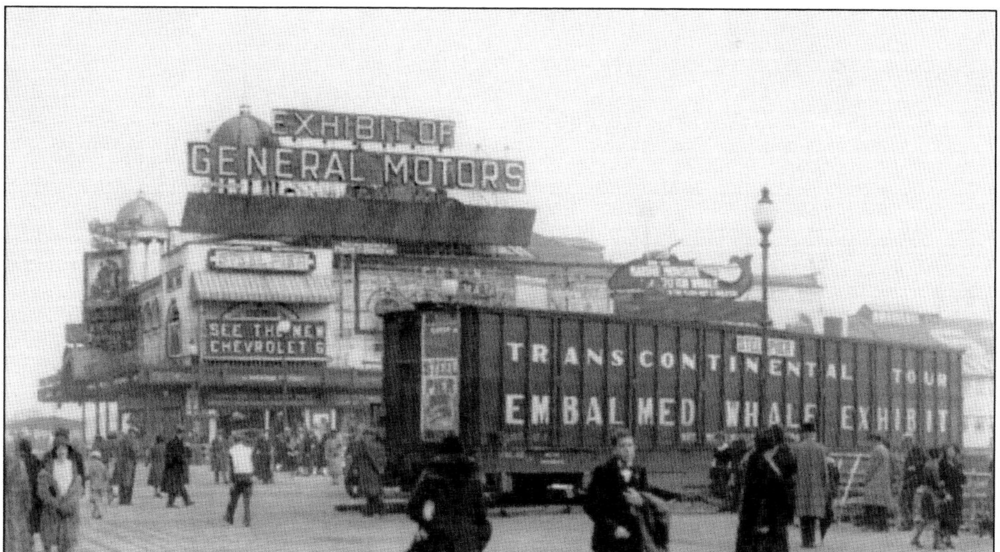

Frank Gravatt's knack of presenting unique animals went over the edge in 1930 and 1931. He bought a 65-foot whale carcass for $15,000 from a state fair in Toronto and shipped the mammal to the pier in 300 gallons of embalming fluid. It was the largest whale ever exhibited in the United States, but the smell made Gravatt think again before he spent so much on an attraction.

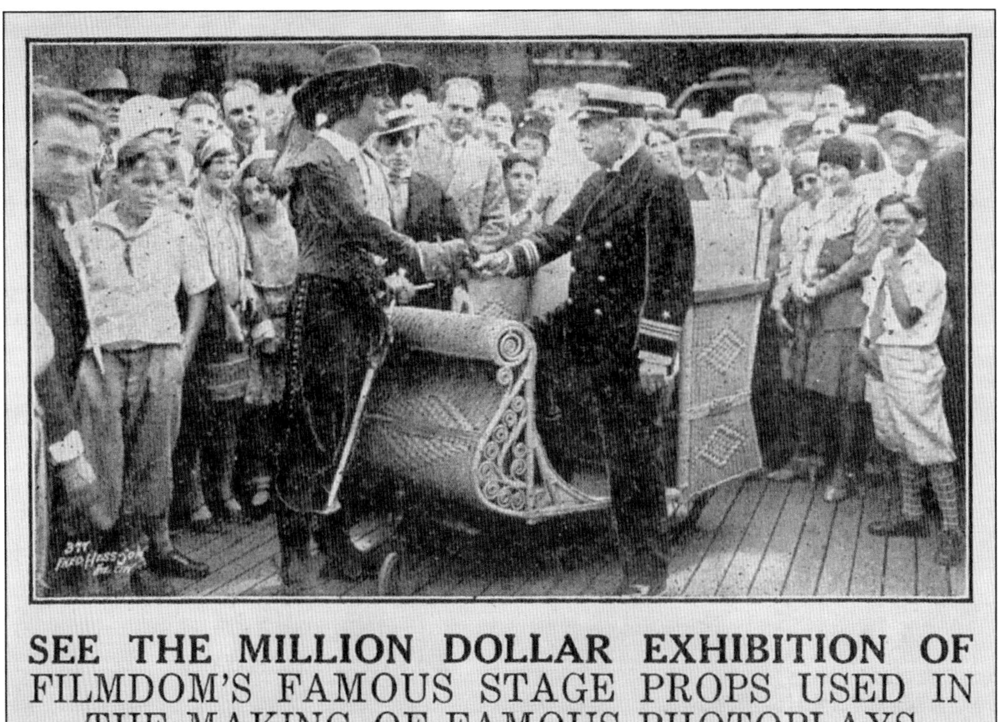

John Philip Sousa (right) meets an actor wearing Douglas Fairbanks's wardrobe to promote the Hollywood display in front of the pier in 1929. Artifacts from Hollywood movies were a very popular exhibit on the pier through the 1930s.

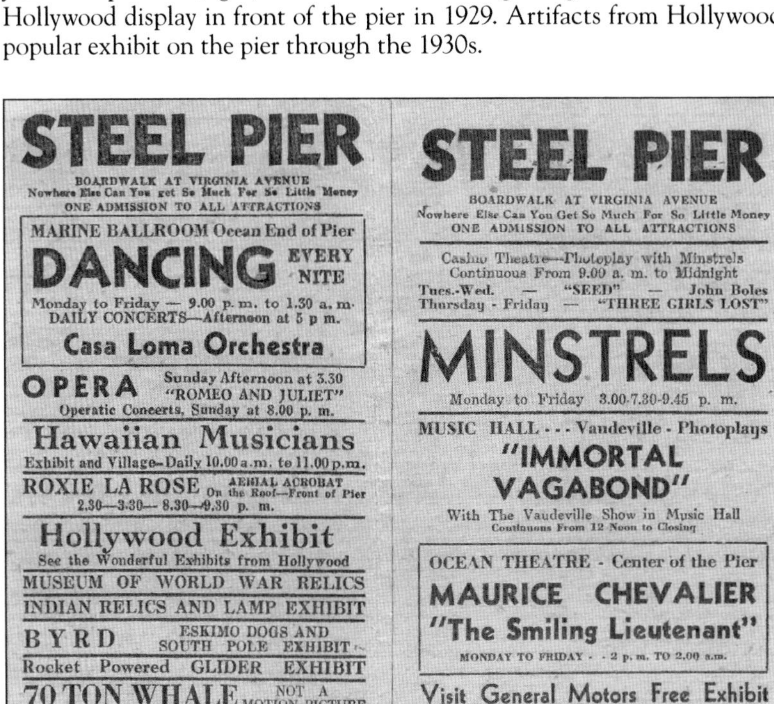

STEEL PIER
BOARDWALK AT VIRGINIA AVENUE
Nowhere Else Can You get So Much For So Little Money
ONE ADMISSION TO ALL ATTRACTIONS

MARINE BALLROOM Ocean End of Pier
DANCING EVERY NITE
Monday to Friday — 9.00 p. m. to 1.30 a. m.
DAILY CONCERTS—Afternoon at 5 p m.
Casa Loma Orchestra

OPERA Sunday Afternoon at 3.30
"ROMEO AND JULIET"
Operatic Concerts, Sunday at 8.00 p. m.

Hawaiian Musicians
Exhibit and Village—Daily 10.00 a.m. to 11.00 p.m.

ROXIE LA ROSE AERIAL ACROBAT On the Roof—Front of Pier
2.30—3.30— 8.30—9.30 p. m.

Hollywood Exhibit
See the Wonderful Exhibits from Hollywood

MUSEUM OF WORLD WAR RELICS

INDIAN RELICS AND LAMP EXHIBIT

BYRD ESKIMO DOGS AND SOUTH POLE EXHIBIT

Rocket Powered GLIDER EXHIBIT

70 TON WHALE NOT A MOTION PICTURE

STEEL PIER
BOARDWALK AT VIRGINIA AVENUE
Nowhere Else Can You Get So Much For So Little Money
ONE ADMISSION TO ALL ATTRACTIONS

Casino Theatre—Photoplay with Minstrels
Continuous From 9.00 a. m. to Midnight
Tues.-Wed. — "SEED" — John Boles
Thursday - Friday — "THREE GIRLS LOST"

MINSTRELS
Monday to Friday 3.00-7.30-9.45 p. m.

MUSIC HALL . . . Vaudeville - Photoplays
"IMMORTAL VAGABOND"
With The Vaudeville Show in Music Hall
Continuous From 12 Noon to Closing

OCEAN THEATRE - Center of the Pier
MAURICE CHEVALIER
"The Smiling Lieutenant"
MONDAY TO FRIDAY - - 2 p. m. TO 2.00 a.m.

Visit General Motors Free Exhibit

This 1931 program card lists all of the exhibits during that year. From the embalmed whale to Indian and world war relics to the South Pole exhibit and Eskimo dogs, Gravatt offered more variety and fascinating attractions than any circus sideshow.

Alvin "Shipwreck" Kelly sits on top of a cupola's 125-foot-tall mast in 1930. Kelly became famous for this stunt during the Depression and made quite a living from it. Eating, sleeping, and even taking a bath seated only on a padded disc from a car brake drum, Kelly broke his own record and descended after 49 days to a crowd of thousands on the boardwalk. He was paid $100 a day, a lofty sum of money at the time.

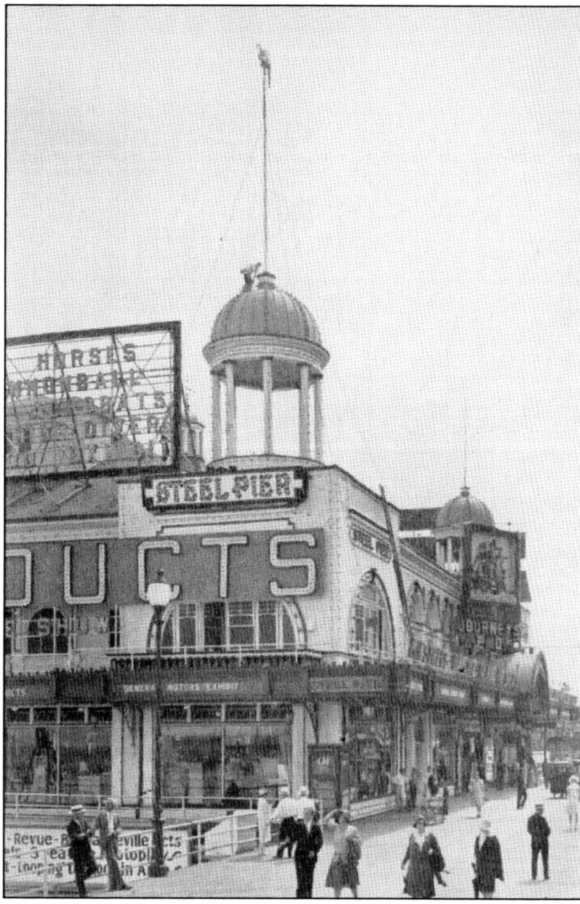

The strangest exhibit of all had to be the presence of author Robert E. Burns in 1934, whose tales of escaping from a Georgia chain gang and exposing its cruelty and injustice became a best seller and a motion picture.

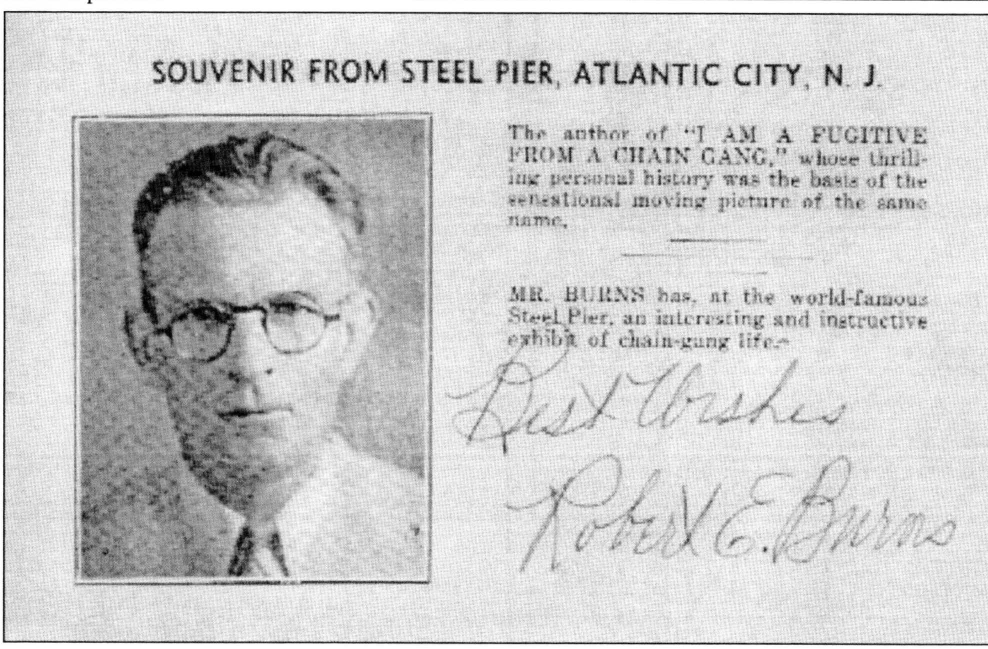

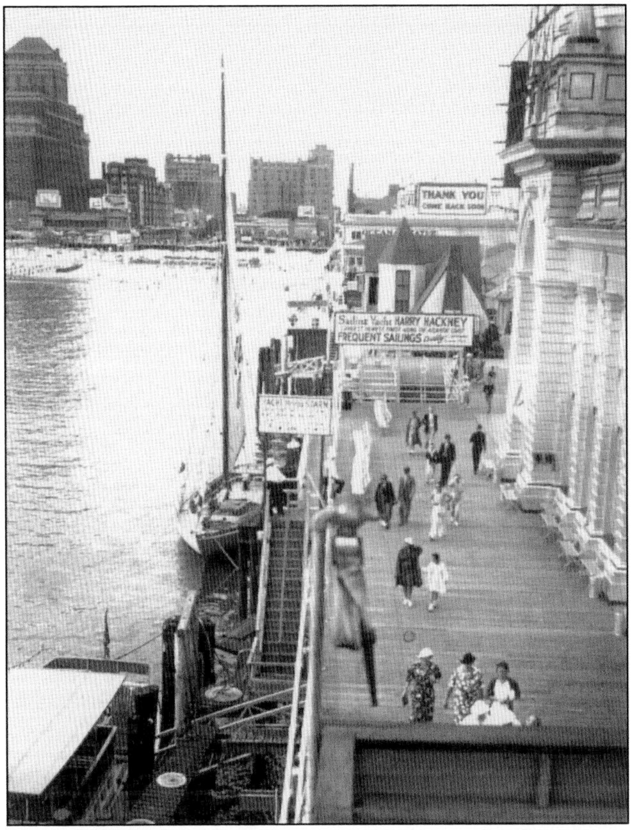

The Home of the Century is seen in the center of the photograph, in front of the Marine Ballroom. Designed by Philadelphia architect William Koelle in 1935, the home was filled each year with the most modern appliances and decorated rooms. It was destroyed in the 1962 storm.

The Home of the Century exhibit was renamed the Victory Model Home during World War II. Many companies made it a priority to promote their products to the huge summer crowds in hopes of increased sales.

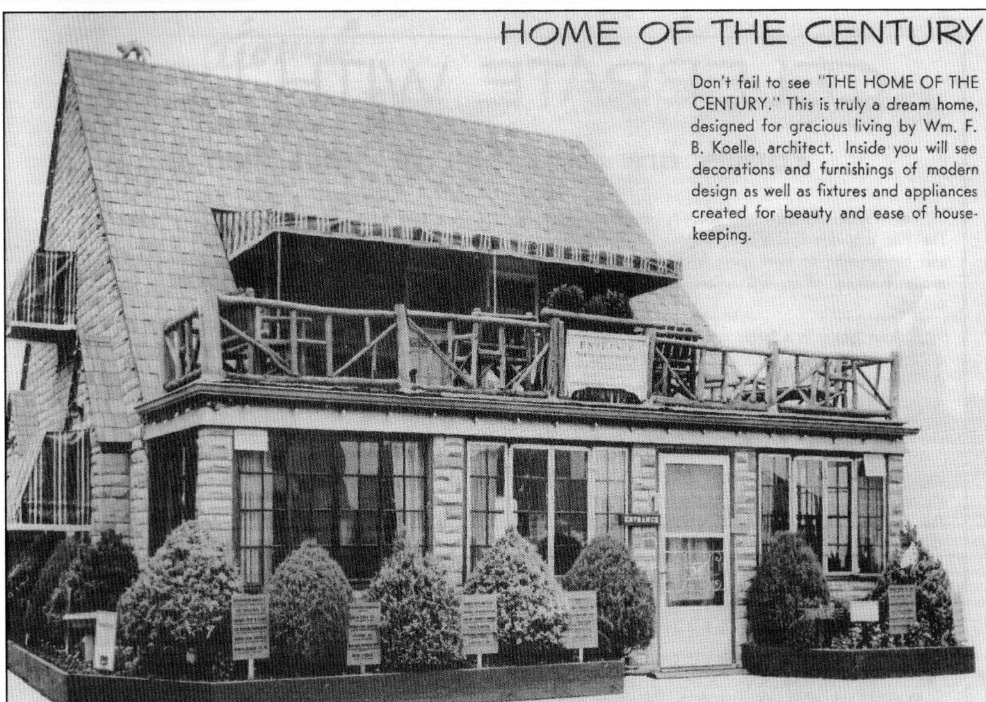

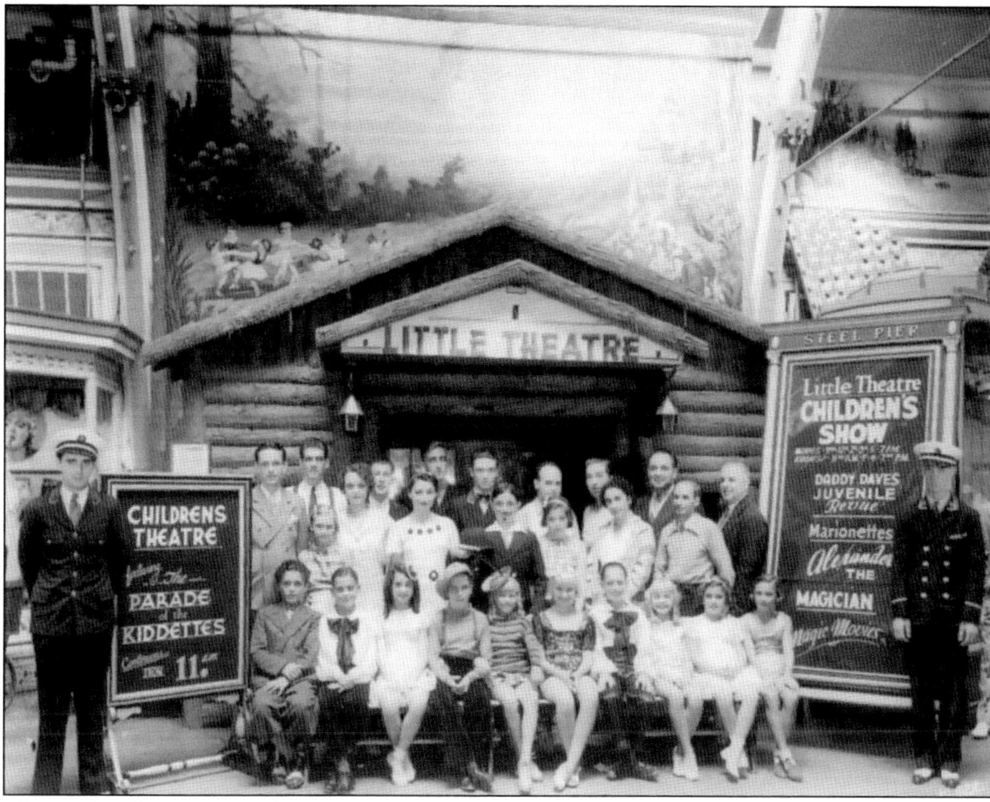

The Little Theatre opened in 1931 for the presentation of shows performed by children and was the only such theater of its kind in the country. "Daddy" Dave Tyson, a former Steel Pier minstrel performer, took over running the activities in 1934.

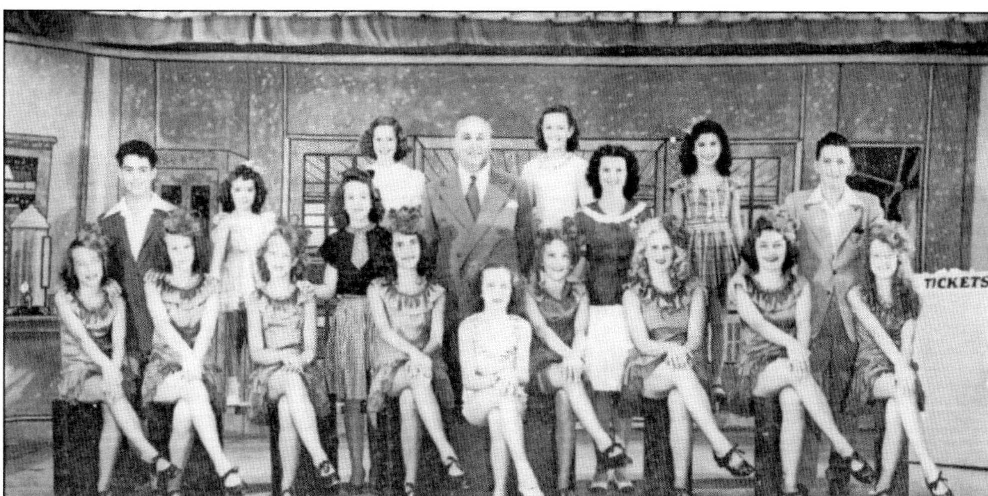

Daddy Dave Tyson poses with a crew of kids who were a part of the Children's Revue. Parents from the Mid-Atlantic states would bring their kids to Atlantic City in the winter months to audition for a lucky spot in one of the weekly programs. The demand for performers was heavy, with four shows scheduled daily, seven days a week.

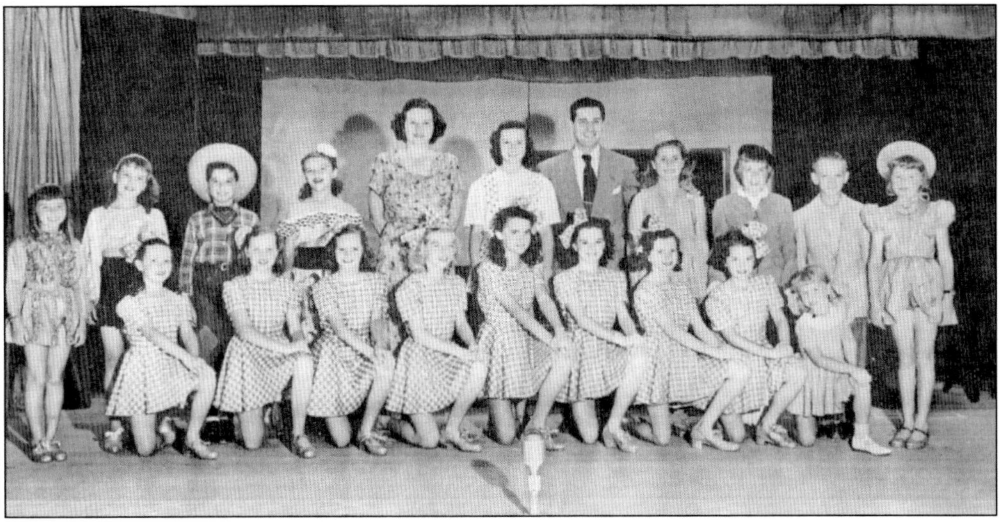

Tony Grant, a former vaudevillian and a proprietor of a dancing school in Wilkes-Barre, Pennsylvania, took over the kids show when Dave Tyson passed away. Here, Grant poses with his "Stars of Tomorrow" in his first full year in charge in 1949.

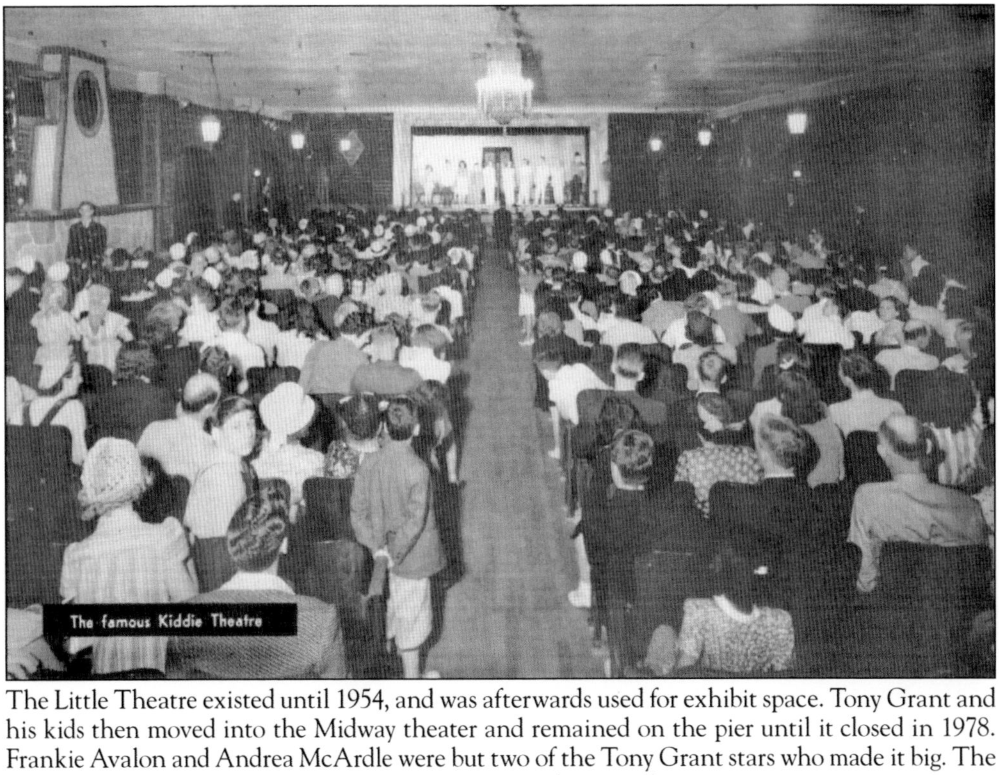

The Little Theatre existed until 1954, and was afterwards used for exhibit space. Tony Grant and his kids then moved into the Midway theater and remained on the pier until it closed in 1978. Frankie Avalon and Andrea McArdle were but two of the Tony Grant stars who made it big. The Little Theatre was renamed Kiddie Theatre for this photograph.

Nine

Rock and Soul

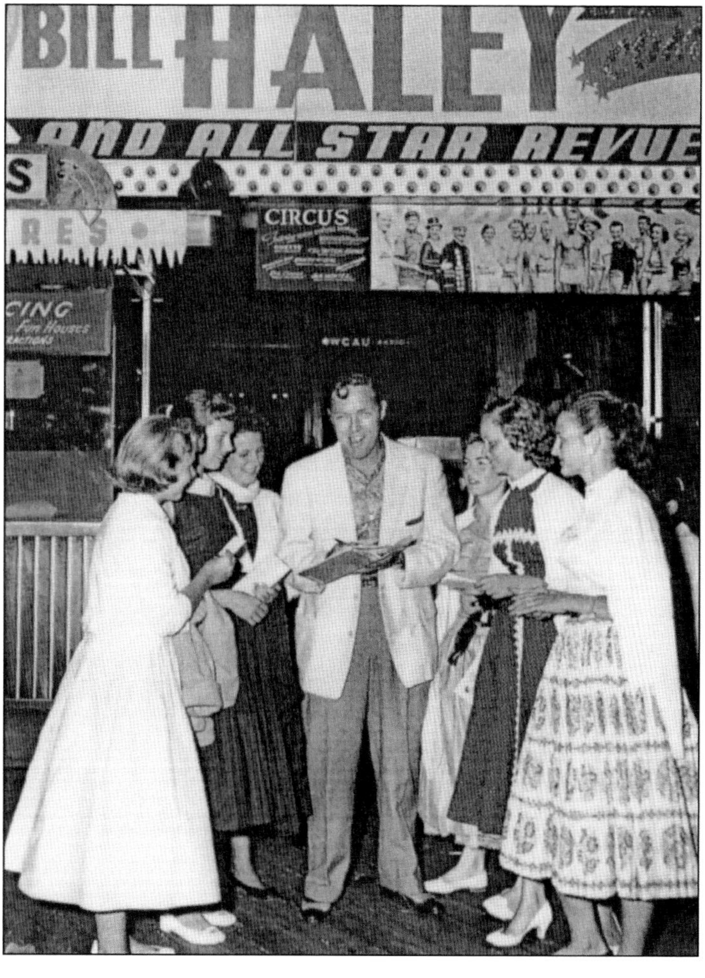

Bill Haley signs autographs for fans at the Steel Pier entrance in 1956. The Hamids fully embraced rock and roll because they knew that teenagers would flock to the pier and pay to see their heroes. Originally, rock bands would play the Music Hall until it was realized that some very popular groups would need the more spacious Marine Ballroom to greet their massive fan base.

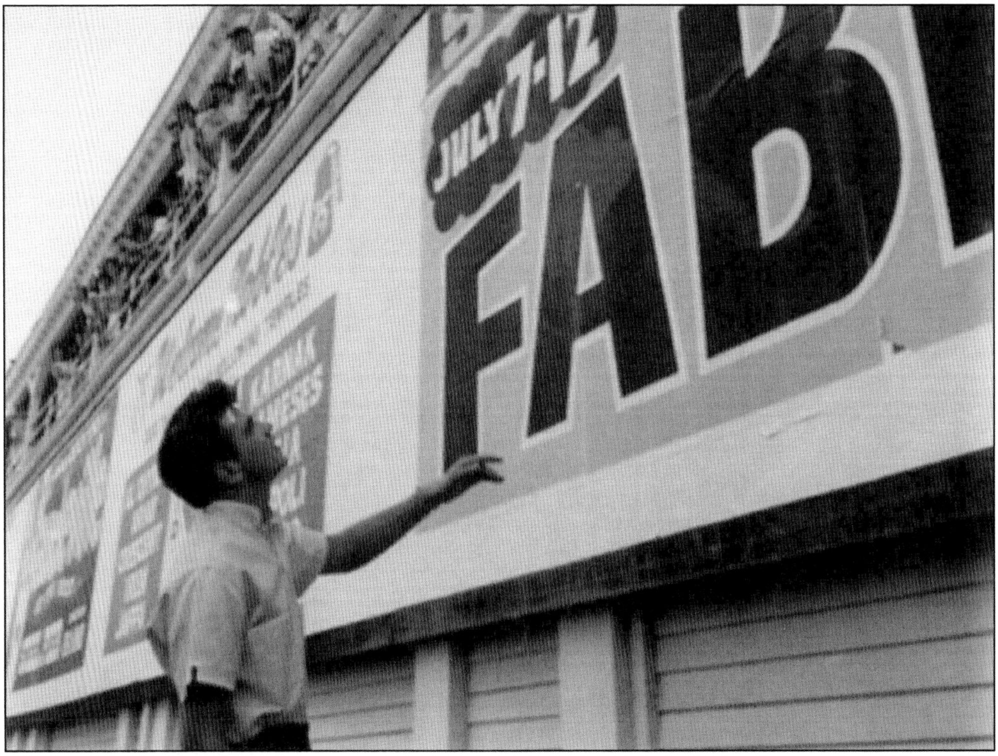

Fabian looks up from the beach to his adoring crowd in 1959. Plucked from the streets of South Philadelphia basically for his looks, the young man was widely recognized as not so much a singing talent as a true teen idol.

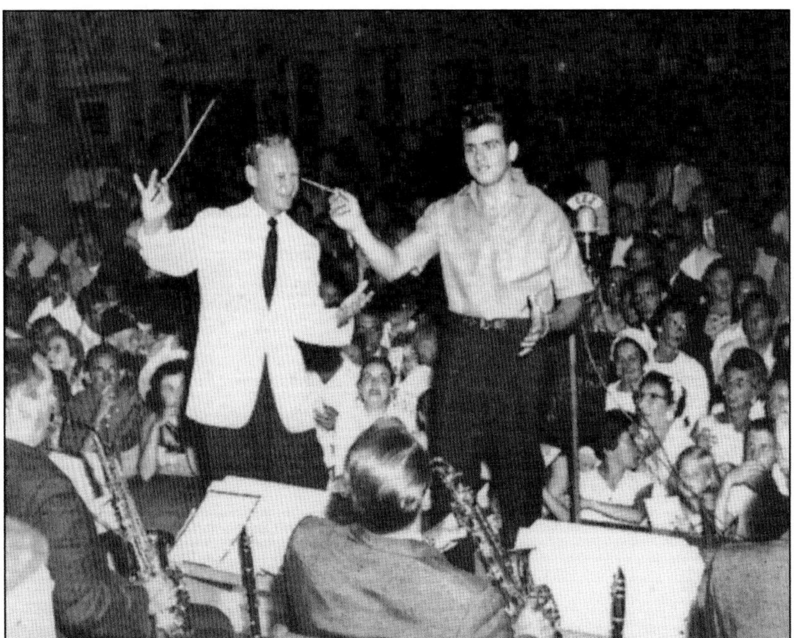

Only on Steel Pier would Fabian conduct with orchestra leader Sammy Kaye. The melding of different musical artists at the same time is what made the pier so unique. Here, the audience is mainly made up of older people who are there for Kaye, not Fabian.

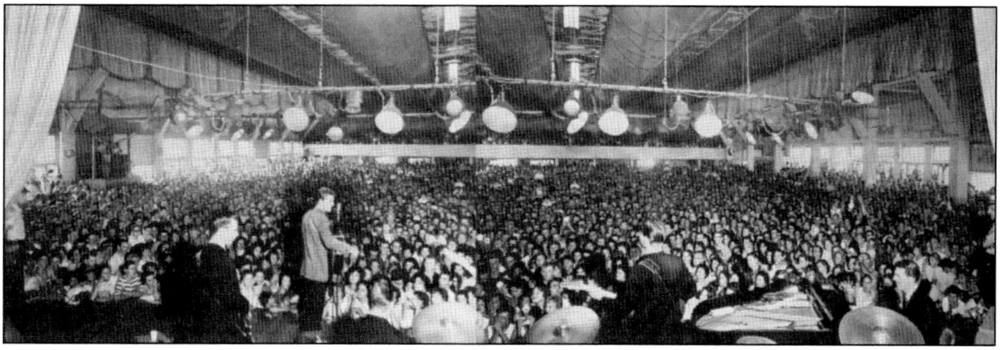

September 1, 1958, is a date that will live in Steel Pier history, when a one-day record of 44,221 people jammed the pier to see Ricky Nelson. It was the first time he had ever played in concert, and, clearly, no one knew how to handle this mass hysteria. Nelson was secretly transferred from the Music Hall to the Marine Ballroom after his first show. It became sheer bedlam as girls fainted and many in the crowd had to be hosed down due to the overbearing heat.

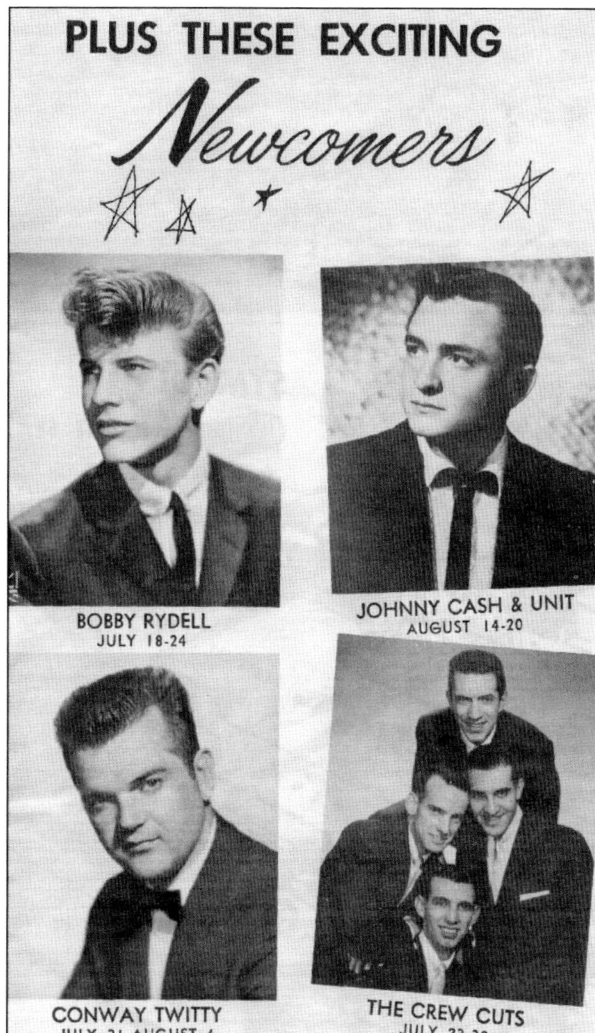

Some newcomers in 1960 include young Bobby Rydell, who went on to play the pier eight times. Johnny Cash and Conway Twitty were pop stars with charted hits who eventually veered toward a country-western sound.

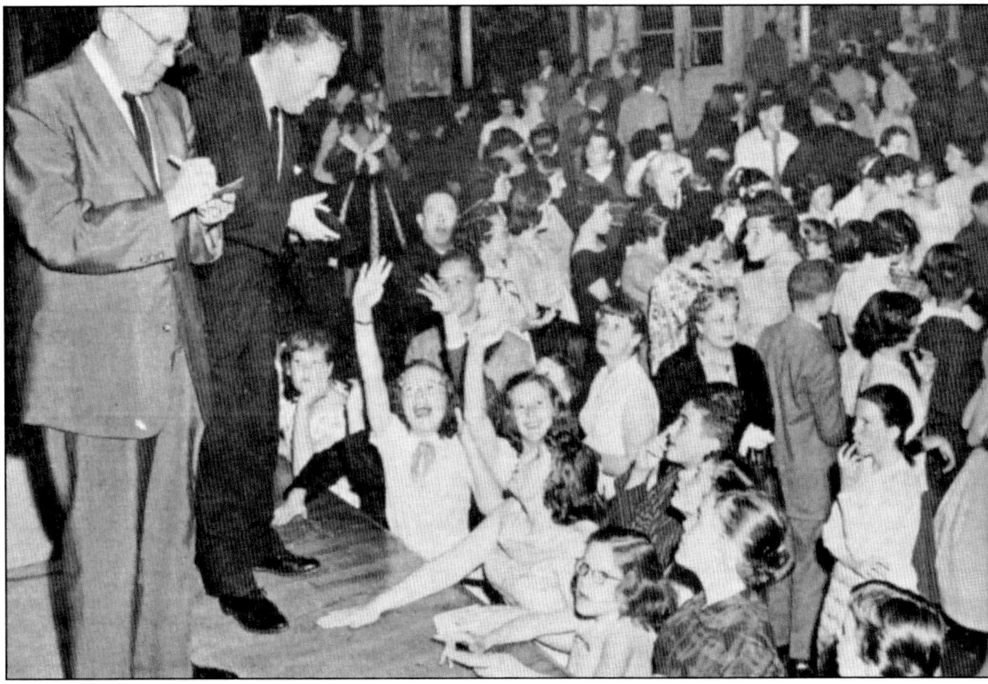

Joe Grady (left) and Ed Hurst were two top-rated disc jockeys from Philadelphia who perfected the American Bandstand format on radio. They began their record hops in the Marine Ballroom in 1958, with Grady leaving after he felt the pier shaking due to the Ricky Nelson riot. Hurst went on hosting his syndicated TV dance show *Summertime at the Pier* until the closing in 1978.

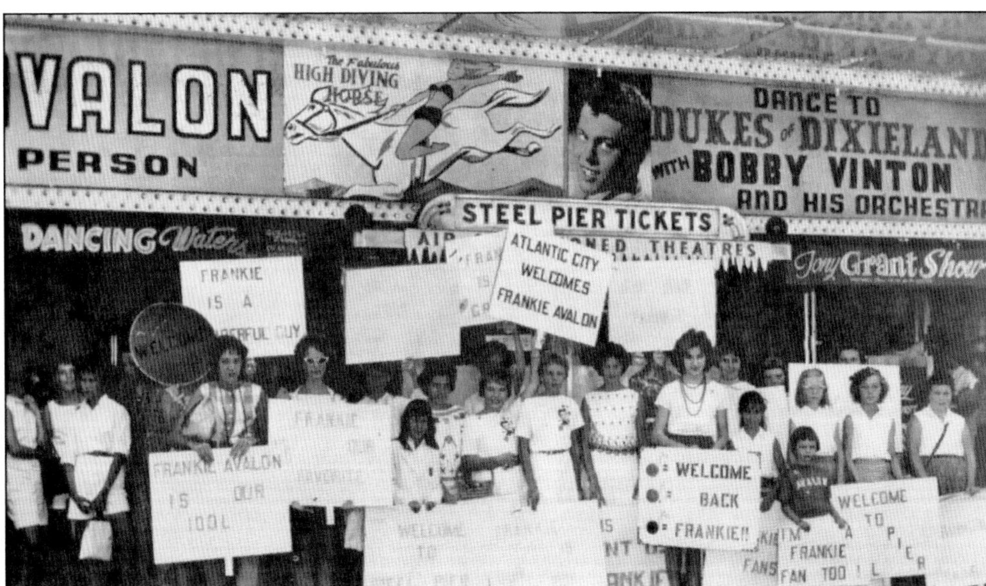

Fans of Frankie Avalon stake out the pier entrance in 1960, awaiting the arrival of their idol. Believe it or not, singer Bobby Vinton was booked at the same time, leading his dance band. Vinton did not commence his successful singing career until two years later.

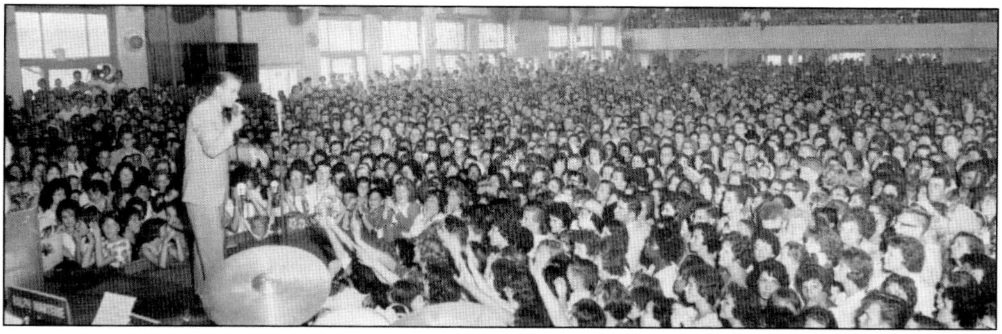

Dick Clark made five different appearances in the Marine Ballroom with his Caravan of Stars, from 1960 through 1964. Some of the hitmakers he brought along included Chubby Checker, Duane Eddy, the Shirelles, Jerry Lee Lewis, Gene Pitney, the Crystals, Jan & Dean, and the Supremes.

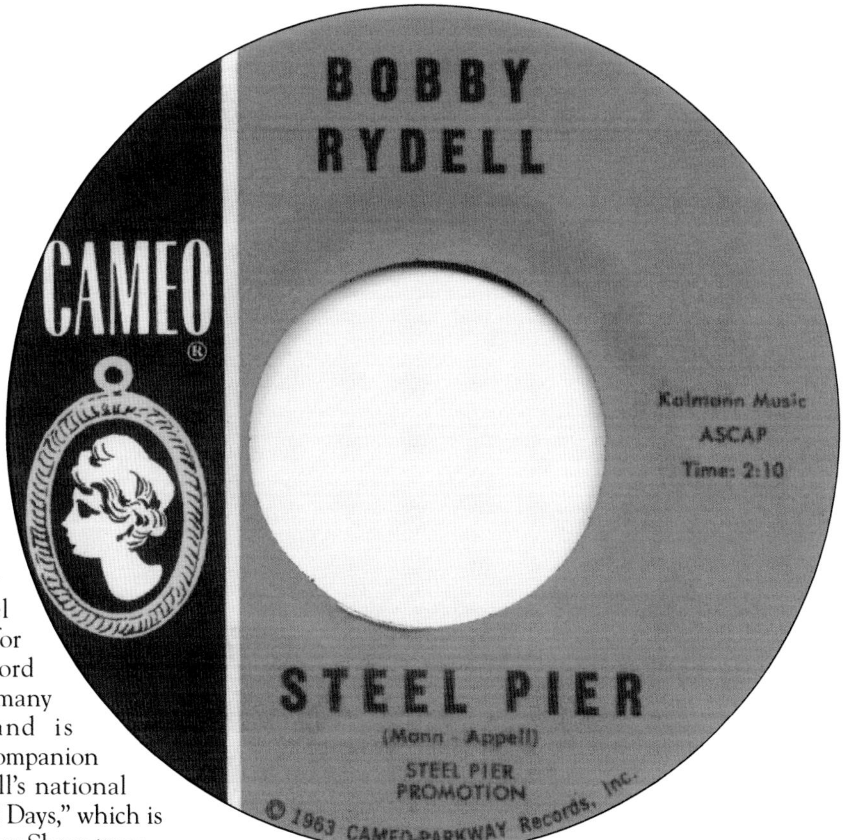

Bobby Rydell recorded a one-sided promo 45 that was only sold on Steel Pier in 1963 for 25¢. The record sold into the many thousands and is considered a companion piece to Rydell's national hit "Wildwood Days," which is about that Jersey Shore town.

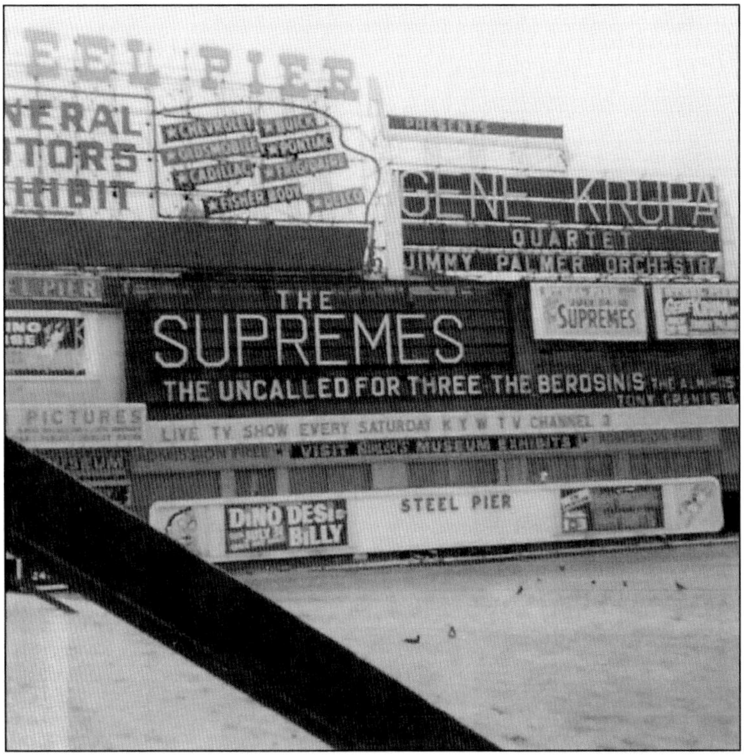

The Supremes played Steel Pier six times—the first with Dick Clark in 1964. This marquee is pictured in July 1966. The ballroom was hosting Gene Krupa. Notice the billing also of "The Uncalled For Three" and "The Berosinis," two of the Supremes' supporting vaudeville acts.

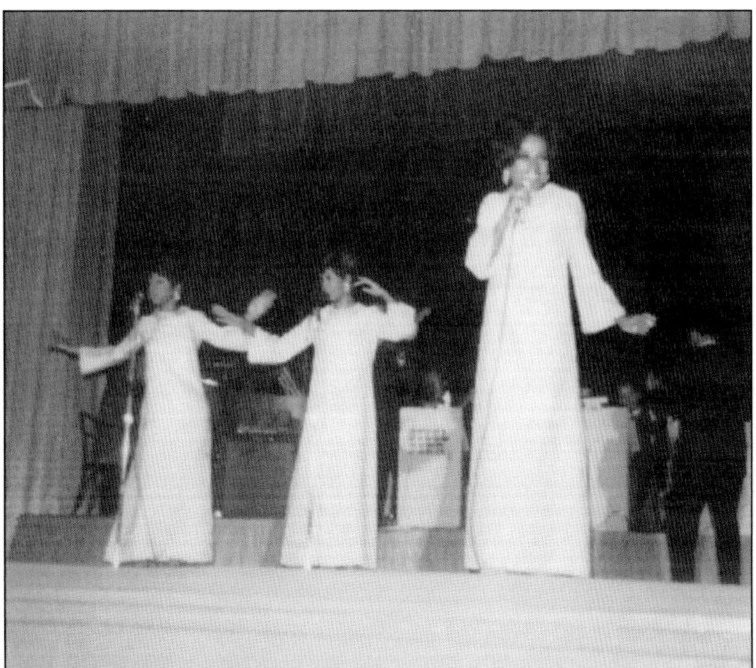

Diana Ross (right) is pictured with Florence Ballard (left) and Mary Wilson on the Music Hall stage in 1967. Ross's name was emphasized prominently on the marquee during this engagement; it was the first time the Supremes had been billed as such.

Pictured are some of the folks who rocked the pier in 1967, including singer Al Martino, who was not rock but did have a number of big hits in the 1960s. Martino appeared on Steel Pier 11 different times.

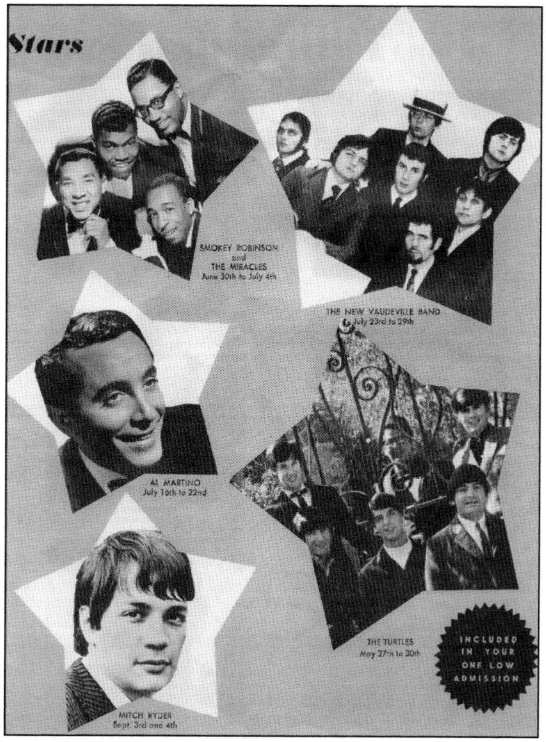

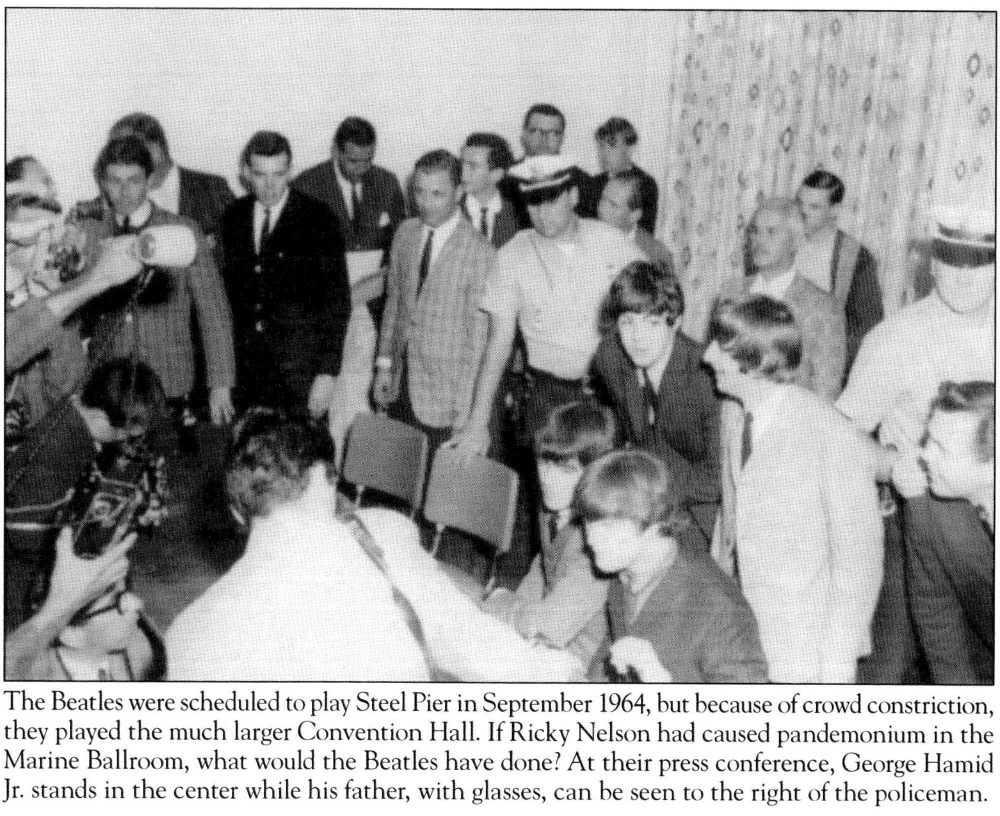

The Beatles were scheduled to play Steel Pier in September 1964, but because of crowd constriction, they played the much larger Convention Hall. If Ricky Nelson had caused pandemonium in the Marine Ballroom, what would the Beatles have done? At their press conference, George Hamid Jr. stands in the center while his father, with glasses, can be seen to the right of the policeman.

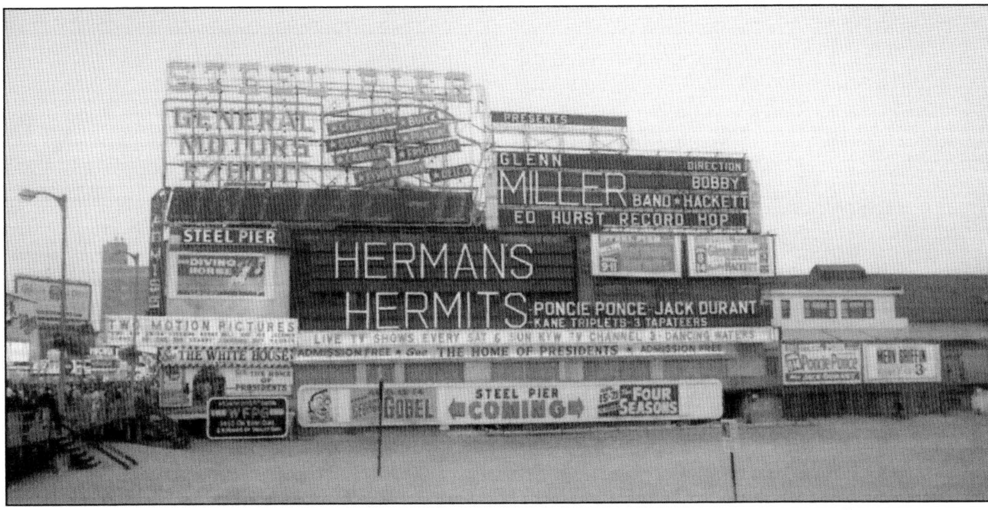

The marquee in August 1965 features Herman's Hermits. Poncie Ponce was a favorite singer-comedian who performed on the pier five times and starred in the television detective show *Hawaiian Eye*. Jack Durant was a former big-time vaudevillian who once played the London Palladium for 16 weeks and broke the house record. He was also half of the acrobatic comedy team Mitchell & Durant.

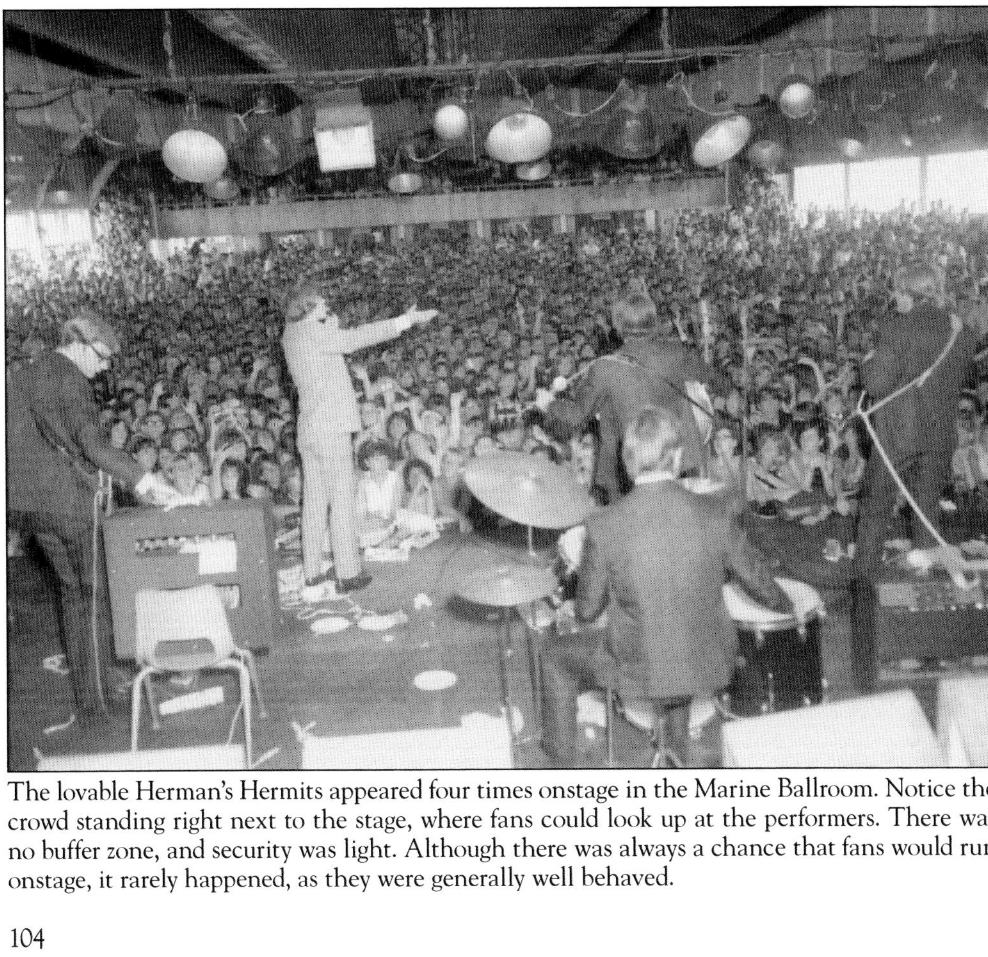

The lovable Herman's Hermits appeared four times onstage in the Marine Ballroom. Notice the crowd standing right next to the stage, where fans could look up at the performers. There was no buffer zone, and security was light. Although there was always a chance that fans would run onstage, it rarely happened, as they were generally well behaved.

The Rolling Stones played two shows in the Marine Ballroom on July 1, 1966, with a supporting cast that included the McCoys and the Standells. The Stones did not have the same status as the Beatles in the early years, and although they were a big deal, they were not icons until a few years later.

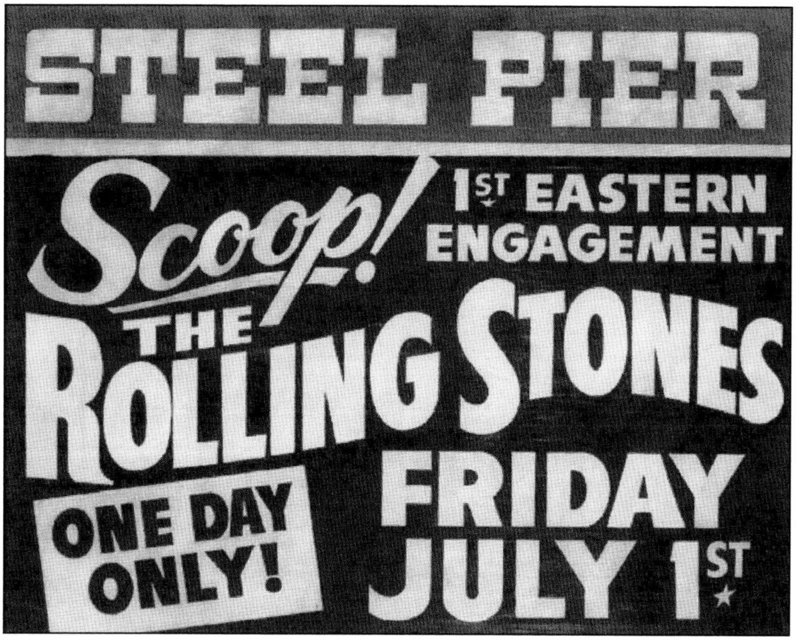

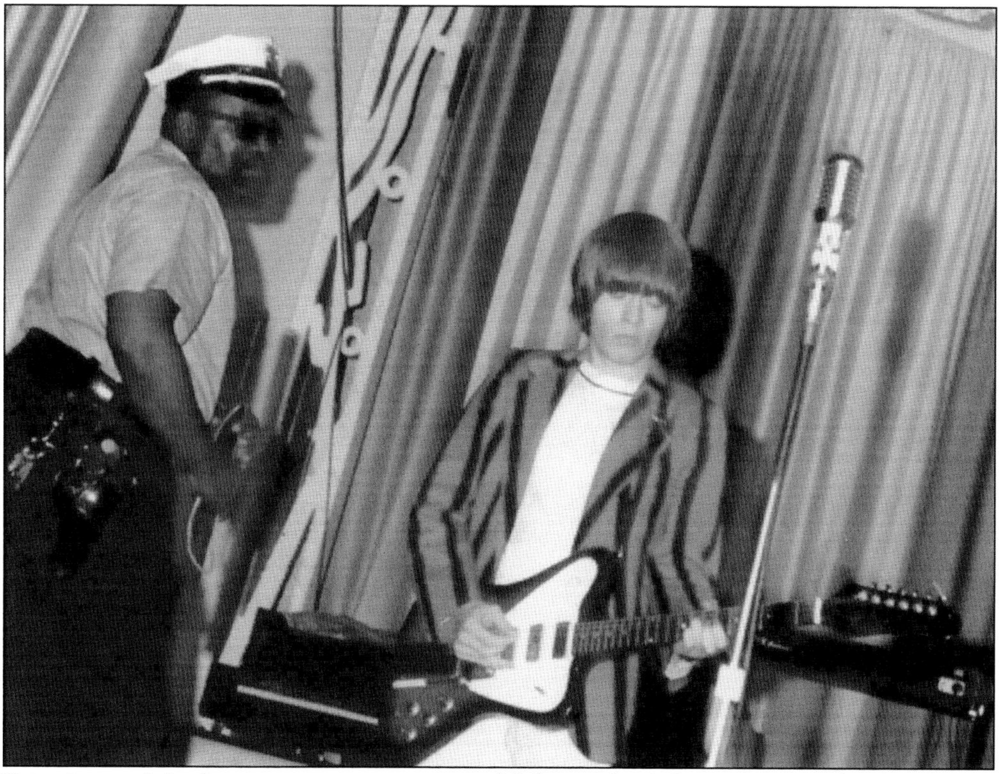

Brian Jones of the Stones strums away as one of Atlantic City's finest is prepared to handle any female fans rushing the stage. Security was tighter for these shows, but the audience was allowed, as always, to stand next to the stage.

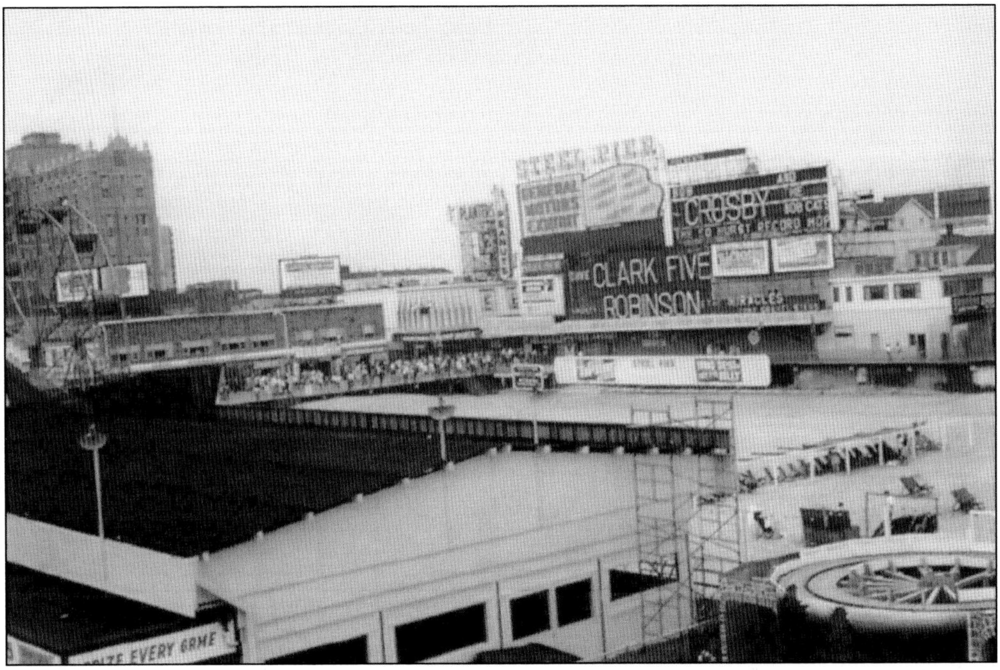

Britain's Dave Clark Five and Motown's Smokey Robinson and the Miracles are both listed on the marquee in July 1967. It was Clark's only appearance on the pier, but Robinson played twice.

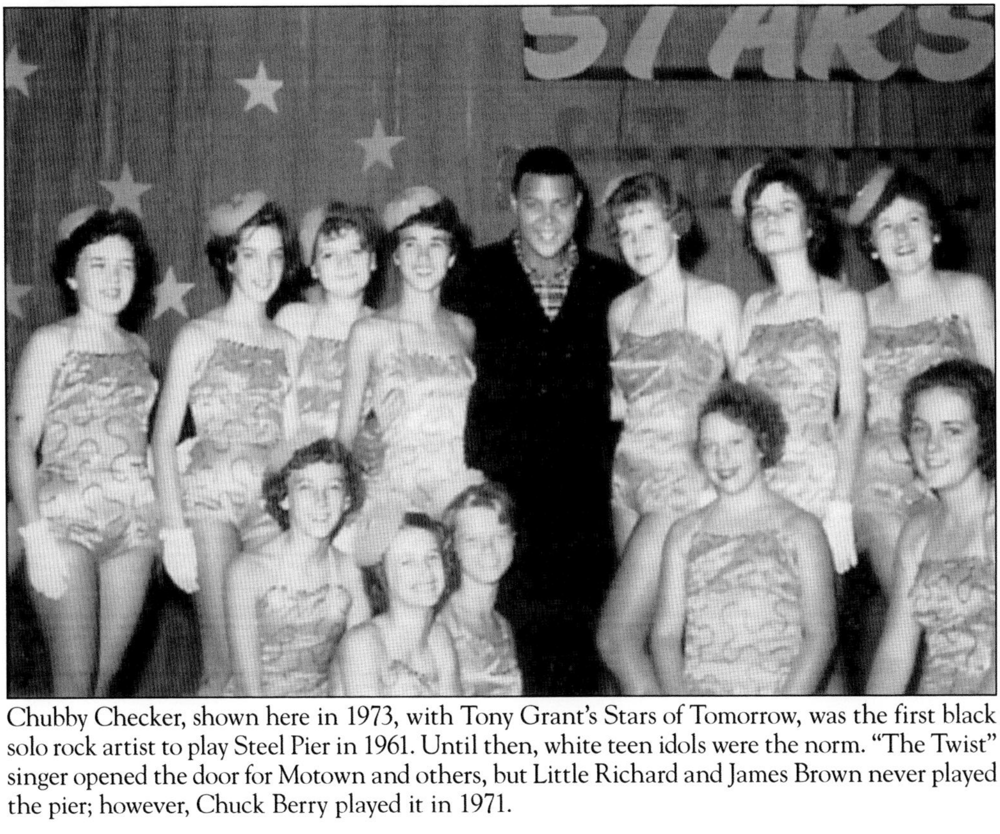

Chubby Checker, shown here in 1973, with Tony Grant's Stars of Tomorrow, was the first black solo rock artist to play Steel Pier in 1961. Until then, white teen idols were the norm. "The Twist" singer opened the door for Motown and others, but Little Richard and James Brown never played the pier; however, Chuck Berry played it in 1971.

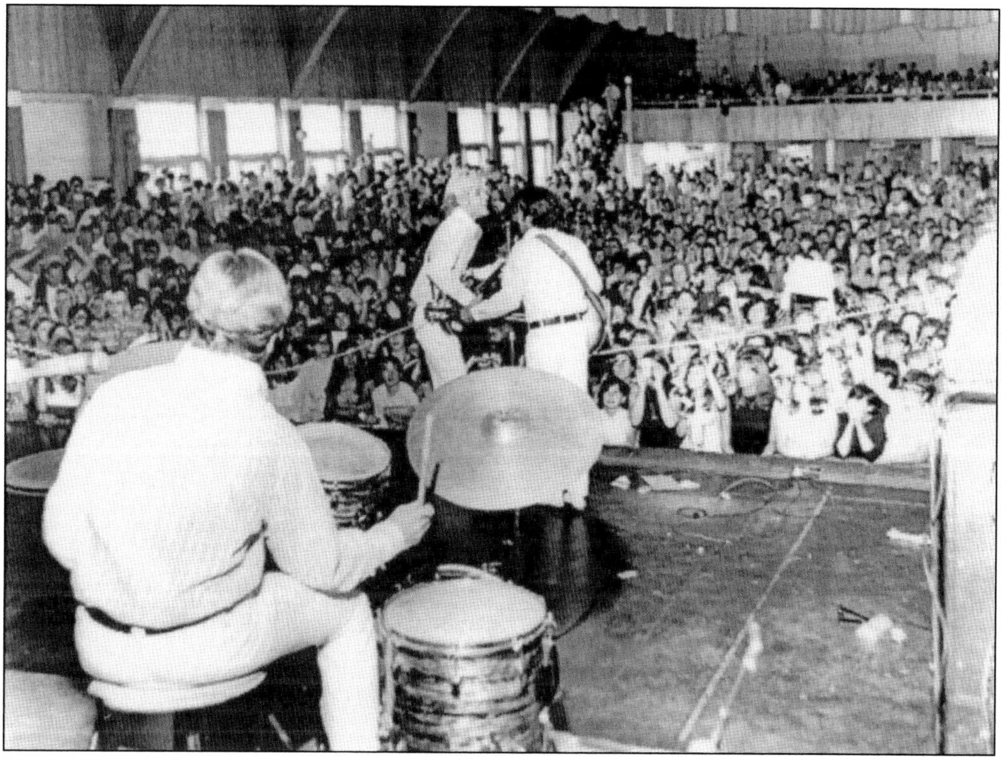

Dino, Desi & Billy included the sons of Dean Martin and Lucille Ball and Desi Arnaz, plus Billy Hinsche, a childhood friend. The group's biggest year was 1965, when it had two Top 40 hits, but when this picture was taken three years later, the young men still had ample fans.

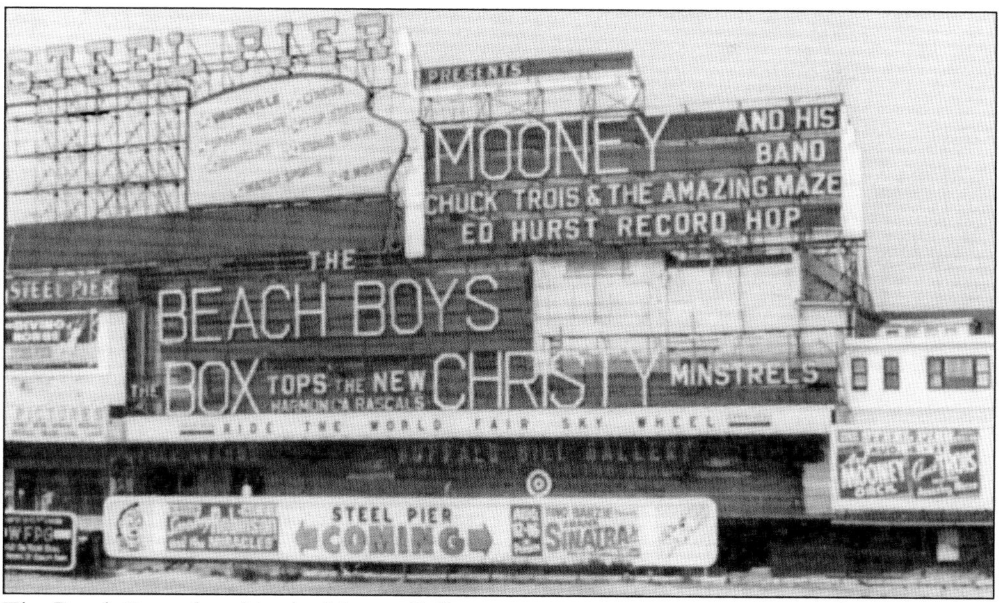

The Beach Boys played in the Marine Ballroom two years in a row, in 1968 and 1969. Also on this bill were the Box Tops, the New Christy Minstrels, and the new Harmonica Rascals, along with Art Mooney's orchestra.

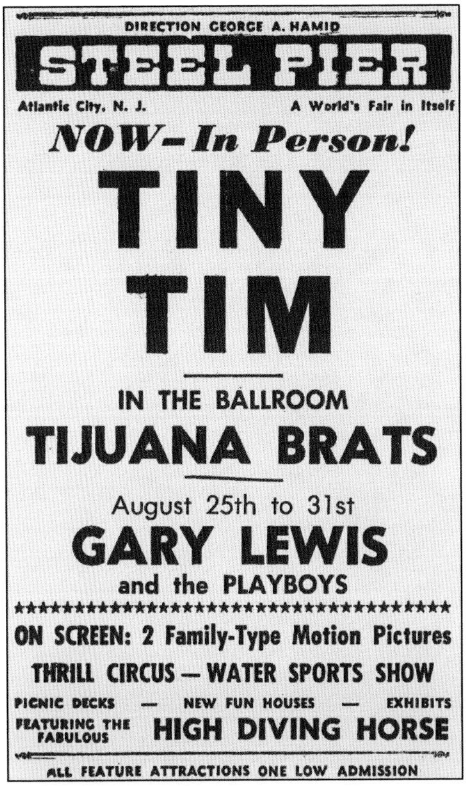

Even the indescribable Tiny Tim appeared in 1969, at the peak of being the hottest act in the country. One-hit wonders were uncannily featured just as their hit peaked.

An example of the one-hit wonder billing would be this 1970 sign promoting two groups, each only known for the hit listed on the sign. Both drew large crowds due to one hit song and never again hit such lofty heights.

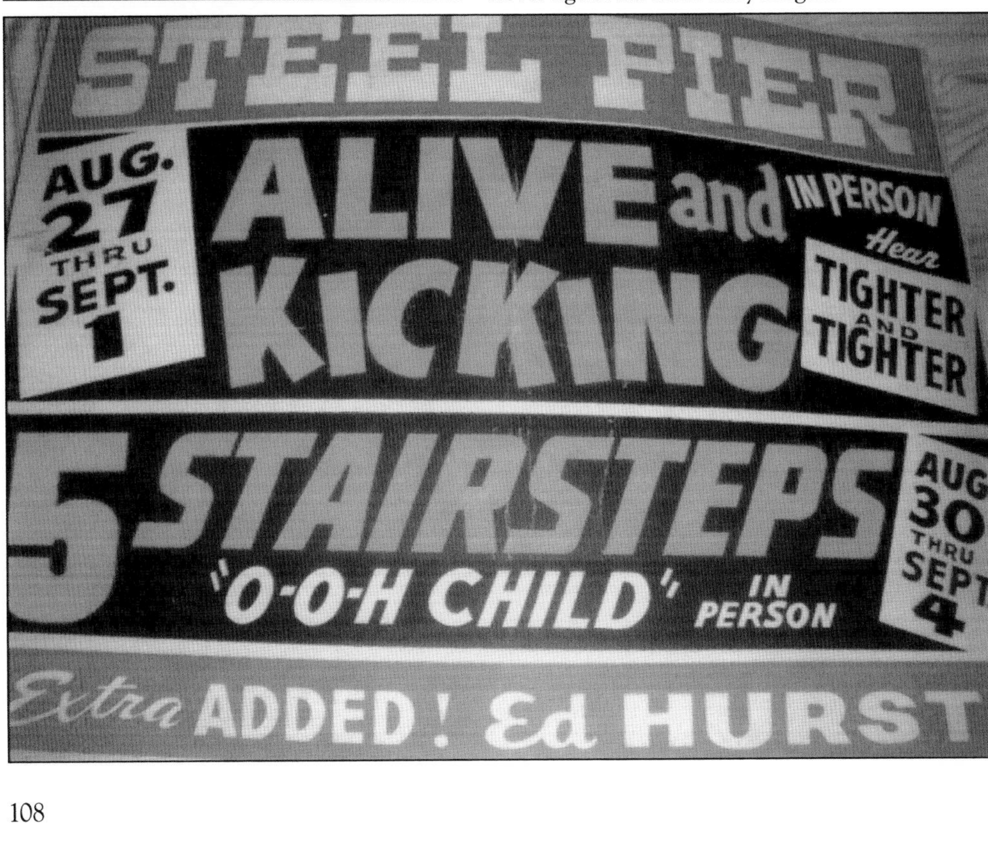

Duane Allman of the Allman Brothers Band plays a solo in the Golden Dome Ballroom in July 1971 as his brother Gregg plays keys and bassist Berry Oakley joins in on the right. Both Duane and Oakley would die in motorcycle accidents a little over one year apart; Duane passed just a few months after this concert. The band was not used to playing short multiple shows per day and found it hard to adjust.

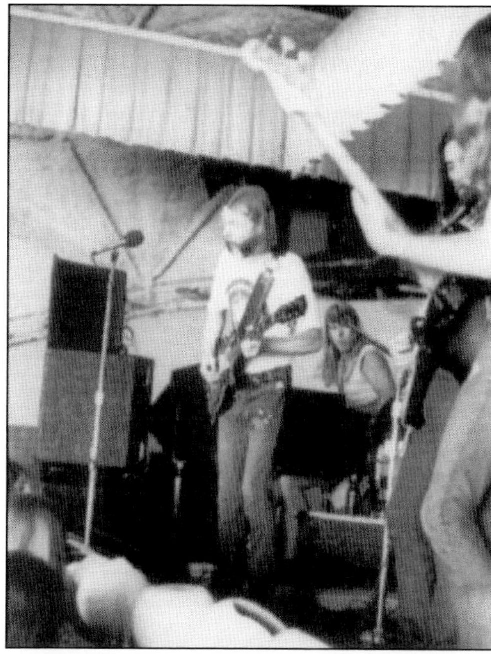

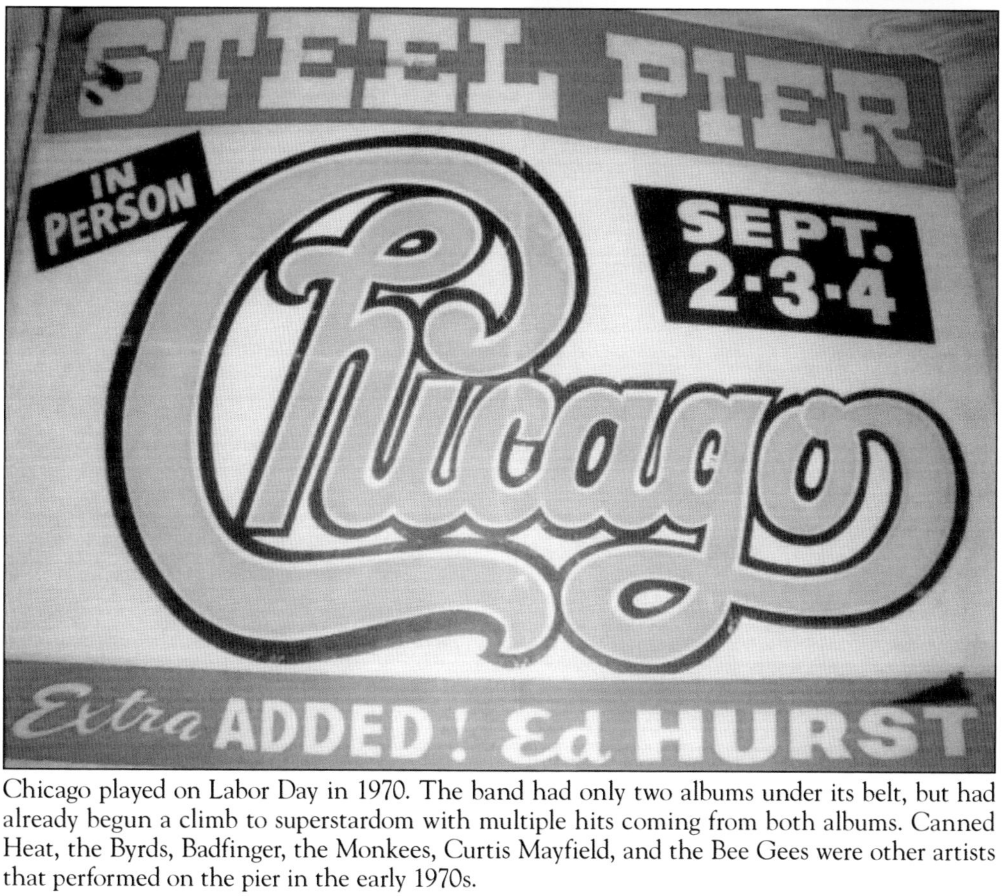

Chicago played on Labor Day in 1970. The band had only two albums under its belt, but had already begun a climb to superstardom with multiple hits coming from both albums. Canned Heat, the Byrds, Badfinger, the Monkees, Curtis Mayfield, and the Bee Gees were other artists that performed on the pier in the early 1970s.

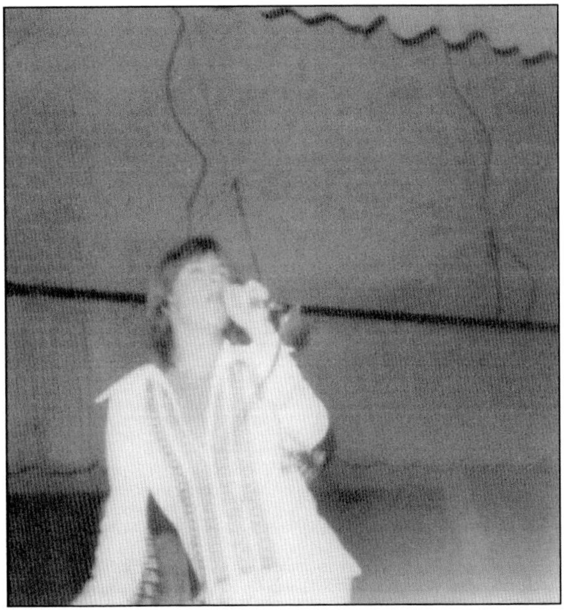

Another wild day on the pier was August 28, 1971, when pop star David Cassidy checked in. Cassidy had almost drawn as many people as Ricky Nelson and was forced to wear disguises just to get around the pier. He was actually quite scared of being noticed, fearful of being swamped and injured by overexuberant fans. (Courtesy of Dave Feller.)

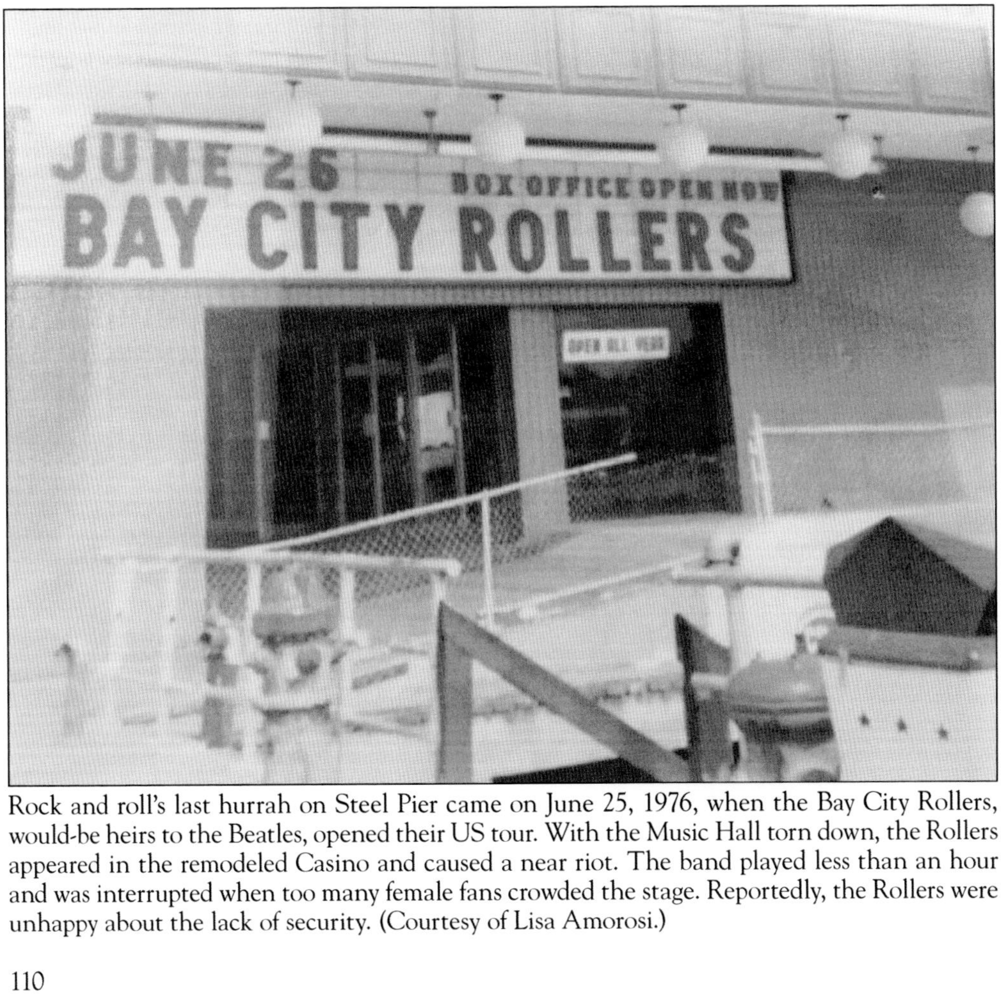

Rock and roll's last hurrah on Steel Pier came on June 25, 1976, when the Bay City Rollers, would-be heirs to the Beatles, opened their US tour. With the Music Hall torn down, the Rollers appeared in the remodeled Casino and caused a near riot. The band played less than an hour and was interrupted when too many female fans crowded the stage. Reportedly, the Rollers were unhappy about the lack of security. (Courtesy of Lisa Amorosi.)

Ten

The Pier Itself

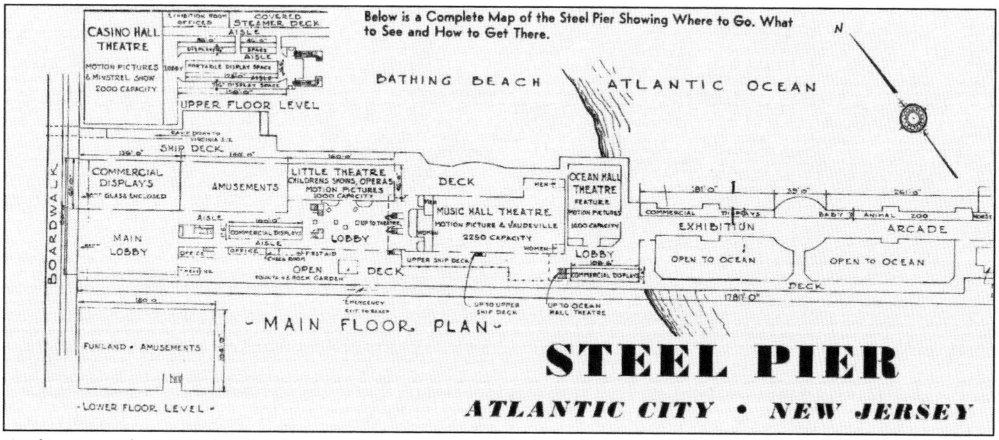

A diagram from 1948 shows the layout of the pier and seating capacities of the theaters. It is astounding from an architectural position how four theaters, concession stands, exhibition halls, and offices are cramped into the boardwalk portion of the pier.

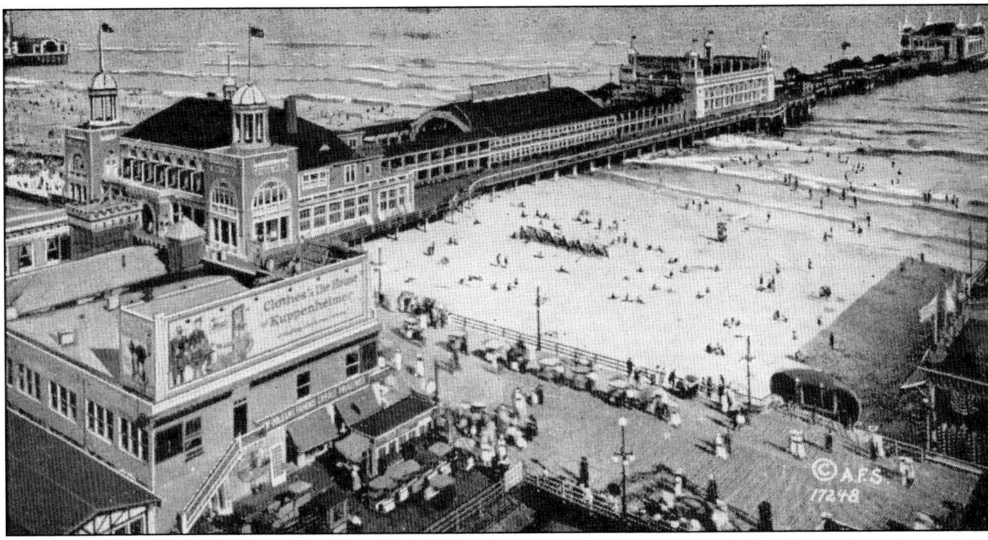

Steel Pier's physical appearance changed greatly during its existence. This long shot from 1916 focuses on the pleasurable simplicity of the structure and the balance of the buildings.

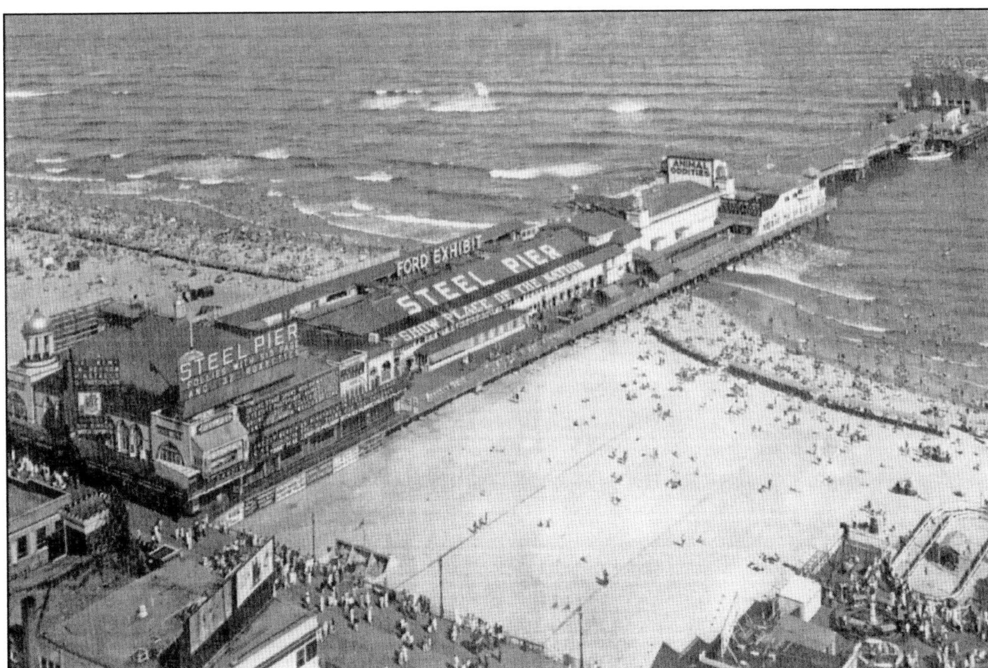

This view from July 4, 1935, shows the improvements and additions by Frank Gravatt, including signage, the closing of the open-air pavilion, and the addition of the Ocean theater. There are more signs advertising products as well as wider walkways.

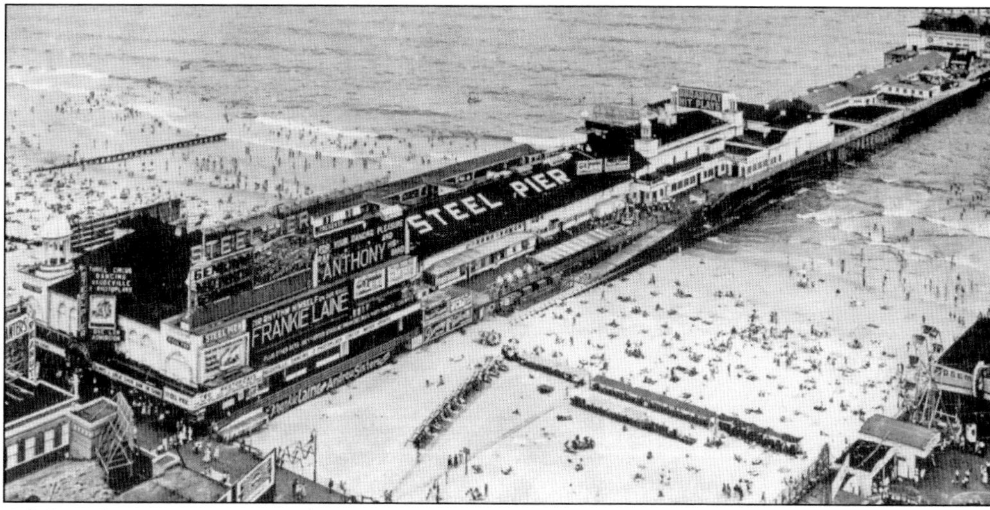

A July 1951 view presents much grander marquees, an exit ramp leading to the beach, searchlights, and an added promenade between the Ocean theater and the ballroom.

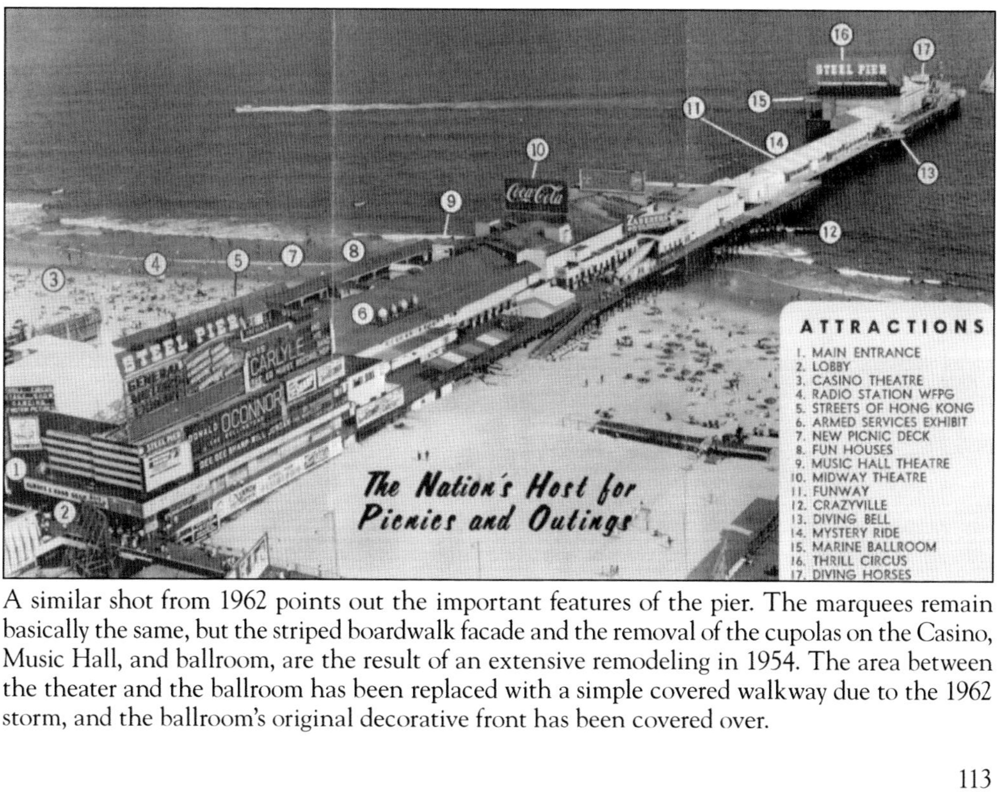

A similar shot from 1962 points out the important features of the pier. The marquees remain basically the same, but the striped boardwalk facade and the removal of the cupolas on the Casino, Music Hall, and ballroom, are the result of an extensive remodeling in 1954. The area between the theater and the ballroom has been replaced with a simple covered walkway due to the 1962 storm, and the ballroom's original decorative front has been covered over.

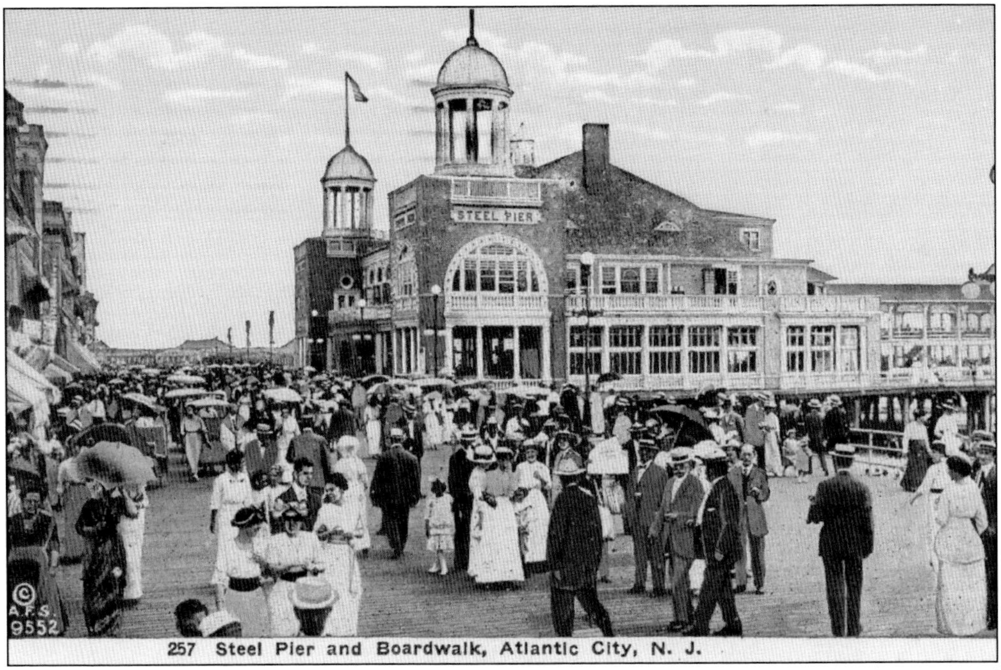

The Casino side of the pier in 1920 is still pretty much the same as the original architecture of 22 years earlier. The lobby and pavilion are open aired, and there is not any signage, except for the pier's name above a rounded lobby window.

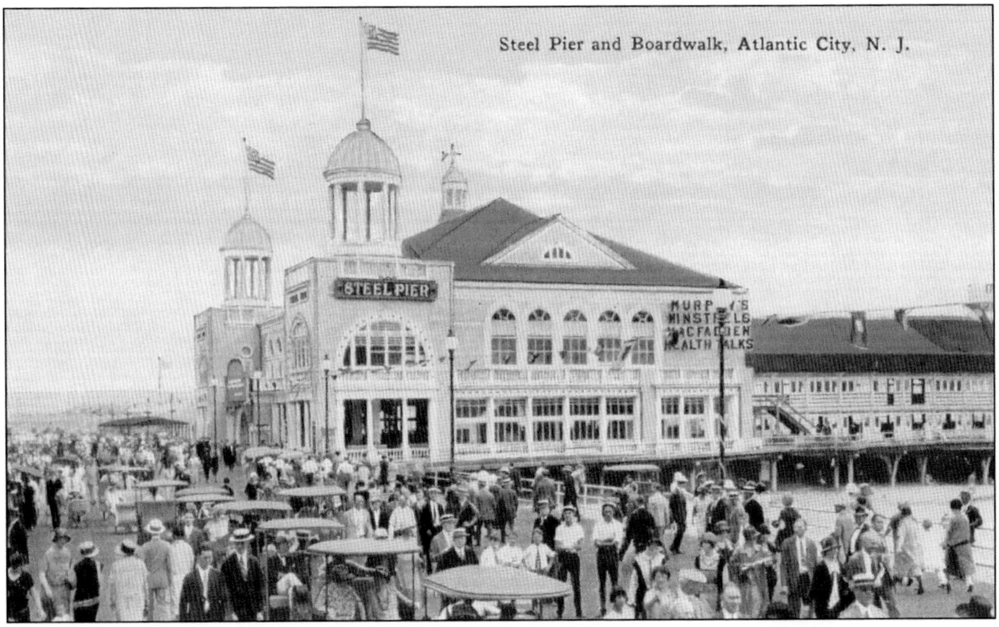

Seen here in 1924, the Casino side presents the subtle changes that have taken place. The second floor of the Casino building has been enlarged, and the pavilion has now been covered and enclosed. A small letter board has been erected, announcing the minstrels and health talks.

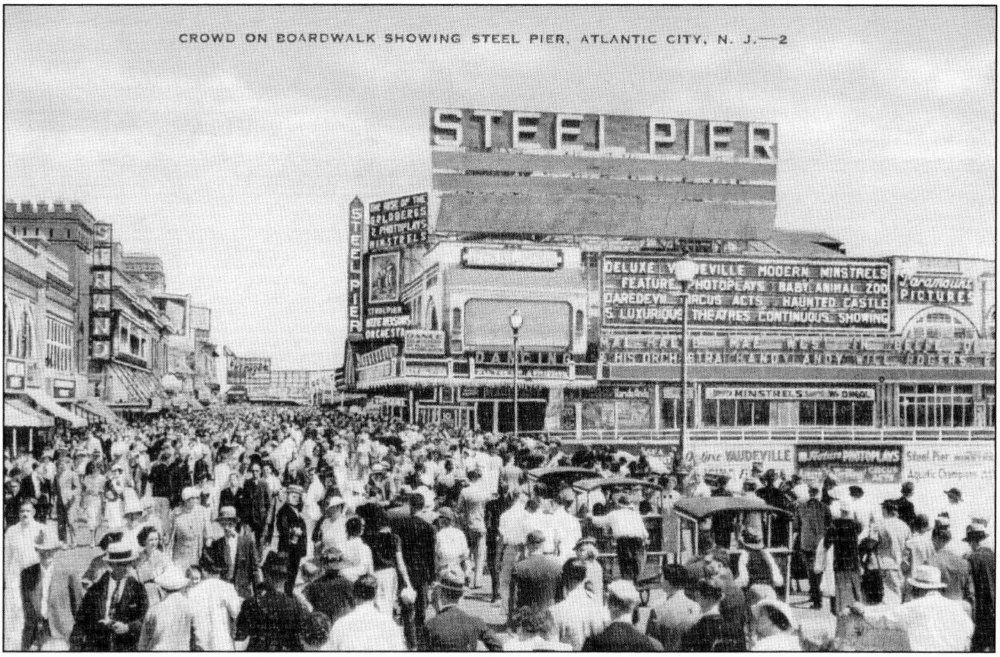

Ten years later, in 1934, the signage on the pier has exploded. It now covers up the majority of the side of the Casino building as it announces the many attractions and entertainment available. An electronic ribbon is now below the huge Steel Pier letters, a marquee has been built, and a decorative montage of smaller signs garnishes the facade above the main entrance.

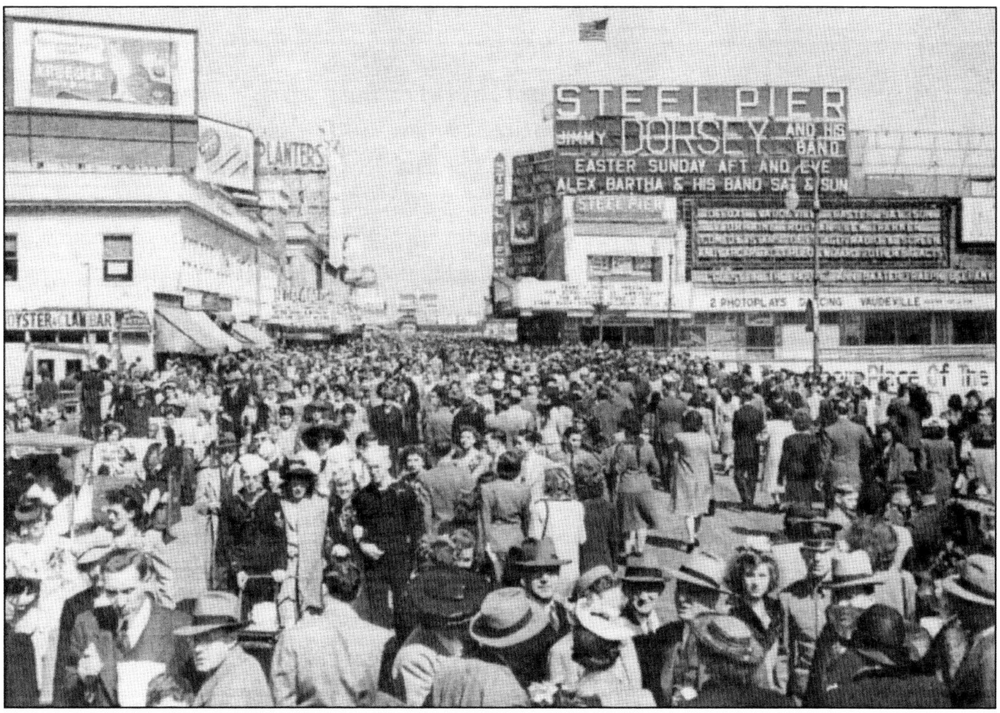

On Easter 1944, the Casino side looks about the same as it did 10 years earlier, except for a new, modern marquee utilizing movie-theater lettering.

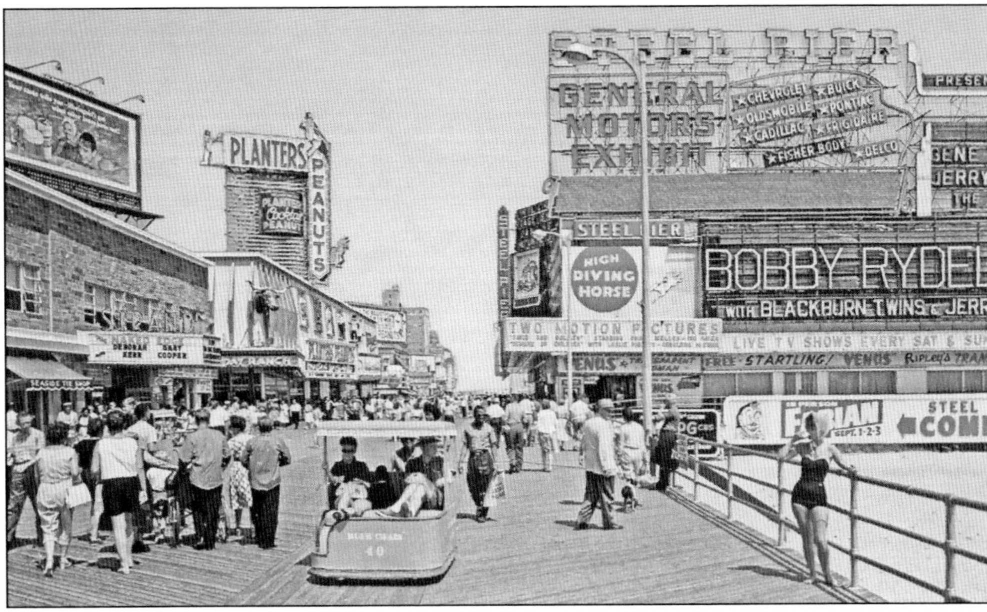

By 1961, with the Hamids firmly entrenched as owners, major physical changes and improvements were made. The signage has grown higher, fitting in ample room promoting the General Motors exhibit. The lettering is bigger and easier to read. However, the marquee and facade signage is still the same.

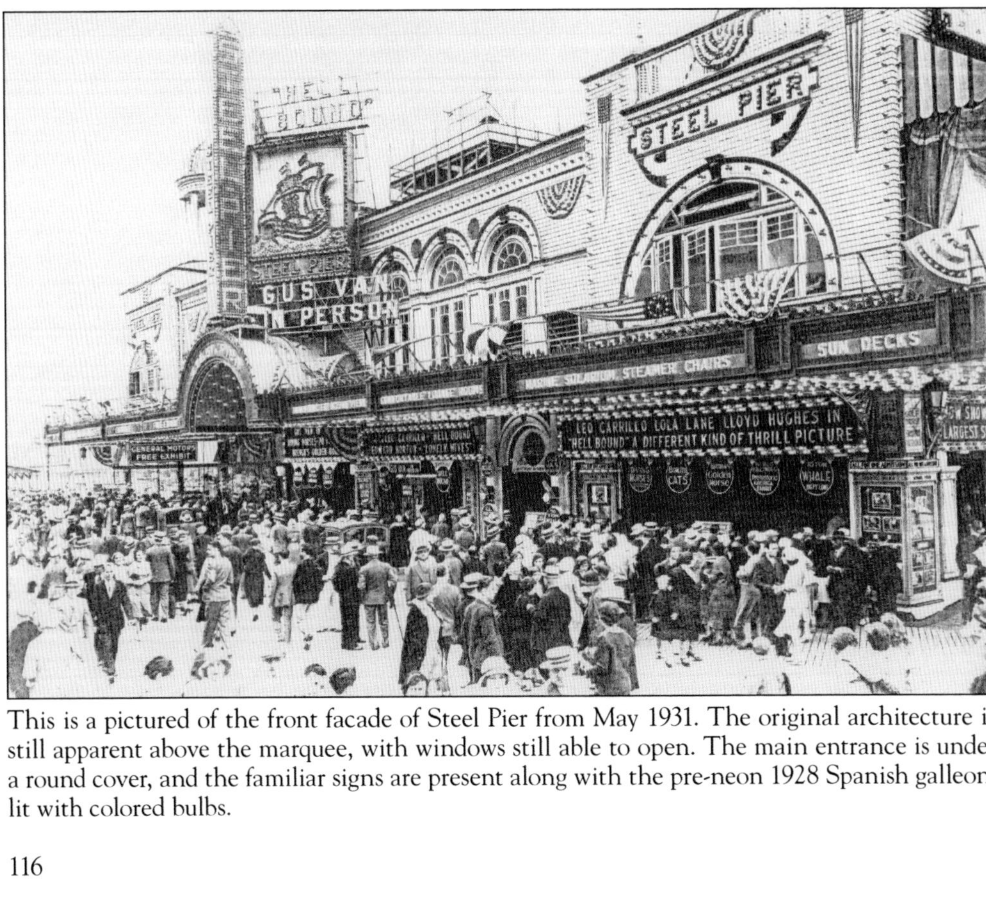

This is a pictured of the front facade of Steel Pier from May 1931. The original architecture is still apparent above the marquee, with windows still able to open. The main entrance is under a round cover, and the familiar signs are present along with the pre-neon 1928 Spanish galleon, lit with colored bulbs.

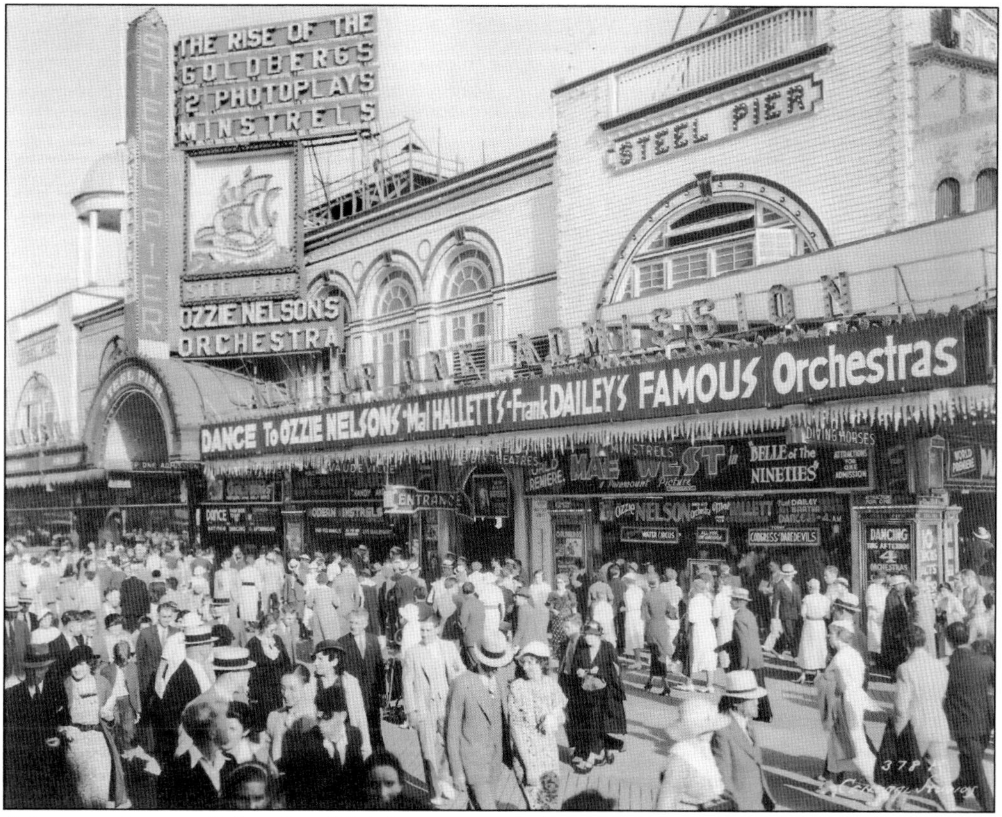

A few years later, on Labor Day 1934, the marquee is beginning to segue from the older, decorative metal to the more modern, streamlined look. The promotional signs below the marquee have now become more graphic, with pictures as opposed to just letters.

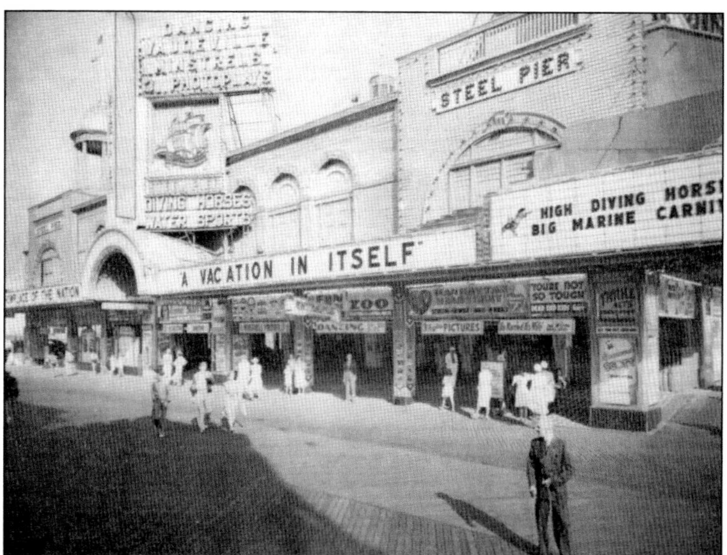

A major change in appearance is apparent in this July 1940 picture, as the pier's facade looks much brighter and more modern. Everything is basically the same structurally, except for the marquee and entranceways, which look more inviting.

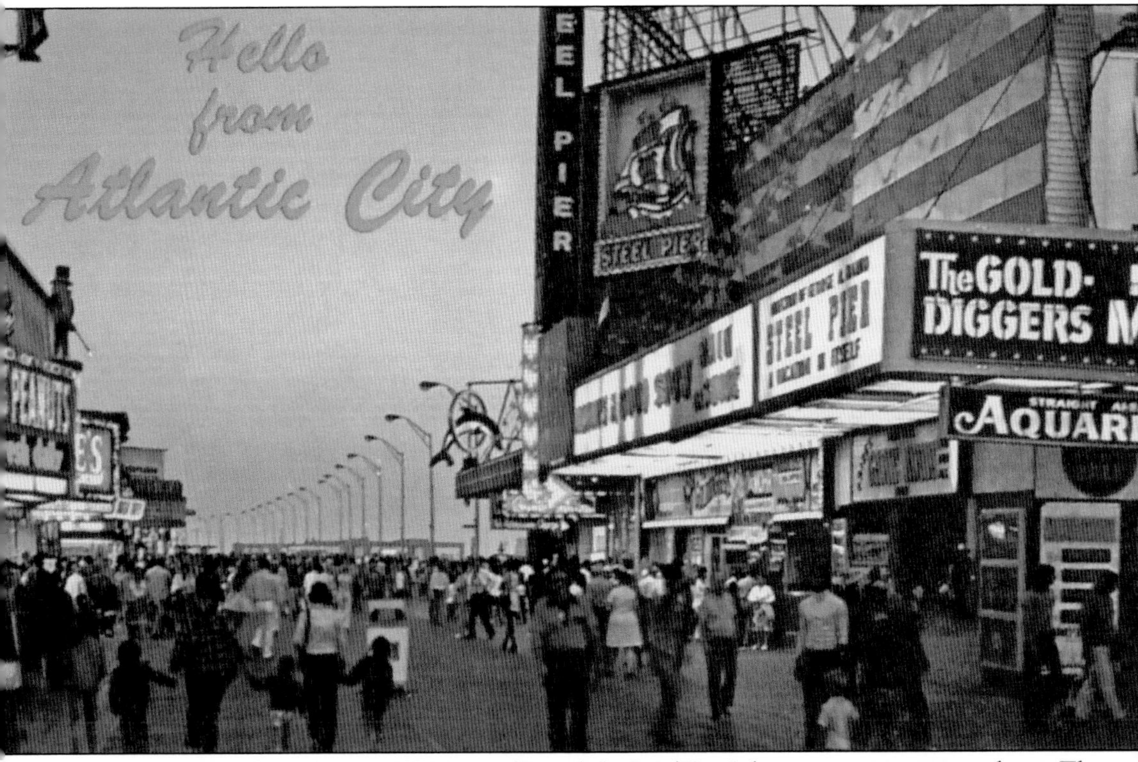

This picture from August 1974 was taken while Steel Pier's last years were approaching. The original front facade still has the remodeled stripe look from 1954, and the marquee has become thicker. The main entrance has lost its round covering and looks nondescript. The Spanish galleon sign is still there, and neon arrows and signs prevail.

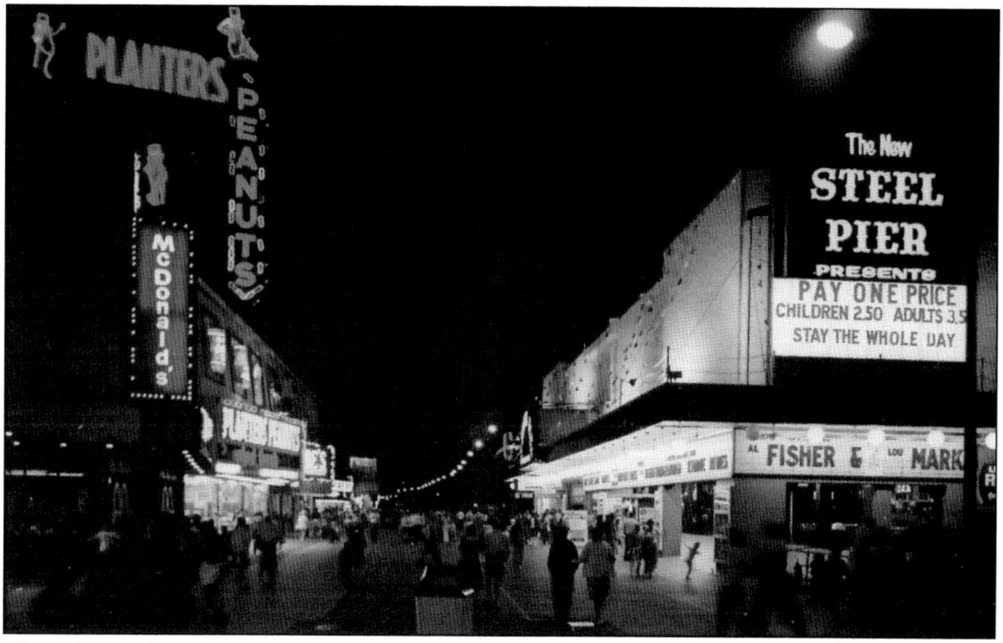

This 1977 nighttime picture is downright depressing. After the major renovations of 1976, a concerted effort was made to totally strip the pier of any signage. The "new" Steel Pier does have a new marquee, and the building looks clean, but it has lost all of the character that made it intriguing and exciting.

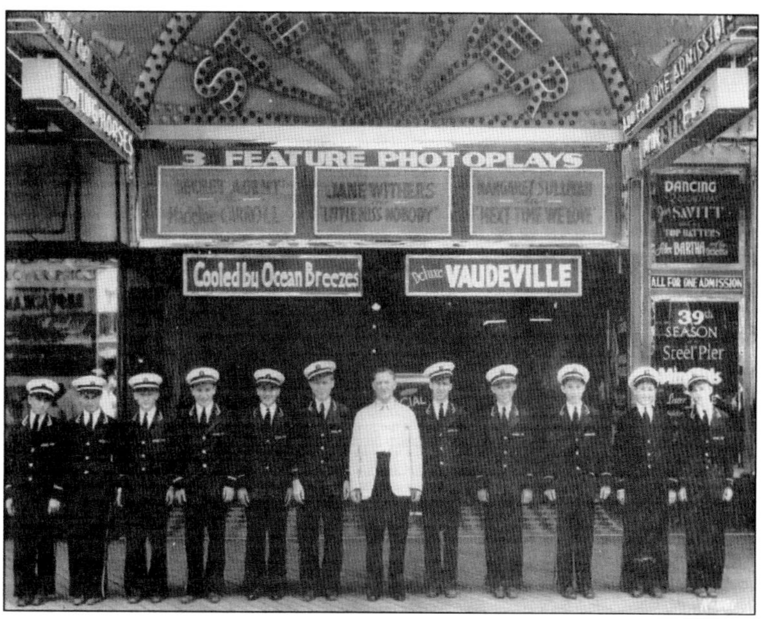

The turnstile boys and front manager James Rock pose in front of the entrance in 1936. All employees wore uniforms and handled the congested crowds with class and respect, a prerequisite enforced by Frank Gravatt.

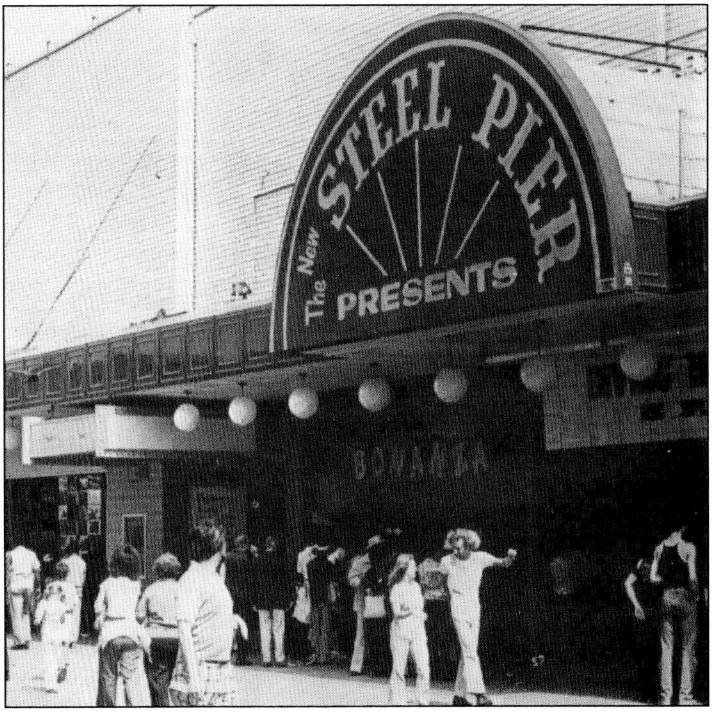

The same entrance is pictured here in 1976. The round covering is still there, modified under the new signage. Forty years later, Steel Pier now exists in an entirely different world of relaxed dress codes, mediocre entertainment, and a public indifferent to the structure's legacy.

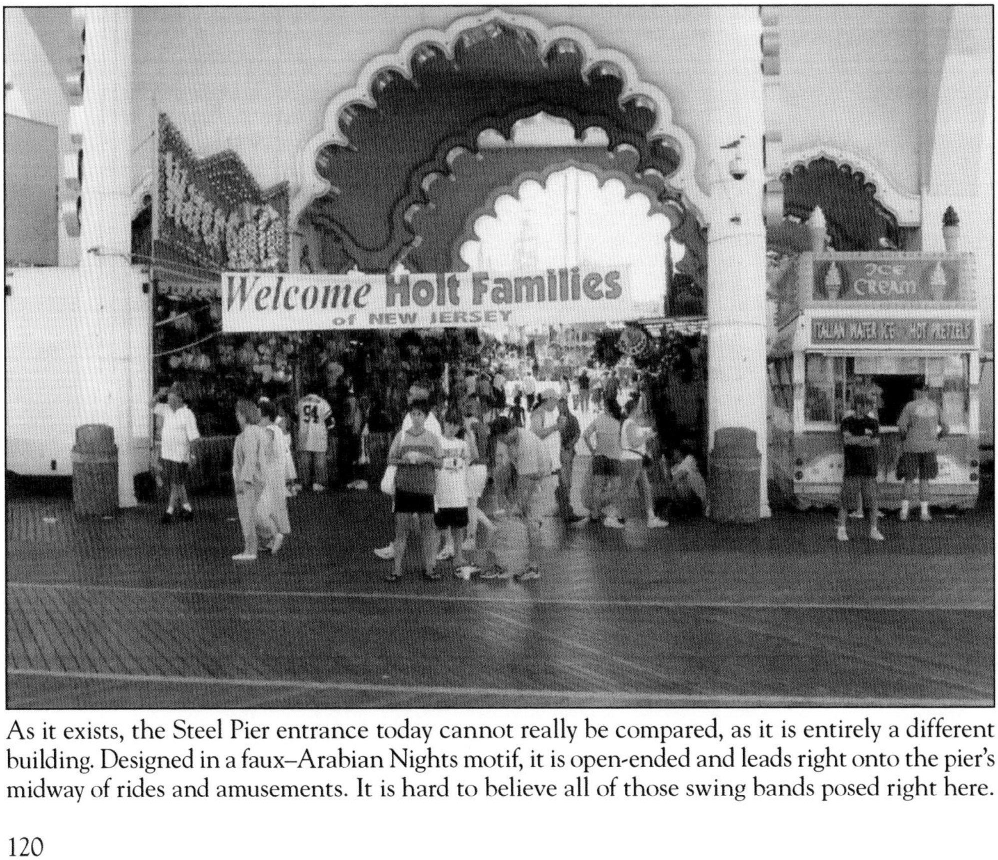

As it exists, the Steel Pier entrance today cannot really be compared, as it is entirely a different building. Designed in a faux–Arabian Nights motif, it is open-ended and leads right onto the pier's midway of rides and amusements. It is hard to believe all of those swing bands posed right here.

Because it was such a large building, the Marine Ballroom could be seen from anywhere on the beach. This picture was taken before the 1962 storm as the Home of the Century stands to the left of the ballroom. Many locals swam around the pier, and some would sneak into the basements of fun houses to bypass admission.

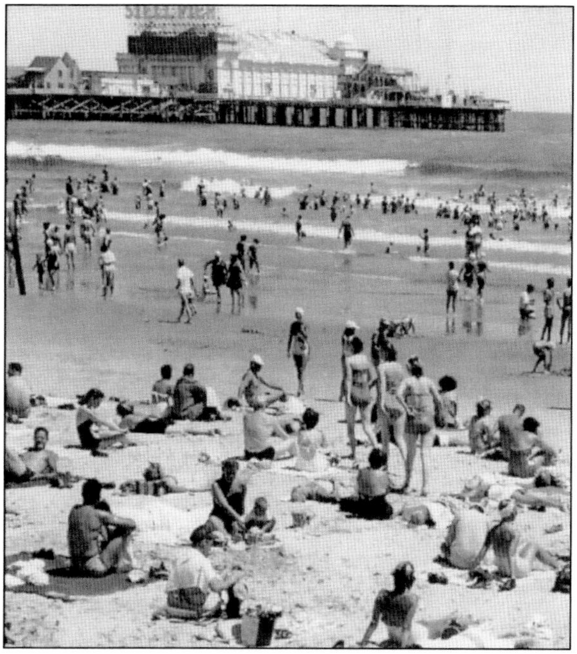

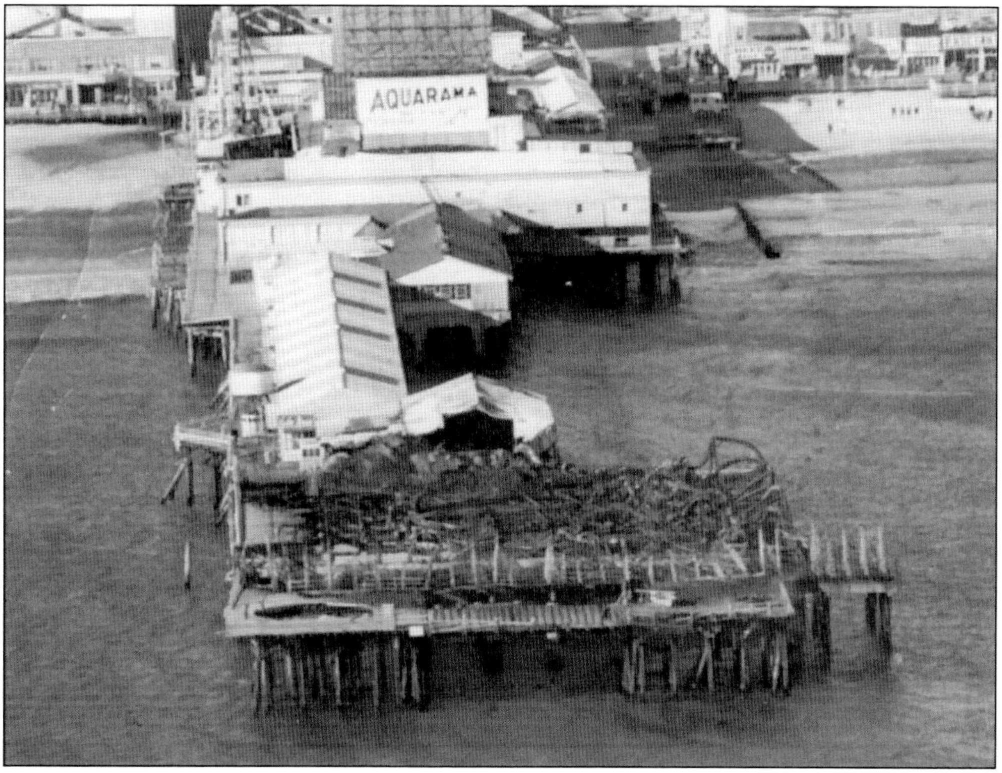

The Marine Ballroom completely burned on December 27, 1969. It was a terrible loss for Steel Pier and Atlantic City, because physically, it could never be replaced. The many memories of the dance orchestras and rock bands that played there before thousands of fans will never be forgotten to those who were present.

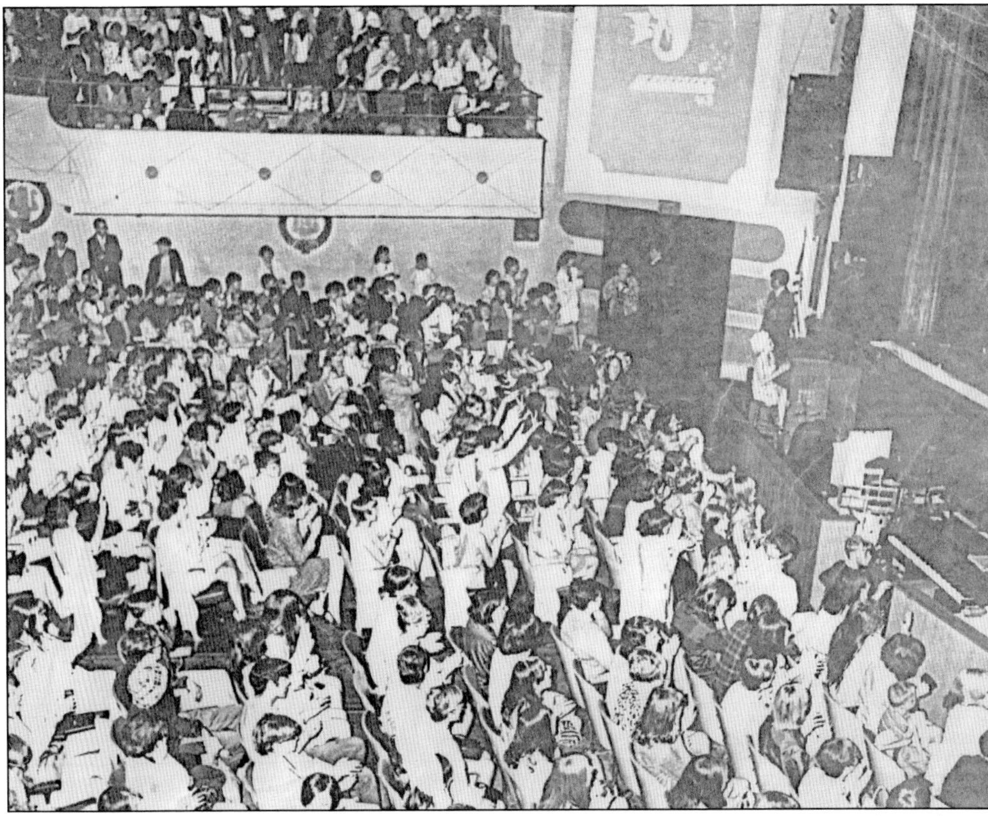

This is a rare side view of the Music Hall, captured from a balcony during the 1960s. The orchestra pit is on the right, and if one could spare some extra change, he or she would be privileged to sit in the first few rows. The balconies were added to a redesigned Music Hall in 1952, with *Billboard* magazine reporting that the seating increased from 3,200 seats to a whopping 4,700; this assertion, however, is disputable.

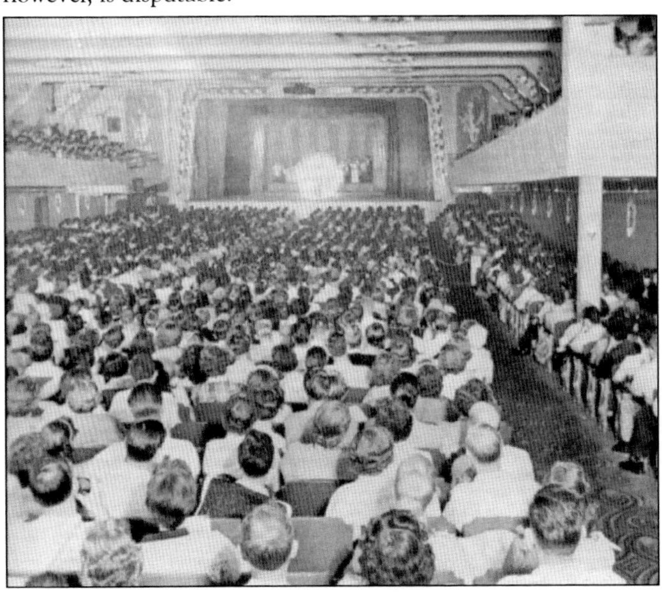

Seen here is another rare view of the Music Hall from a decade earlier. The balconies were built with poles that situated some seats with an obstructed view of the stage. Because the theater was so large, the headliner must have looked very tiny from the seats farther in the back.

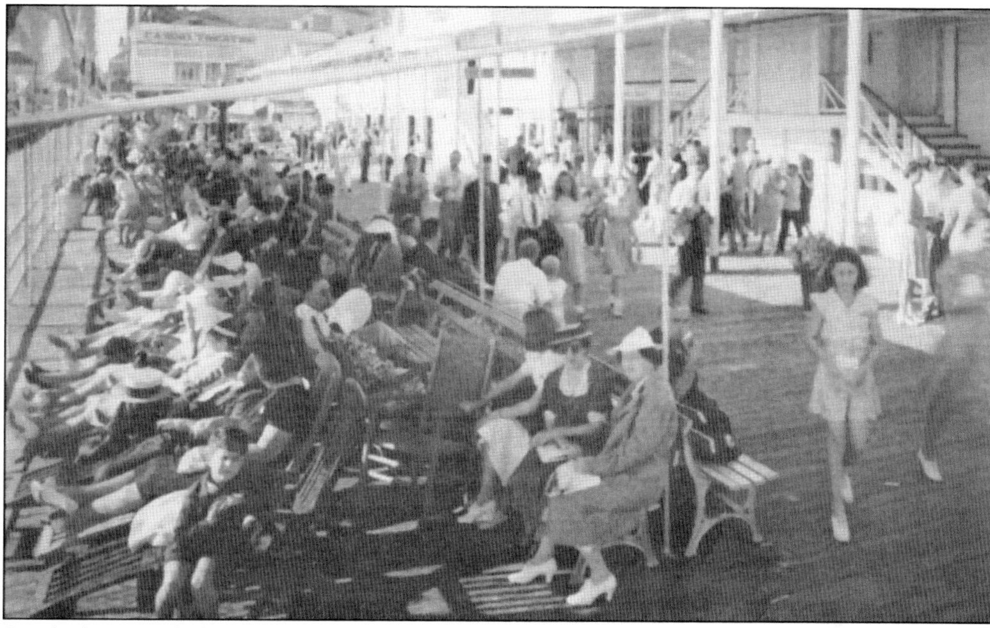

Sundecks prevailed over most of the pier and visitors could relax on either side. This scene is on the south side next to the Music Hall. There was never a time constraint on the pier, as one could stay all day and night for the one price. Many people would bring a bag lunch, place it on a picnic table for later consumption, and find it exactly where it was left, untouched.

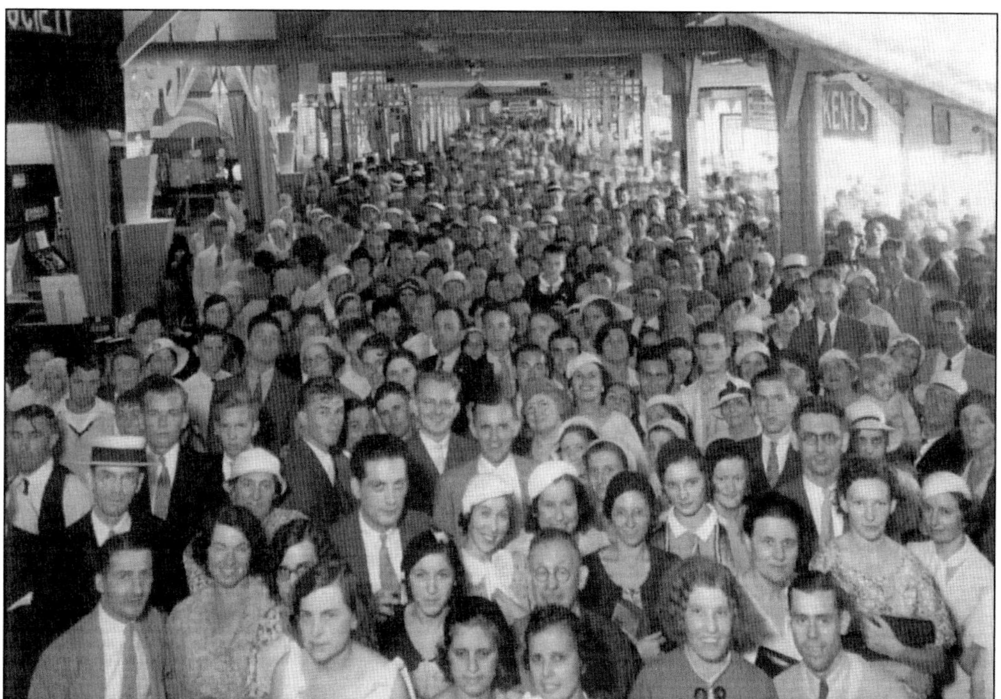

A jammed Marine Arcade from 1936 presents a very busy area full of exhibits, concession stands, and small activities for those going to and from the Ocean theater out to the Marine Ballroom.

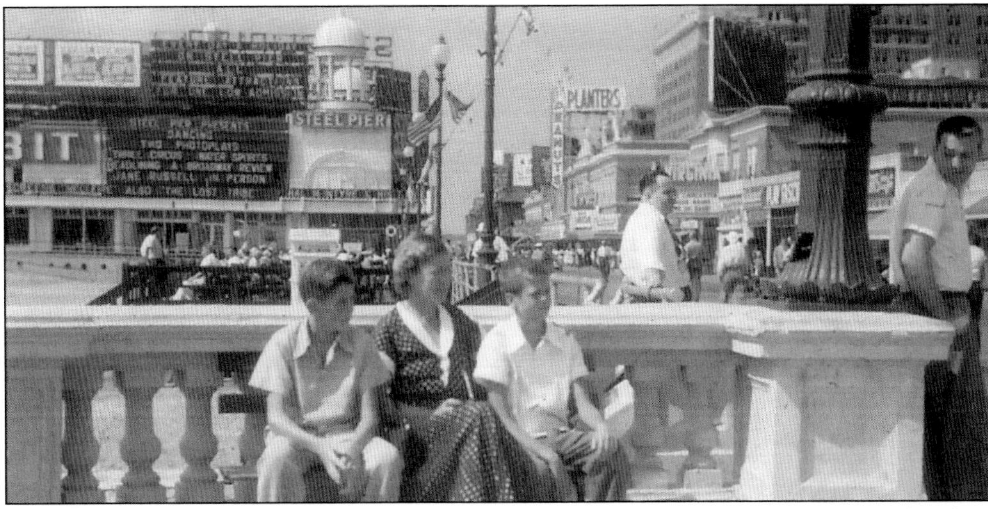

An unidentified woman and her two sons take a breather in 1949, with the pier's north side in the background. The signage was not as large as that on the Casino's south side. In fact, it was miniscule in comparison. The Boardwalk Virginia theater can be seen behind the man in the right center of the photograph.

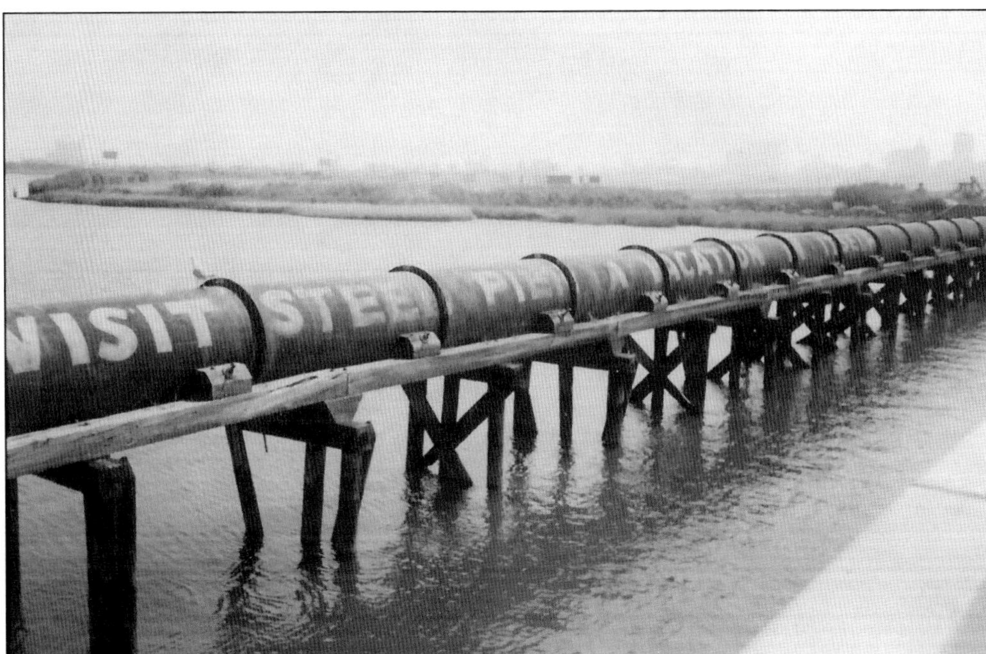

Because Steel Pier advertised literally everywhere, a few remnants of painted signs were discovered into the early 1990s. Here, a water pipe outside of Atlantic City advertises something that had not yet been rebuilt.

The destruction of the Music Hall in late 1975 was on par with the burning of the Marine Ballroom. This historic theater, which held over 2,000 seats (depending on the source), was the home to the last continuous vaudeville in the United States. (Courtesy of Terri Tyrrell.)

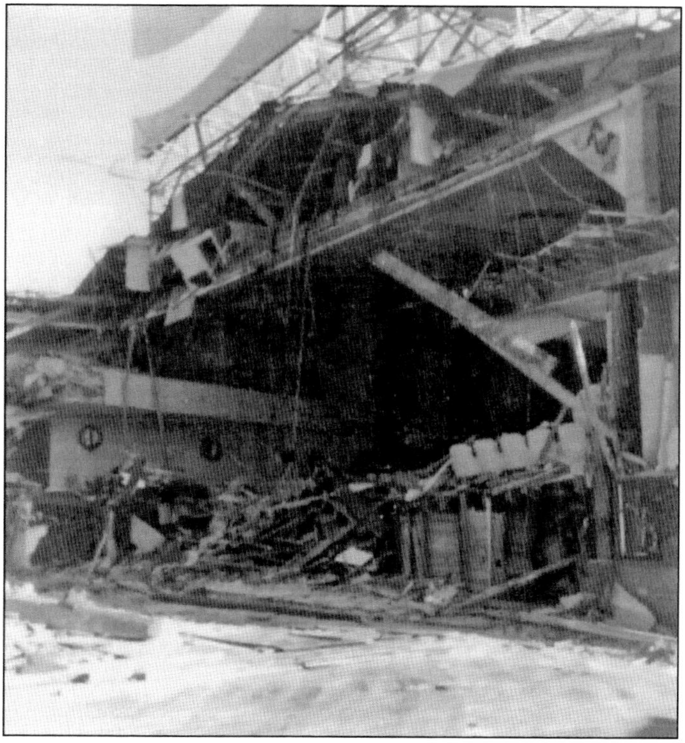

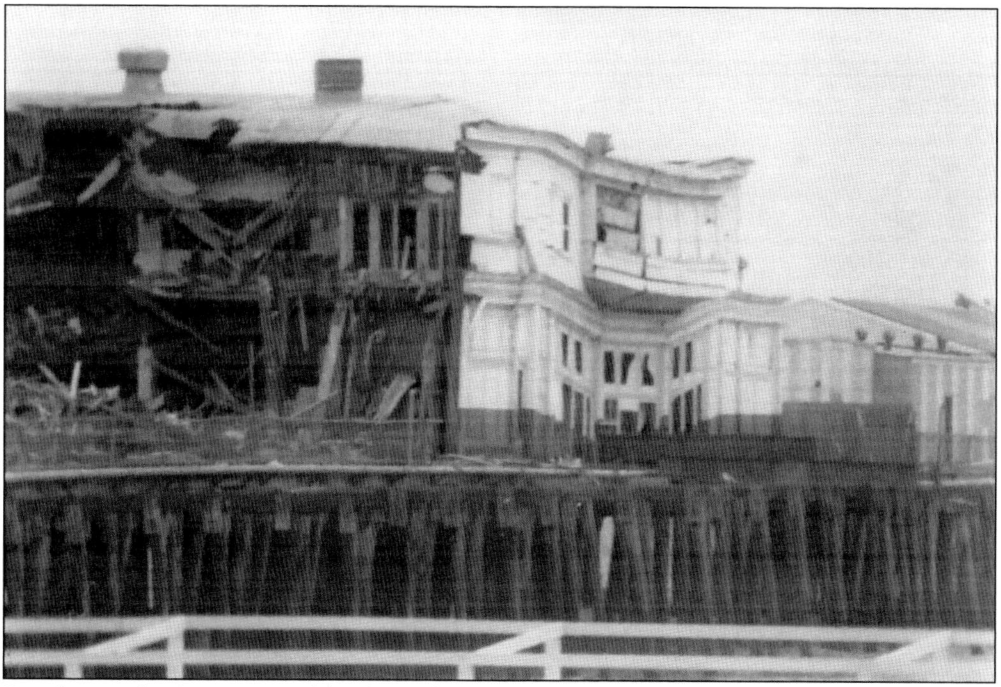

Seen here is the destruction of the Ocean/Midway theater in 1975. The Ocean Hall was built and opened by Frank Gravatt as a state-of-the-art motion picture theater in May 1929. Live Broadway plays were staged in 1949 and 1950 but were not successful. It remained a movie theater until its end. (Courtesy of Terri Tyrrell.)

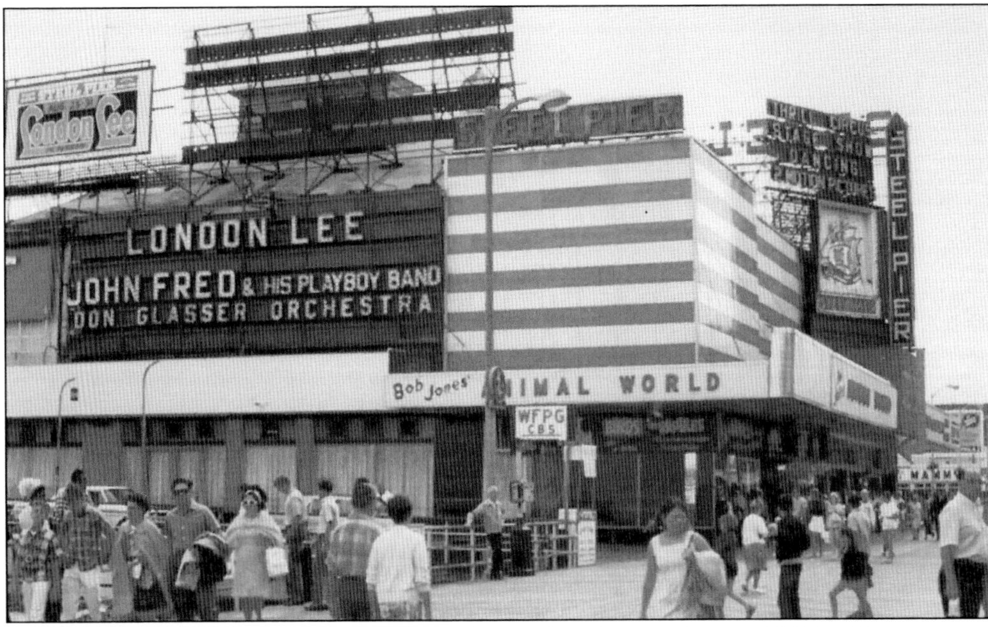

This scene shows the northern side of the Casino building in August 1968, with a marquee announcing comic London Lee and another one-hit wonder, John Fred and His Playboy Band. "Judy in Disguise (With Glasses)" was their big hit, and they came to the pier as that was being played on radios all over the United States.

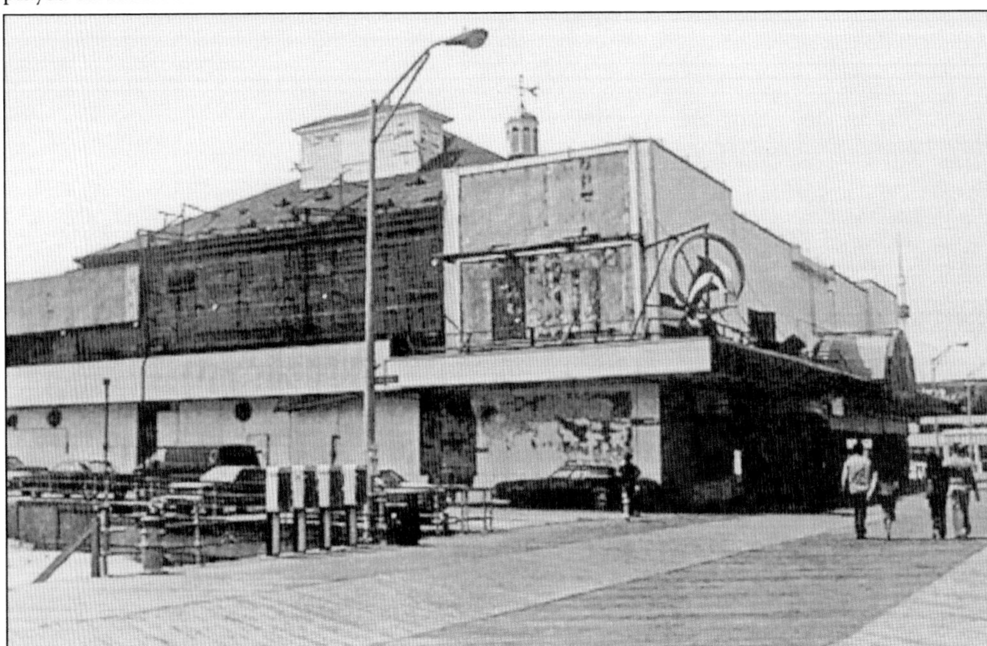

This 1982 look at the same scene shows a decaying and vacant building. Resorts International, the organization that opened up Atlantic City's first casino hotel, owned Steel Pier at this point and did not know what to do with it. Only the front of the building was open, offering arcade games. The cars parked on the side are vehicles belonging to employees of radio station WFPG, which was still on the pier. Other than that, Steel Pier sat as a memory.

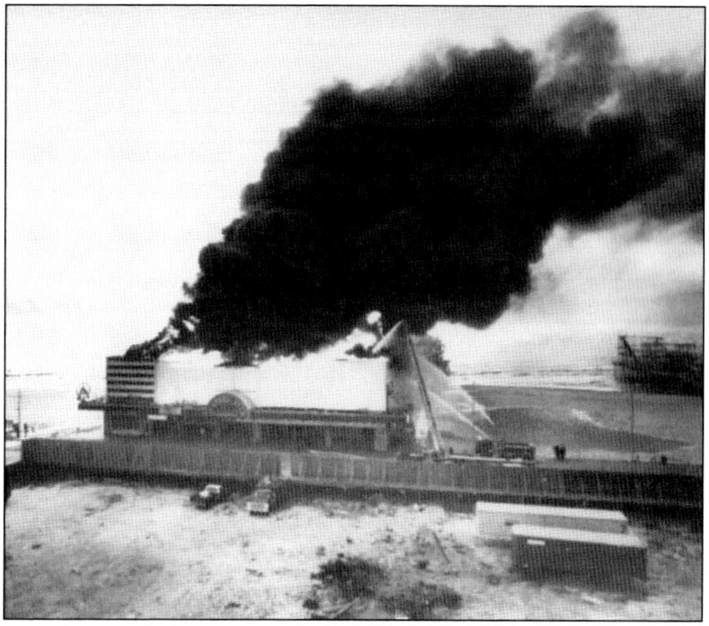

Steel Pier's last act was on December 10, 1982, when an arsonist destroyed the structure. The original Casino building and arcade, on that boardwalk location at Virginia Avenue for 85 years, were gone. Not only were the buildings vacant, but so was the lot across from the pier. Planters Peanuts, Fralinger's Salt Water Taffy, other stores, theaters, and various buildings were demolished for the building of the Trump Taj Mahal casino and hotel.

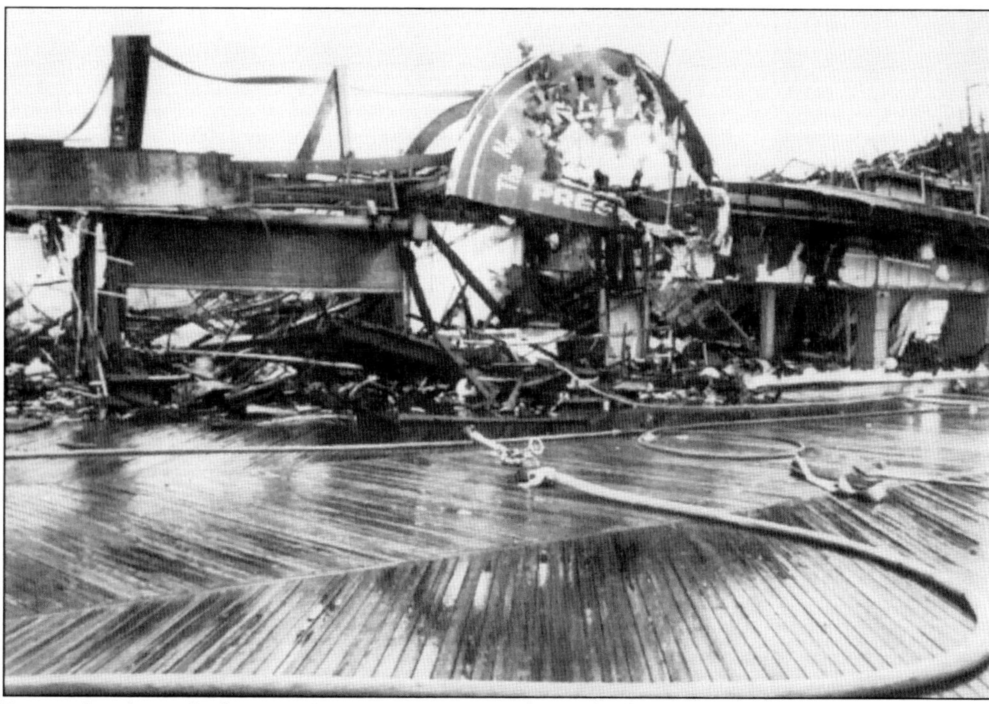

Pictured is the end of an era. However, a new Steel Pier, built on thick concrete pilings, opened June 15, 1992, in the same exact location. Pier operators Anthony and William Catanoso steadily added rides and amusements on the new pier for a new generation of fun-seekers. The Catanosos bought the pier from Trump Entertainment on August 3, 2011, for $4.25 million, with major plans to gradually add buildings and bring back a bit of the original Steel Pier atmosphere. Although much shorter than the original pier, Steel Pier still lives on in Atlantic City and brings joy to young and old.